Total Value Development

How to Drive Service Innovation

Series on Technology Management*

Series Editor: J. Tidd (University of Sussex, UK)   ISSN 0219-9823

Published

*The complete list of the published volumes in the series can be found at
http://www.worldscientific.com/series/stm

SERIES ON TECHNOLOGY MANAGEMENT – VOL. 26

Total Value Development

How to Drive Service Innovation

Frank M Hull

Cass Business School and
Fordham University Graduate School of Business-Executive Education

Chris Storey

University of Sussex, UK

Imperial College Press

ICP

Published by

Imperial College Press
57 Shelton Street
Covent Garden
London WC2H 9HE

Distributed by

World Scientific Publishing Co. Pte. Ltd.
5 Toh Tuck Link, Singapore 596224
USA office: 27 Warren Street, Suite 401-402, Hackensack, NJ 07601
UK office: 57 Shelton Street, Covent Garden, London WC2H 9HE

Library of Congress Cataloging-in-Publication Data
Names: Hull, Frank, author. | Storey, Christopher David, author.
Title: Total value development : how to drive service innovation /
    Frank M. Hull (Cass Business School and Fordham University Graduate School of Business-
    Executive Education, USA) & Christopher David Storey (University of Sussex, UK).
Description: New Jersey : Imperial College Press, [2016] |
    Series: Series on technology management ; vol. 26
Identifiers: LCCN 2015042689 | ISBN 9781783267132 (hc : alk. paper)
Subjects: LCSH: Total quality management. | Value. | Customer relations. | Industrial management.
Classification: LCC HD62.15 .H857 2016 | DDC 658.4/063--dc23
LC record available at http://lccn.loc.gov/2015042689

British Library Cataloguing-in-Publication Data
A catalogue record for this book is available from the British Library.

Desk Editors: Chandrima Maitra/Mary Simpson

Typeset by Stallion Press
Email: enquiries@stallionpress.com

Printed in Singapore

PREFACE

This book provides a significant conceptual and empirical contribution to the understanding and practice of business model innovation (BMI). Business models define the way companies create and deliver value for customer while retaining a portion for growth and profit. Enterprises pursuing BMI develop novel value creation architectures and original value propositions.

In the recent years, scholars have devoted a growing attention on innovation at the business-model level.[i] There is no single consensus definition of a business model, but David Teece suggests at the core is the: "design or architecture of the value creation, delivery, and capture mechanisms" (p. 127).[ii] Thus a business model should be able to link two dimensions of firm activity — value creation and value capture. Value creation and capture are linked by what is sometimes called value delivery.[iii] According to Teece, the "business model" defines the way the company creates and delivers value to customers, and then captures a portion of this value to make profit and growth. Organizations which pursue this type of innovation develop novel value creation architectures and original revenue models, more than focus just on new products or new services. BMI involves the integration and adaptation of capabilities, and the exploitation of these novel combinations to create and capture value in new ways.[iv] However, studies focusing on the relationships between capabilities, BMI and firm performance are rare.

Schneider and Spieth argue that BMI "is simultaneously about the (re) deployment and usage of existing resources and capabilities to develop new value offerings or forms of value creation... the question of 'how' to use resources has been less considered" (pp. 415).[v] Despite the increasing number of investigations in the field, much remains to say. First, most of studies on BMI are conceptual or case-based,[vi] while quantitative investigations are limited. Second, and the most important, these contributions have primarily addressed the capture and the monetization stage, rather than its value creation architecture.[vii] These contributions highlight the relevance of the issue, but often then they emphasize the client side, while they do not deepen under which conditions an innovative "back-end" architecture may foster the competitive advantage and lead to a superior performance. In other words, literature has focused too much on the downstream options, but studies of the upstream or "back-end" of BMI are less common.

O'Mahoney and Vecchi found the relationship between intangible assets and productivity to be higher in R&D — and skill-intensive contexts.[viii] Organizations require a diversified portfolio of resources, including both tangible and intangibles, to combine technological assets with other resources and capabilities, to create value. Demil and Lecocq investigated the dynamics created by the interactions of the different building blocks of business models.[ix] Sustained value creation instead relies on successfully shaping, adapting, and renewing the underlying business model of the company on a continuous basis, which comprises the rationale of how an organization creates, delivers, and captures value.[x] Denicolai *et al.* revealed the exploitation of tangible and intangible assets as complementary building blocks which compose the business model.[xi] Such complementary assets are central to the delivery of value, by leveraging monetizing opportunities, for example: "Systems integrators, platforms, and multi-sided markets share what is sometimes referred to as a business ecosystem. For managers, the ecosystems perspective holds the promise of opening up the wider entrepreneurial and collaborative space that a new technology affords, and provides room for novel business models to succeed".[xii]

Such a systems perspective of BMI is needed which comprises the rationale for how organizations create, deliver, and capture value. Exploiting a diversified portfolio of resources, both tangible goods and intangible services, boosts value creation opportunities. Many business models entail the exploitation of tangible and intangible assets as complementary building blocks. Combination of complementary assets is central to the delivery of value by leveraging monetizing opportunities by system integration that found the relationship between intangible assets and productivity to be higher in R&D and skill-intensive contexts. Such studies underscore the importance of intangible knowledge as well a tangible assets for creating highly valued outputs.

The central argument of this book is that value is created by better integrating product and service offerings to provide superior customer experiences. The model draws upon components of quality management and concurrent engineering, to develop a composite model for co-developing products and services. The model consists of three groups of practices, early cross-functional collaborative *organization*, flexible but disciplined *processes*, and enabling *tools/technologies* (OPT), which individually and through interaction are associated with superior performance. It builds on earlier work which separately examined the development of product and services.[xiii] The composite model presented in this book is derived from, tested and validated by two statistical studies and the efficacy of the component practices is demonstrated by qualitative evidence from numerous case studies, workshops, and consultancy projects.

The focus on the specific practices and tools which create options for BMI, independently and in combination, by better integrating product and service development and delivery represents a significant contribution and agenda for innovation research.[xiv]

Joe Tidd
Professor, Technology & Innovation Management
SPRU (Science Policy Research Unit), University of Sussex, U.K.

Notes

i   For example, Casadesus-Masanell, R., and Ricart, J. E. 2012. Competing through Business Models, *Handbook of Research on Competitive Strategy*, 460–491; Gambardella, A. and McGahan, A. M. 2010. Business-Model Innovation: General Purpose Technologies and their Implications for Industry Structure, *Long Range Planning*, 43, 262–271; Zott, C., Amit, R., and Massa, L. 2011. The Business Model: Recent Developments and Future Research, *Journal of Management*, 37, 1019–1042.

ii   Teece, D. J. 2010. Business Models, Business Strategy and Innovation, *Long Range Planning*, 43, 172–194.

iii   Casadesus-Masanell, R. and Ricart, J. E. 2010. From Strategy to Business Models and onto Tactics, *Long Range Planning*, 43, 195–215.

iv   Gambardella, A. and McGahan, A. M. 2010. Business-Model Innovation: General Purpose Technologies and their Implications for Industry Structure, *Long Range Planning*, 43, 262–271.

v   Schneider, S. and Spieth, P. 2013. Business Model Innovation: Towards an Integrated Future Research Agenda, *International Journal of Innovation Management*, 17(1), 1340001–1340034.

vi   Casadesus-Masanell, R. and Ricart, J. E. 2010. From Strategy to Business Models and onto Tactics, *Long Range Planning*, 43, 195–215; Koen, P. A., Bertels, H. M. J. and Elsum, I. R. 2011. The three faces of business model innovation, *Research-Technology Management*, 54, 52–59.

vii   Desyllas, P. and Sako, M. 2013. Profiting from Business Model Innovation: Evidence from Pay-As-You-Drive Auto Insurance, *Research Policy*, 42, 101–116; Witell, L. and Logren, M. 2013. From Service for Free to Service for Fee: Business Model Innovation in Manufacturing Firms, *Journal of Service Management*, 24, 520–533.

viii O'Mahony, M. and Vecchi, M. 2009. R&D, Knowledge Spillovers and Company Productivity Performance, *Research Policy*, 38, 35–44.

ix   Demil, B. and Lecocq, X. 2010. Business Model Evolution: In Search of Dynamic Consistency, *Long Range Planning*, 43, 227–246.

x   Osterwalder, A. and Pigneur, Y. 2010. *Business Model Generation: A Handbook for Visionaries, Game Changers, and Challengers*: wiley. com.

xi   Denicolai, S., Ramirez, M. and Tidd, J. 2014. Creating and Capturing Value From External Knowledge: The Moderating Role of Knowledge-Intensity, *R&D Management*, 44(3), 248–264.

xii   Baden-Fuller, C. and Haefliger, S. 2013. Business Models and Technological Innovation, *Long Range Planning*, 46, 419–426.

xiii Tidd, J. and Hull, F. 2003. *Service Innovation: Organizational Responses to Technological Opportunities and Market Imperatives*. Imperial College Press: London; Tidd, J. and Hull' F. 2006. Managing Service Innovation: The need for Selectivity Rather than 'Best-practice', *New Technology, Work and Employment*, 21(2), 139–161.

xiv   Tidd, J. and Thuriaux-Alemán, B. 2015. Innovation Management Practices: Cross-Sectorial Adoption, Variation and Effectiveness, *R&D Management*, doi: 10.1111/radm.12199.

ACKNOWLEDGMENTS

Paul Collins, University of Washington, who co-discovered the synergistic troika at the operating core of the composite model

Theodore Caplow, Columbia University, for profound models of organization design and insights into how human factors affect operations

Philipp Drost, UBS, whose work at Fordham University helped translate industrial practices into the language of services

Jerald Hage, University of Maryland, whose appreciation for the organic form of organization design provided a key building block for this book

Beth Hirschhorn, formerly VP at Chase Bank, who systematically deployed best practices from the composite model

Marco Lisi, European Space Agency, for helpful insights about innovation

Cesar Rego, University of Mississippi, for editorial comments

Gary Rosen, VP of Varian Semiconductor, whose deployment of the composite model proved extraordinarily successful

LIST OF ABBREVIATIONS

Total value development (TVD)
Early simultaneous influence (ESI)
Organic team structure (OTS)
In-process dynamic controls (IDC)
Computer information technologies (CIT)
New service development (NSD)
Quality function deployment (QFD)
Total quality management (TQM)
Computer automated design/manufacturing (CAD/CAM)
Product life cycle management (PLM)
Transformational assurance process (TAP)
Define, measure, assess, improve, and control (DMAIC)

LIST OF FIGURES

LIST OF TABLES

INTRODUCTION

Total Value Development

Total Value Development (TVD) provides a framework to help businesses innovate and derive greater value from the services they offer. The challenge for devising innovative business models is how to optimize customer experience, the ultimate arbiter of worth. A myriad of enterprises compete for the attention and money of customers by developing varied offerings. However, most enterprises develop either goods or services, but seldom both simultaneously. Although some corporations sell both services and goods, offerings from each sector are usually conceived separately, developed in segregated units, and sold either individually or in ad hoc bundles. To the extent customers commingle goods and services in their experiences, segregating development by sector misses opportunities for optimizing value by designing holistic offerings.

The thesis of this book is that a "composite" model of development is sufficiently robust for developing goods and services simultaneously. The dual capability of this model provides opportunities for collaboratively developing holistic offerings integrating service and goods for customers from the outset. If offerings integrating services and goods enhance customer experiences, innovative business models may exploit the robustness of the composite model to gain competitive advantage.

The composite model hybridizes earlier forms of enterprise design to achieve development systems capable of multitasking to optimize customer value in terms of innovative features as well as cost. The model, which is based on the principles of Total Quality Management (TQM) and concurrent engineering, argues for simultaneous collaboration by all relevant stakeholders in value creation at the conceptual outset of development. This book explores opportunities for business creation by providing customers with more holistic experiences by developing innovative offerings integrating goods and services cost-effectively.

To realize robust development capabilities of the composite model, however, usually means transforming mechanistic bureaucracies, which are internally focused on internal operating efficiencies, into more organic enterprises open to flexible options. Therefore, actions recommended for creating the capability of TVD arise from the enactment of a scenario depicted in Figure 1.

The composite model is shown as the immediate driver of performance which is measured not only as differentiating features, but also delivery operations which are critical for many kinds of services augmenting customer experiences. The model comprises three domains of practice dealing with organization, process, and tools/technologies (OPT). Red two-way arrows denote synergistic interactions among these essential elements which enable the achievement of cost-effective innovation if deployed synergistically in development operations.

Organic team structure (OTS) is a prerequisite for the composite model because people from different functional groups must be organized to innovate. In bureaucratic structures, which is a characteristic of most large-scale enterprises, each function performs a specialized task within a hierarchy before handing work off to the next. Cross-functional teaming system is antithetical to serial development operations in mechanistic bureaucracies. Therefore, champions of transformation are necessary to help lead integrated teams for developing new kinds of customer value.

Enterprise adopting a strategy of innovation obtains more benefit from the composite model because of the cross-fertilization of ideas among heterogeneous functions. The more radical the development undertaken, the greater the benefits of early collaboration by multiple functions along the value stream using flexible processes and enabling tools and technologies.

1. Environment	2. Adaptation	3. Strategies	4. Structure		5. Performance
Dynamism	NSD Function	Innovation & Knowledge	Transformation to Organic Team Structure (OTS)	Composite Model & Integrated Value Development	Differentiation & Delivery

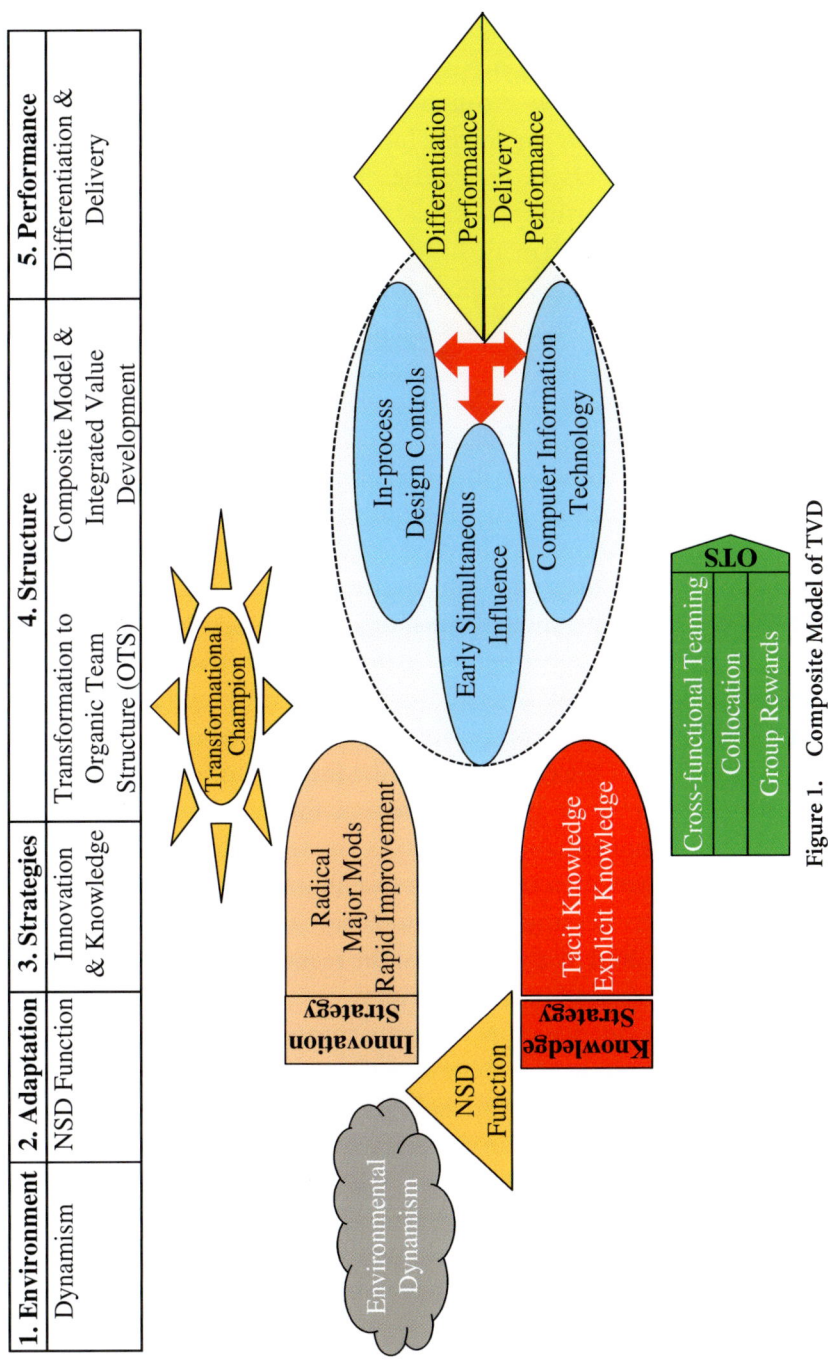

Figure 1.   Composite Model of TVD

Knowledge is an increasingly competitive differentiator in customer offerings. Elements of the composite model are designed to exploit both explicit knowledge, such as through tools and technologies, and/or tacit knowledge by organically organizing human capital from the outset of the development cycle. Service enterprises that reconnoiter their environments and adapt by forming an explicit new service development (NSD) function are higher performers. Enterprises which operate in static environment or fail to recognize the need for transformation from mechanistic bureaucracy to a more organic, composite model of development are low performers.

Evidence supporting the TVD framework is provided by *qualitative* and *quantitative* evidences. Qualitative evidence from case studies illustrates how many leading service enterprises organized cross-functional collaboration for NSD in lieu of serial operations within bureaucratic hierarchies. A user group of renowned service enterprises in the New York area shared best practices with one another during hosted visits. Round-table discussions, conferences, workshops, and special MBA classes were conducted on how to improve service productivity. The information and experiences about new NSD shared in these forums are included in case illustrations to profile the composite model of development in operation. Cases illustrations of the composite model from goods companies are also provided to demonstrate the robustness of the principles of concurrent methods of development.

Pseudonyms are often used in the case illustrations. However, companies studied in services and goods industries are listed in the Appendix, Research Methods and Analysis, so that the readers may have an idea of the kinds of enterprises used in case examples.

Quantitative evidence supporting the composite model is provided by two parallel studies, one of 100 industrial corporations followed by a parallel survey of 70 service enterprises in the greater New York area.[i] Similar results from the goods and services analyses suggest that the composite model is sufficiently robust for trans-sector development of holistic customer offerings. Exploiting its robustness offers prospects for devising innovative business models achieving competitive advantages not only by economies of scale, but also by developing holistic offering integrating services and goods to enhance total customer value.

Correlation coefficients are shown in the text and tables to establish associations between practices and performance outcomes. Coefficients range from 0.0 to 1.0, which indicates perfect co-variation. Levels of statistical significance show the likelihood that associations are due to chance alone. The probability that a relationship is due to chance is less than one in a hundred is designated by double asterisks (**), probabilities of less than one in twenty by a single asterisk (*). Moderated regression analyses used in the quantitative studies as well as the qualitative methods are provided in the Appendix: Research Methods and Analysis.

Structure of the Book

Section A — TVD systems: Axioms and images

Value is determined by holistic customer experience in which goods and services are intermingled. A framework for TVD deploys robust operating system so that goods and services may be co-created simultaneously. A composite model of development operations synergistically integrates three sets of practices dealing with the OTP. Case examples show how to deploy this troika of practices separately and in synergistic combination. Five axioms provide compelling logic for the composite model which is based on the principles of quality management and concurrent engineering. A total of 10 images depict facets of the composite model to illustrate how enterprises may be transformed from a serial, bureaucratic operation into a concurrent system for optimizing total value.

Section B — Evidence for advantages of a composite model

To create total customer value, a systems approach is required for transforming diverse inputs into holistic outputs. The composite model synthesizes practices from earlier forms of business operation to create business systems with greater capabilities for developing innovative customer offerings cost-effectively. In particular, the efficiencies of mechanistic bureaucratic forms are hybridized with innovative organic forms of operation.

The troika of practices of the composite model are detailed and measured in two parallel statistical studies, one of goods and the other of services. The three sets of practices include early collaborative organization, flexible but disciplined processes, and enabling tools/technologies. The troika of practices individually and synergistically predict performance in both the goods and services samples. The axis of the composite model, the positive impact on performance due to synergy between organization and process was observed in both analyses. However, synergy between tools/technologies with the organization and process was observed in the service sample only among enterprises pursuing a strategy of radical new development.

These parallel statistical findings, coupled with qualitative evidence from case studies, provide evidence that the composite model is sufficiently robust for developing customer offerings holistically integrating goods and services simultaneously. This capability provides a springboard for the consideration of innovative business models for optimizing customer value.

Section C — The synergistic elements of the composite model

The foundation of the composite model is the organization of cross-functional collaboration from concept to delivery. The epitome of concurrent practice is early simultaneous influence (ESI) by multiple functions in development decisions at the concept phase where opportunities for innovation and cost avoidance are greatest. In serial, non-concurrent systems of development, engagement by downstream functions, such as manufacturing and customer service, is often only after the bulk of consequential decisions have already been made.

A prerequisite for early simultaneous engagement is transformation from a mechanistic bureaucracy to OTS. Cross-functional groups are formed, rewarded as a group, and well collocated to the extent feasible. To retain the efficiencies of mechanistic bureaucracies, formal procedures are rendered into In-process Dynamic Controls (IDC) that may be flexibly adapted to specific development operations. Computer Information Technologies (CIT) not only provide analytical capabilities for virtual designs, but also enable asynchronous communications among cross-functional team members as well as continual updating and improvement of processes.

Section D — Configuring investment in human capital to optimize value

Investment in diverse forms of human capital is required for developing new customer offerings. But which of the 10 different functions make the greatest contributions? When is deployment of each function optimal: concept, pre-launch, or post-launch? How the contingencies of innovation strategy and type of knowledge exploited affect differential value of functional contributions is explored using moderated regression analyses. The role of each of the 10 functions in adding value predicting variation in differentiation and delivery performance is reported as an index of three factors: (1) variation explained by correlations, (2) the contingency of radically new development, and (3) the exploitation of tacit vs. explicit knowledge. The role of each of the the 10 functions is described and profiled to guide enterprises in configuring their investment in human capital to boost value added.

Section E — Championing transformation for TVD design capabilities

Service enterprises that respond to dynamic changes in their environment are higher performers than those which do not. One way high performers adapt is by creating an executive position to proactively take responsibility for NSD. By contrast, low performers are more likely to rely on ad hoc developments often lead by functional departments. To lead the transformation of service development from serial bureaucratic operations to concurrent systems often requires a champion of change to realize TVD capabilities.

Champions help institutionalize NSD as a cross-functional endeavor. Otherwise, the development system will default back to mechanistic bureaucracy. Champions face difficult choices in attempting to create innovative designs that are developed in-house. Therefore, a variety of options are described ranging from intrapreneurial ventures to external launches.

The need for transforming service development into operations with more dynamic capabilities is driven in part by understanding how to add value by building outwards from customer experiences. Innovative designers increasingly co-create experiences in collaboration with their customers. A customer-centric perspective in development opens up a variety of design options because the solution as experienced is the objective. How the solution is developed and delivered and by whom is often irrelevant from the customer perspective. Champions of transformation need to leverage voice of the customer in helping enterprises design offering fulfilling unmet needs.

Transformational Workbooks

Workbooks provide readers with guidance for envisioning and realizing high-performance systems for NSD. First, readers benchmark their enterprises against best practices in services and/or goods databases. Second, worksheets enable readers envision more capable development systems. Third, a transformational assurance process provides guidance for prioritizing closure of gaps between "As Is" and "Should Be" development systems. Fourth, criteria for formulating a winning value proposition are profiled. A key is identifying ways of enhancing holistic customer experiences. A checklist is provided on the kinds of human capital required for realizing radically new offerings. Alternative paths for exploiting the robust capabilities of the composite model are explored. To institutionalize concurrent practices within an existing enterprise, an intrapreneurial venture may stimulate change. In some situations an external venture may need to be launched. Whatever modes are used, however, opportunities for exploiting new business models are likely to be greater if the all stakeholders in the value stream have simultaneous input and services and goods are collaboratively developed to the extent appropriate.

Notes

i   The quantitative results from the New York study were subsequently reinforced by a follow-on study of 39 enterprises in London. See Tidd, J. and Hull, F. 2003. *Service Innovation: Organizational Responses to Technological Opportunities & Market Imperatives*, London: Imperial College Press.

CONTENTS

SECTION A
TOTAL VALUE
DEVELOPMENT SYSTEMS:
AXIOMS AND IMAGES

CHAPTER ONE

TOWARDS A FRAMEWORK FOR TOTAL VALUE DEVELOPMENT

Overview

This chapter provides a typology of four kinds of value development systems that vary in the extent to which goods and services are integrated in customer offerings from the outset of development. The thesis is that innovative business opportunities may be exploited by simultaneously integrating goods and services in the holistic development of customer offerings. A composite model of development operations is introduced as robustly capable of concurrently developing goods and/or service offerings because it melds the strength of multiple kinds of practice into an integrated system. To exploit the capabilities of the composite model, two divides need to be crossed. The first is between stakeholders at upstream vs. downstream ends of the value development continuum. The second is the integration of development by functional specialists in services and goods which are typically housed in separate administrative units. Crossing these two divides generates opportunities for devising innovative business models offering customers greater holistic value.

1.1. Introduction

A Total Value Development (TVD) framework helps connect dots of knowledge for integration into holistic customer offerings. Making interconnections in large-scale bureaucracies is difficult, however, because people with knowledge about any given dot are often functionally divided from one another in hierarchically organized departmental units. To optimize creative combinations offering customers unique value, business systems need to be redesigned so that constructive collaboration occurs up-front among knowledgeable stakeholders and continues throughout the development cycle. This book proposes a framework for TVD to foster purposive cross-fertilization of ideas among diverse stakeholders possessing knowledge in specialized domains.

The TVD framework focuses particularly on integrating knowledgeable people separated by two kinds of divisions. The *first* divide is between those at the front-end of the value development stream and those at the back-end whose actions are largely delimited by decisions already taken. Large-scale bureaucracies mechanistically splinter job responsibilities into sequentially defined roles along assembly-line stages segregating upstream and downstream functions. Role differentiation in developing value is almost always an inevitable consequence of the structuring of activities in large-scale enterprises so that people perform specialized roles sequentially instead of collaboratively.[i] This mechanistic approach is cost efficient but at the expense of innovation. A common presumption is that specialized functions such as R&D are required for creating value at the conceptual phase of development whilst people with relatively lower knowledge-based skills enact downstream roles such as manufacturing or service delivery. However, segregation based on brains vs. brawn neglects the value of knowledge of downstream functions resulting in suboptimal conceptualization and realization of customer offerings.

To transcend the first divide, collaboration among up and downstream stakeholders needs to occur early in the decision-making cycle. The TVD framework builds multifunctional engagement up-front so that value is added relatively more simultaneously than sequentially. The cornerstone of concurrency is early involvement of downstream functions such as manufacturing and customer service at the outset of the development cycle. Concurrent product development adapts many of the principles of quality management to focus like a laser beam on

> Downstream functions, such as customer service, need to collaboratively participate with the development team in design decisions at the concept phase

simultaneously integrating actions adding value along all points of the development stream.

Evidence for the advantages of simultaneous engagement by all relevant stakeholder functions up-front and throughout the development cycle is provided not only by analyzing data on service enterprises, but also goods industries. Results of analysis demonstrate that a "composite" model of development is effective for performance improvement in both sectors. The principles of total quality management (TQM) and concurrent engineering are of proven benefit for developing products in good industries.[ii] But the same principles also apply to systems for developing value in services as well. Case studies provide qualitative illustrations of the composite model in both the goods and service sectors.

The *second* divide is between the knowledge of people in goods and services sectors. The prevailing assumption is that goods and services are fundamentally different because of differences in intangibility and other factors. Consequently, many enterprises presume that distinctive operating systems are needed within each sector for developing customer offerings. Diversified industrial corporations usually segregate those responsible for developing new products from those engaged in New Service Development (NSD). Governments often contract with goods companies to supply engineered products which civil agencies are responsible for using to deliver public services.

The result is that many goods are designed with services as an afterthought. Conversely, many service operations develop offerings principally focused on intangible features with little up-front consideration of the extent to which customer value is based on physical accoutrements enhancing user experiences. The term "bundling" is often used to refer to offerings combining goods and services. While such combinations represent a step toward TVD, a more encompassing notion is to integrate goods and services from the outset so that offerings are based on holistic customer experiences.

Integrating goods and services from the outset in development is possible because the TVD framework is so robust that a single system may simultaneously

> The robust capabilities of the composite model enables the simultaneous development of customer offerings integrating services and goods from the outset

handle the collaborative development of goods and/or services. Enterprises in both sectors deploy essentially the same trio of building blocks in development systems dealing with *organization, process,* and *tools/technologies.* Organization involves fostering collaboration among diverse functions throughout the value stream starting at the outset. Process means that bureaucratic procedures are rendered into flexible guidelines for development teams subject to the exercise of human judgment rather than inviolate rules. Tools and Technologies includes not only the use of computer-aided design, but also electronic communications among team members and capabilities for easily updating processes. Synergies among this troika make higher levels of development capability achievable in both goods and services. The generic framework enables development operations to simultaneously develop customer offerings integrating goods and services. Transcending the sectoral divide provides competitive advantages to the extent that holistic offerings offer customers more value than ad hoc bundles of services and goods.

Holistic offerings may enhance the experiences of customers in daily life where goods and services are often commingled. The importance of service is underscored by views originally expressed by Aristotle — *Happiness consists in the activity or use rather than the mere possession of a characteristic.*[iii] In a service economy people frequently enjoy the experience of using objects without the nuisance of ownership. This trend is manifest in the growth of rentals of all kinds, e.g., ZIP cars, Uber, temporary offices spaces, time shares, and Amazon Web Services.

Many customers purchase goods and services from separate sources that are interactively linked in life experiences. If enterprises developing goods and/or services would take a customer perspective, might they be better able to architect offerings providing more holistic customer value? The TVD framework offers the prospect of breaking down barriers bureaucratically segregating people with specialized knowledge about goods and services.

1.2. Integrating Knowledge Along the Value Stream

Collaborative decision-making by up and downstream functions from the outset and throughout the development cycle drives innovation and

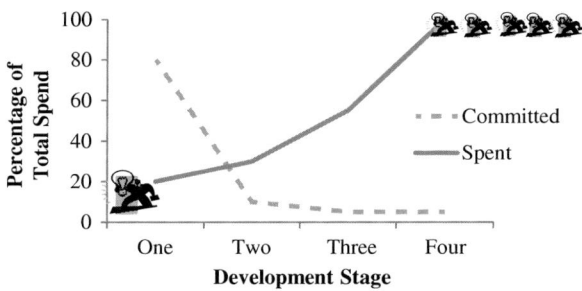

Figure 1.1.   Committed Spend by Development Stage

productivity. In many goods and service enterprises, over 80 percent of ultimate cost of developing physical products is often determined during the initial phase of the product development cycle.[iv] As illustrated in Figure 1.1, the great bulk of costs are committed by decisions made early-on in the development cycle where the concept of the customer offering is defined. Although the expenditure of actual funds at the initial phases is relatively low, it rises exponentially to peak at phase five as manufacturing and/or delivery operations ramp-up to full scale.

In large-scale enterprises, the assignment of people to develop customer offerings is usually a significant decision not only because creative talent is scarce for the initial phase, but also because future funds must be tentatively reserved should development be carried to fruition. This initial phase is of outsized importance for connecting dots of knowledge. The opportunities for cross-fertilizing ideas are greatest at the concept phase. An open-funnel at the outset means that many design options may be explored up-front because the costs and risks of assessing alternative combinations of features and resources are relatively low. Early simultaneous participation by downstream functions such as manufacturing and service in decision-making enables enterprises to integrate knowledge needed for optimizing customer value from concept to delivery.

People with diverse dots of knowledge need to collaborate on ways of re-architecting the design and delivery of customer offering prior to actual development. After the concept phase, changes to design architecture become progressively more costly for several reasons. People engaged at the front-end have already funneled design options into a narrowed array of alternatives. Decision-making processes entail an emotive as well as rational closure necessary for forward progress from the concept to realization. Once development operations are launched, reexamination of early decisions is often expensive. The cost of redesign may be especially high in goods industries where physical materials may require rework. However, the cost of change in materials is often relatively small in proportion to the expenditure of human capital. So the cost of late changes in terms of human capital and emptions applies more or less across both the goods and services sectors.

After developed offerings proceed to manufacturing and/or delivery to customers, the cost of change is usually much greater. In goods industries, physical products must be recalled or reworked in the field. In services, especially those associated with tangible features, costs of change may also be considerable. However, late phase changes risk opportunity costs by affecting customer retention regardless of sector.

The fact that opportunities for innovation and precluding costly late changes are largely determined at the front-end argues strongly for early simultaneous influence by diverse functions along the value stream, especially those typically engaged only at the end in serial development systems, such as manufacturing and/or customer service. A person assigned to generate innovative solutions to customer needs by precluding back-end problems may be less than 1/5th as effective as one engaged at the front-end. Ideas and actions by functions at the back-end are largely constrained by prior decisions.

1.3. Desegregating Goods and Services

A composite model provides the foundation for designing TVD systems not only by integrating the work of up and downstream functions, but offers the prospect of developing holistic offerings integrating goods and services. The opportunity for realizing TVD depends not only on redesigning value development systems, but also challenging some of the presumptions about differences in goods and services. A barrier to holistic thinking about optimizing value creation is the contrast between "engineering-centric" vs. "service-centric" mindsets. From a systems perspective, however, operations dealing with things, data, and people cut across the

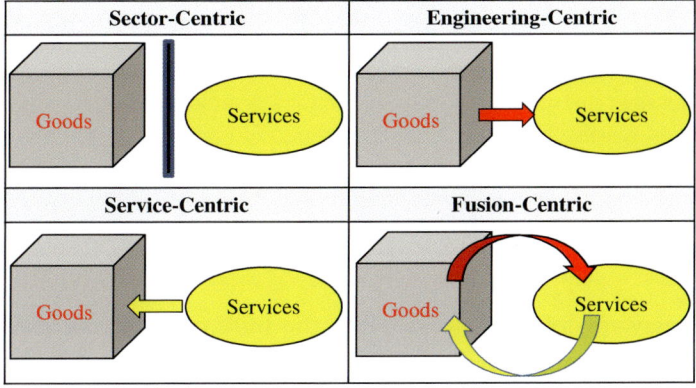

Figure 1.2.   Value Creation Systems

goods vs. services divide.[v] The TVD framework offers the prospect of a fusion-centric mind set for fostering holistic development of customer offerings integrating goods and service features from the outset of development as illustrated in Figure 1.2.

1.3.1. *Sector-centric value creation system*

Many enterprises are relatively sector-specific. On the one hand, some manufacturers ship goods to customers with little or no follow-on interaction. On the other hand, some services, especially those valued because of intangible knowledge, often focus on experiences in dynamic interactions between providers and customers with relatively little reliance on physical accoutrements.[vi] Enterprises providing customers with sector-specific offerings may add the most value by sticking to their knitting, so to speak. The notion of focusing on core competencies is generally considered a good practice especially as a corrective for many instances where diversifications have gone awry. Continually building improvements in design and delivery of extant offering may be the best path for profitability in many enterprises that provide relatively traditional or standardized offerings that mature in the definition of their value proposition.

Actions for Sector-specific Enterprises
Define and continually reinforce core competencies so that what differentiates the offerings of your enterprise relative to competition is understood internally as well as by customers. Clarity of focus optimizing the unique capacities of an enterprise may be the best approach even if customers supplement purchases from enterprise by buying complementary goods and/or services from another. Design of customer offerings need to focus on a clearly delineated value proposition.

One may speculate, however, that the bulk of customer experiences involve some degree of commingling of goods and services. To the extent that customers have to make purchases of goods from one enterprise and services from another to optimize their experiences, business opportunities may be missed. Goods companies might sometimes provide more valued offerings by diversifying downstream toward customers. Some service enterprises may enhance the value of their offering by bundling it with goods. Alternatively, fusion-centric enterprises may provide customers with holistic offerings integrating goods and services from the outset.

1.3.2. *Engineering-centric value creation system*

A common assumption is that development of goods is far more impersonal than the development of services. However, some services deal relatively more with data than people. For example, many financial services transform data in ways that are even more amenable to impersonal automation than the manufacture of physical goods. Service enterprises offering value based on explicit knowledge may rely principally on codified protocols and relatively mechanistic modes of impersonal communication with customers.[vii] Many services are developed and offered with insufficient attention given up-front to customer experiences. Some service organizations treat the people like commodities congruent with an engineering-centric perspective.

Within goods industries, the dominant coalition is often engineering-centric and sometimes neglectful of the people side of business, including the experiences not only of their customers, but even their own employees.

A mechanistic model of organization design has proved efficient for standardized, large-scale tasks in a wide variety of enterprises. The engineering mindset is sequential partly due to tangibility. Make the goods, and then service them. Many goods embody explicit knowledge in fixed packages so that transactions terminate at point of sale.

Actions for Diversifying Goods Enterprises
Form a cross-functional group responsible for NSD. Sell services enhancing customer experiences with physical objects so that experiences in using rather than owning objects is the principal source of perceived value. Integrate interpersonal as well as data services with products so that customer experiences transcend physicality. Infuse knowledge of customer experiences at the concept phase in the design of customer offerings. Simultaneously engage multiple functions to help engineers and other technical functions such as IT deploy *design for experience.*

1.3.3. *Service-centric value creation system*

A presumption is often made that service enterprises are relatively more people-focused than goods industries. For some services, interpersonal exchanges with people in delivery processes may be tantamount to the product itself, especially for offerings valued because of tacit knowledge. A people-centric approach for creating value is relatively more viable for intangible services that are delivered interpersonally over extended periods of time. Many service companies add value by catering to the idiosyncrasies of individual customers.

Some goods companies retain a relationship with customers even after initial sale of product. Many industries have found that customer empathy helps design products catering to the human experiences. Such enterprises are typically organized along relatively more organic than mechanistic design rules to foster innovation.[viii] Indeed, one of the strongest correlations with innovative success in goods companies is observing how customers use their products in actual practice. The value in some goods industries is enhanced by tacit knowledge transmitted through interpersonal exchanges, such as customized adaptations by field staff or follow-on face-to-face help in stores provided by Apple, Viking Ranges, Tiffany's, etc.

> **Actions for Diversifying Service Enterprises**
>
> Envision value creation throughout the life cycle at the outset so that customer experiences are considered at product creation phases. Design products in ways to enhance intangible as well as physical dimensions of customer experience during use, e.g., low cost of operation, easy maintenance, upgradability, replacement, and end of life disposal. Use *design for service* methods at the outset engaging diverse stakeholders by observing experiences customers have in using physical products.

1.3.4. *Fusion-centric value creation system*

Designing goods for service and/or services to exploit the benefits of goods provides a way of optimizing total value creation. Although the mix of goods and services in customer experiences varies enormously, it is how well they play together in the experience of customers that makes for competitive differences. The fusion-centric approach extends the composite model to include up-front collaboration between those responsible for good and services. Goods companies can deploy customer-centric methods such as Design for Service at the outset of their development cycle by using anthropological methods to understand how buyers experience the use of their products. Service companies can not only augment customer experiences with goods, but also collaborate in their design to optimized user experiences. Design for X (manufacturability, serviceability, etc.) is a proven approach frequently used in goods industries and is robust enough for application in the design of customer offerings holistically integrating services and goods.

A "fusion-centric" approach may simultaneously integrate engineering and service-centric approaches to the extent that the segregation of goods and services in management practices is an unnecessary artifice. An engineering view of value creation often underestimates the extent to which services may enhance the value of goods, e.g., car repairs. By contrast, a

> Design for X methods provide a way of interactively developing customer offerings fusing manufacturability for reducing defects with serviceability for enhancing physical as well as subjective experiences of users

people-centric view may underestimate the extent to which physical objects are intertwined with the creation and delivery of value to customers, e.g., buildings, instruments, computers, etc. A "fusion-centric" approach provides a common system for optimizing customer benefit by developing holistic offerings integrating goods and services at the outset of the creation cycle.

A four-fold schema is summarized below. A brief profile of alternative perspectives on value development systems suggests that a holistic approach to development may transcend some of the mental barriers associated engineering vs. service-centric perspectives. A systems approach to value creation based on the principles of concurrency may foster more integrative development regardless of the dominant mindset. A fusion approach may transcend the goods vs. services divide regardless of the bundle.

Fusion-centric Actions

Develop value propositions for customers based on reciprocal relationships between tangible and intangible modes of value integrated throughout a life cycle of use. Build broad-based multi-functional teams with representatives capable of concurrently designing holistic offerings optimizing integrative offerings of goods and services. Ensure value creation teams consider integration of all relevant dimensions of value: data, people, and things. Foster interpersonal relationships among stakeholders in goods and services based on reciprocal integration at various phases of the conceiving and realizing the value of holistic customer offerings. Design physical features in ways that not only conform to standards of engineering quality, but also to new benchmarks of intangible customer experiences. Build trans-sector teams to *design for total value.*

1.4. Bridging the Chasm between Goods and Services

Integrating the development of goods and services with a generic framework is helpful for three reasons. *First,* opportunities for trans-sector diversification are underexploited. The TVD framework offers the prospect for greater realization of collaboration between the sectors. *Second,* barriers to cross-functional integration in large-scale development systems are similar regardless of sector. The composite model offers a way of integrating diverse perspectives to achieve creativity whilst at the same time containing costs. *Third,* research on development systems is polarized. The great bulk of literature on development systems has been in goods industries. Yet the need for research on NSD is great because services employ many times more people than goods industries and are often relatively more profitable.

1.4.1. *Optimizing trans-sector diversification and integration*

When defining the customer offerings at the concept phase, many goods companies omit input from downstream functions such as manufacturing engineering, suppliers, logistics, and various support services such as maintenance, feature upgrades, replacement, etc. This lack of a life cycle perspective suboptimizes customer experiences because of post-sale defects and suboptimal user experiences. Numerous industrial corporations have fulfilled gaps in markets by aggressively complementing their physical products with services for the products they sell, e.g., automobiles, computers, jet engines, etc. Many have found servitization to be highly profitable. For example, GE Aerospace makes far more profit from servicing than manufacturing jet engines. However, many of goods companies lack a people-centric approach and neglect the experience of customers.

Some of the gap in the marketplace for people-focused offerings has been exploited by service companies. For example, service enterprises have filled many market niches by offering follow-on maintenance to customers who purchased stand-alone goods. Some goods companies essentially terminate their relationship with customers after sale of their manufactured product which represents lost potential for diversification by vertically integrating downstream toward customers. Bundling occurs, but perhaps far less frequently than is possible and often as an afterthought.

Some service enterprises provide physical goods as an integral part of their offering, such as cell phones, ATMs, airplanes, etc. However, some service providers remain very people-centric and may miss opportunities for enhancing the value of their offerings by adding physical accoutrements. Regardless of whether coordination of goods and services is handled by hierarchically organized units within a single corporation or by market contracts between separate legal entities, opportunities abound for providing customers with a more integrated experience throughout a life cycle of use, from concept to consumption.

1.4.2. *Overcoming bureaucratic barriers*

Cross-functional integration is needed for improving capabilities for value creation in large-scale systems regardless of sector. Growth in size predictably results in hierarchically differentiated labor in large systems regardless of sector. Procedural controls are typical in large-scale bureaucracies because job responsibilities are splintered into defined roles analogous to an assembly-line process. Mechanistic systems are efficient for developing standardized customer offerings but ineffective for generating innovation.

To create new kinds of value, organic systems evolved as an alternative to mechanistic bureaucracies for creating more innovative offerings although at relatively high costs. To achieve low cost and innovation simultaneously, hybrid systems evolved mixing the advantages of mechanistic and organic systems. The composite model, a kind of hybrid system, integrates diverse perspectives to achieve creativity whilst at the same time containing costs. This book proposes extending the cross-functional teaming dimension of the composite model to encompass the collaborative development of offerings integrating goods and services.

1.4.3. *The academic divide*

Research on value development systems is generally split into two camps, one in goods, and the other in services. Although over 80 percent of the publications on value creation have been on product development of goods, over 80 percent of jobs in advanced industrial economies are

> Focusing on how to create value for which customers are willing to pay may help integrate disparate research on development operations in goods and services

in services.[ix] However, NSD has been less systematically researched than in goods industries. Ways in which the creation of value in the two sectors is like and unlike needs to be better understood. NSD remains among the least studied and understood topics in both the service management and the innovation literatures. Greater effort is needed to understand the unique characteristics of NSD and to "discredit the belief that new services happen as a result of intuition, flair, and luck".[x] This book attempts to contribute to an emerging literature on how NSD system design affects innovation performance in service enterprises.

1.5. A TVD Framework

As shown in the following diagram, the composite model of development operations provides a hub for flows along the value steam as well as a nexus for the integration of stakeholders in goods and services. Early simultaneous influence, the cornerstone of the composite model of development operations, is a practice capable of bridging the divide between up and downstream function. From a systems perspective, the same generic phases of development are generally applicable to both goods and services: conceptual input, throughput development, and delivery (with customer feedback). Therefore collaboration development of goods and/services may occur along largely parallel tracks from concept to customer which makes function-centric offerings feasible. The TVD framework provides collaborative paths for reciprocal collaboration among four groups of internal employees: up and downstream functions as well as stakeholders in goods and services.

The customer is the focal point of value creation. Each group in a concurrent system of development should have indirect if not direct interchanges with them. Optimizing experiences for which customers are willing to pay is the ultimate object of early collaboration. These parallel tracks are illustrated in Figure 1.3.

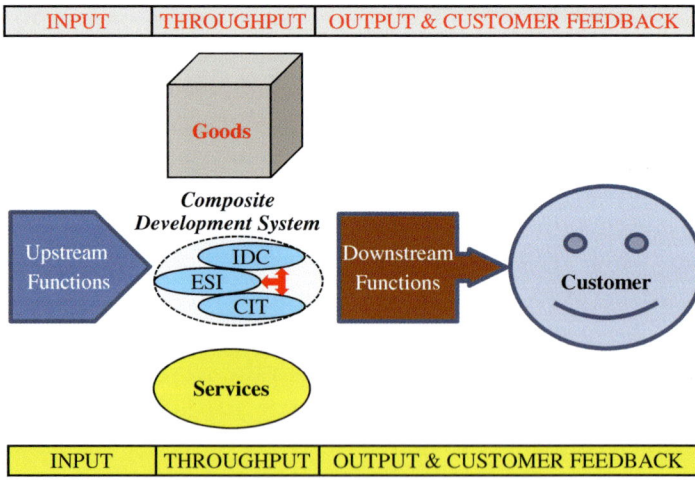

Figure 1.3.   Parallel Tracks for Developing Customer Offering: Integrating Goods and Services

The composite model of development is shown as an operations system with three synergistic components dealing with organization, process, and tools/technologies. The organization of early collaboration is its cornerstone. The composite model provides not only human interconnections for generating innovative ideas, but also benefits from its synergistic axis with process for bounding costs. The effectiveness of the operating system is enhanced by tools and technologies which also enable asynchronous communications and continually updated processes. The composite model of development provides a means for systematically connecting dots of knowledge in a disciplined manner to optimize value. The TVD framework ensures that the model includes stakeholders for goods and/or services as appropriate for creating holistic value.

1.5.1. *Leveraging TVD for business model innovation*

The TVD framework provides an approach for re-architecting value creation systems so that stakeholders in goods and services collaborate throughout the life cycle to optimize customer experiences. TVD provides an opportunity for rethinking the segregated development of offering in goods and services. Recent studies have suggested that business model innovation may be more effective if a diversified portfolio of resources is exploited, including both tangible and intangibles, to create new kinds of value.[xi]

The benefit from business model innovation should be greatest for services, which represent a far larger segment of industrialized economies than goods. Yet the deployment of concurrent methods in services lags behind established industrial practices. One reason is because service enterprises are less likely to form a team of cross-functional stakeholders for creating new kinds of value. Services can enhance capabilities for creating value by adopting proven practices in goods industries with appropriate adaptations. By diversifying into goods, services can further enhance the value of their offering. Goods industries have much to learn from services that cater to

> Opportunities for profitable business model innovation abound if developers architect heterogeneous inputs to configure holistic offerings integrating services and goods

customer experiences. Engineering-centric companies often fail to design customer offerings optimizing total value. Business models synergistically combining the potential of integrating goods and services in holistic offerings would seem to offer a win–win proposition for the enterprises and the customers they serve.

Notes

[i] Blau, P., Falbe, M., McKinley, C., and Phelps, W. T. 1976. Technology and Organization in Manufacturing, *Administrative Science Quarterly*, 21, 20–40.

[ii] Gerwin, D. and Susman, G. I. (Eds.). 1996. Special Issue on Concurrent Engineering, *IEEE Transactions on Engineering Management*, 43(2), 118–123; Gerwin, D. and Barrowman, N. J. 2002. An Evaluation of Research on Integrated Product Development, *Management Science*, 48(7), 938–953.

[iii] Rifkin, J. 2001. *The Age of Access: The New Culture of Hypercapitalism, Where All of Life is a Paid-For Experience*, Tarcher: New York.

[iv] Clausing, D. P. 1994. *Total Quality Development*, ASME Press: New York.

[v] Collins, P., Hage, J., and Hull, F. 1988. Technical Systems: A Framework for Analysis, in Bacharach, S. and DiTomaso, N. (Eds.), *Research in the Sociology of Organizations*, JAI Press: Greenwich, Vol. 6, pp. 81–100.

[vi] Storey, C. and Easingwood, C. 1998. The Augmented Servicing Offering, *Journal of Product Innovation Management*, 15, 335–351.

[vii] Storey, C. and Hull, F. 2010. A Value Contingent Model of Service Product Development, *Journal of the Service Management*, 21(2), 140–161.

[viii] Burns, T. and Stalker, G. M. 1961. *The Management of Innovation*, Tavistock: London.

[ix] Johne, A. and Harborne, P. 2003. One Leader is Not Enough for Major New Service Development: Results of a Consumer Banking Study, *The Service Industries Journal*, 23(May), 22–39.

[x] Menor, L. J., Tatikonda, M. V., and Sampson, S. E. 2002. New Service Development: Areas for Exploitation and Exploration, *Journal of Operations Management*, 20(2), 135–157.

[xi] Baden-Fuller, C. and Haefliger, S. 2013. Business Models and Technological Innovation, *Long Range Planning*, 46, 419–426; Demil, B. and Lecocq, X. 2010. Business Model Evolution: In Search of Dynamic Consistency, *Long Range Planning*, 43, 227–246; Grönroos, C. and Helle, P. 2010. Adopting a Service Logic in Manufacturing: Conceptual Foundation and Metrics for Mutual Value Creation, *Journal of Service Management*, 21(5), 564–590.

CHAPTER TWO

A TVD FRAMEWORK FOR DIFFERENTIATING CUSTOMER OFFERINGS

Overview

An effective operating system for developing customer offerings is a key asset business enterprises require for competitive differentiation. The hub of the Total Value Development (TVD) framework is a composite development system. The troika of elements of the composite model is explained in operational terms. Case examples illustrate the model and the deployment of key practices. Five axioms are profiled to depict the logical underpinning of the model which is based on concurrent methods of development. These axioms are common sense principles based on proven experiences which provide generic guidance for achieving TVD.

2.1. Operational Elements of the Composite Model

Large-scale enterprises are built from a trio of building blocks dealing with organization, process, and tools/technologies. Each block bundles diverse practices. The composite model ameliorates practices from these building blocks in specific ways so that hybrid bonds may be forged between antithetical practices of the mechanistic vs. organic types of system.[i] Synergy

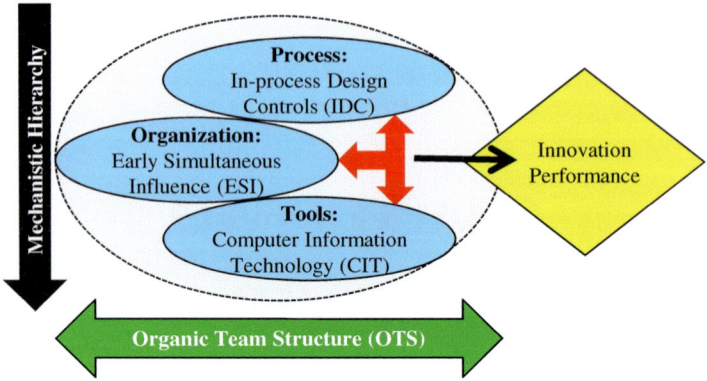

Figure 2.1.   The Composite Model of Development Operations

from these hybrid bonds enables enterprises to achieve cost-effective innovation in developing customer offerings as indicated by the two-way arrows among the troika in Figure 2.1.

The troika of developmental practices in the composite model integrate forces from two vectors. The downward force of the hierarchical vector of mechanistic bureaucracy is mitigated partially by OTS, a horizontal vector integrating up and downstream functions along the value creation flow.

The axis of the composite model is a synergistic bond between practices drawn from the building blocks of organization and process. The cornerstone is the organic organization of cross-functional teams exemplified by the practice of Early Simultaneous Influence (ESI). All stakeholders in the development system are engaged from concept to customer delivery as cross-functional collaborators. Participation by downstream functions at early phases provides opportunities for cross-fertilizing ideas for innovative features that can be realized cost-effectively.

Process provides complementary discipline for translating ideas about customer offerings into reality. Process provides teams with flexible guidance enabling them to exercise human judgment within boundaries. The cost efficiencies associated with mechanistic procedures may be achieved by In-process Design Controls (IDC). Adapting to dynamic situations rather than rigidly proceeding lock-step as though on an assembly-line allows teams to achieve greater effectiveness by using best known methods in ways that optimize capabilities for developing innovative offerings cost-effectively.

Tools and technologies represent the third building block. CIT provides capabilities for designing and transforming inputs into outputs. Ancillary benefits include electronic communications among organizational team members and continual adaptation of processes to ensure they are enabling rather than rigidly coercive.

Interactions among the troika of building blocks enable composite systems to achieve high performance levels. The combinatory effects of the building blocks exceeds the sum of each separate effect, e.g., one plus one equals more than two. Synergies amongst the troika enables development systems to provide customer offerings delivering advantages in cost and innovation simultaneously.

The composite model is illustrated by cases studies of development systems in services and goods companies. To the extent practices driving performance are similar in both sectors, a common development system may be used for generating value that transcends the putative divide between goods and services. Qualitative research suggests that the composite model is robust and capable of supporting simultaneous development of goods and services in holistic offerings.

2.1.1. *Organization: ESI*

The "O" in the troika deals with the organic structuring work. In mechanistic systems performing relatively standardized kinds of tasks, roles are delimited and specific to phases of an assembly-line sequence so that those responsible for delivery, such as manufacturing and/or customer service, are engaged only at the back end after crucial decisions have already been made. Mechanistic systems are best suited for efficiently designing and developing relatively standardized quantities of similar offerings. To develop innovative offerings, however, OTS, is needed for fostering creativity. In organic organizations, role responsibilities are enlarged so that communications cut across hierarchical lines of authority to enable cross-functional collaboration among diverse specialists along the value stream from concept to delivery.

Organic structures are reliant upon teams. Yet connotations of the word "team" vary enormously. Therefore, the spearhead of the composite model is a form of cross-functional teaming that proactively engages downstream functions, such as manufacturing and customer service, at the outset of development where the most consequential decisions are made affecting subsequent realization of customer value. Upstream engagement of downstream functions is only feasible on a platform of an OTS which entails the reorganization of work to foster collaboration among functions along the horizontal value stream at the base of the organization. ESI is a vector of influence partially countervailing the top-down authority of those at the apex of mechanistic hierarchies.

2.1.2. *Process: IDC*

The "P" in the troika deals with controls for structuring work activities. In mechanistic systems bureaucratically prescribed procedures are inviolate rules associated with cost efficiencies in stable, standardized operations. By contrast, controls in organic organizations are less detailed because functionally specific procedures inexactly apply to collaboration among diverse stakeholders performing complex, uncertain tasks. Whilst a *laissez-faire* approach unfetters constraints on innovative ideas, a disciplined focus is also needed for structuring development operations. Therefore, composite development systems refashion mechanistic procedures into processes providing cross-functional teams with flexible guidance. Development processes in composite systems entail emergent, ad hoc tailoring of knowledge to achieve dynamic objectives.

IDC melds the discipline of mechanistic controls with organic teaming to apply best-known development practices contingent upon the targeted characteristics of the project. Flexible processes are important for guiding development activities so that optimal methods are evaluated in terms of fitness for purpose. Instead of automatically prescribed standard procedures such as rigid stage-gates, cross-functional team members in composite development systems use enabling processes to shorten cycles and mitigate potentially costly risks by reusing knowledge about best practices along the entire value chain. The adaptive flexibility of IDC teams achieve purposive innovation cost-effectively.

2.1.3. *Tools: CIT*

The "T" in the troika stands for Tools and Technologies which are important for designing, developing, and delivering customer offerings. Information technology helps with the design and development of customer offerings as well as the transformation of inputs to outputs. Historically, most tools and technologies have been deployed in ways congruent with mechanistic systems, such as assembly-line types of operation. The advent of programmable automation, however, provides alternative choices. On the one hand, people in organic organizations may pioneer innovative capabilities of new tools and technologies with relatively few constraints. On the other hand, mental as well as physical value creation activities may be managed by computer programs serving as mechanistic substitutes for bureaucratic controls. For example, some corporations deploy product life cycle management systems to direct and monitor the activities of employees in product development much like assembly-line operatives.

In composite development systems, CIT is not only used for visualization of virtual prototypes, but also in operations throughout the entire life cycle for realizing values including manufacture, delivery, and service. In sum, CIT not only provides design capabilities, but also enables diverse functions to communicate electronically and processes to be continually adapted for targeted purposes. The synergistic effects of CIT enable more effective organizational teaming and continually updated processes. However, the competitive advantage offered by tools and technologies *per se* is often limited because of their declining price and widespread availability.

2.1.4. *The composite model: A synergistic troika of practices*

A prerequisite for the emergence of a composite model is an infusion of organic practices fostering horizontal collaboration in mechanistic bureaucracies, the structural backbone of industrial economies. The mechanistic vector is hierarchically organized in contrast to OTS which threads interpersonal relationships among people in diverse functions across hierarchical lines of authority. ESI builds interdependencies among functions along the horizontal value creation flow, from upstream development of the concept to the delivered customer offering. However, the organic vector is reliant on so-called "dotted-line" relationships powered by influence rather than direct authority. Melding these antithetical forms of organization design is analogous to attempting to mix oil and water as a stable solution. But it is precisely the synergistic benefits of this catalytic combination that provides the crux of competitive advantage for the composite model. The integration of two antithetical forms of enterprise design, the mechanistic and the organic, enables composite systems capabilities for developing customer offerings optimizing innovation as well as cost-effectiveness, thereby generating top line profits and bottom line savings simultaneously.

> High performance systems achieve more output per unit of input because of catalytic interactions exemplified in the composite model

2.2. Illustrations of the Model at Work

Case studies help us understand how development actually occurs in composite systems. Almost all the cases are selected from enterprises included in representative samples of goods and services quantitatively analyzed in subsequent chapters. The benefit of case studies is that we can more readily understand what practices enterprises deploy and how they relate to performance advantages.

Illustrative cases summarized below focus on three kinds of advantage of the composite model for differentiating customer offerings. *First,* the synergistic design of the composite model achieves cost-effective innovation by melding the discipline of flexible controls with the cross-fertilization of ideas for creativity. *Second,* up-front collaboration by diverse stakeholders throughout the value steam precludes defects adversely affecting customer experiences. *Third,* the robust capability of the model for developing both goods and/or services offers enterprises opportunities for integrating tangible and intangible assets in holistic offerings.

Each of the troika of components of the composite system of development operations is highlighted in one or more cases studies. Cases illustrations also show how the troika systemically interacts synergistically as a composite. An example from the goods sample is presented in parallel with one from the service sample. One objective is to show how concurrent practices operate by fostering purposive collaboration between up and downstream functions. Another objective is to illustrate the extent to which capabilities of the composite model have the potential for holistically integrating the development of goods services.

Each case is selected to illustrate not only how the composite model operates, but also the potential for simultaneously integrating goods and services in relatively more holistic offerings. The cases illustrate the model, but also their synergistic interactions as a composite:

2.2.1. *ESI case examples*

(A) *Goods*

A new product development group in an aerospace corporation included over 120 staff members but only a single representative from the manufacturing and service functions. The dominant coalition was engineering-centric with manufacturing and service issues largely considered after designs had been accepted by customers. The lack of strategic alignment among functional groups resulted in product designs being thrown over walls with little reciprocal interactions. The lack of concurrent engagement by down-stream functions increasingly became a business liability as the manufactured cost of their engines was amongst the highest in the industry largely because of late stage changes to the design. Similarly, their percentage of revenue from post-launch services was amongst the lowest among competitors. To improve performance, the corporation began beefing up attempts to enforce compliance with its stage-gate development procedures. Although the procedures specified input from downstream functions, authentic information was often lacking because of the detailed complexity of requirements for entering and exiting stage-gates. The corporation subsequently began investing millions in deploying a product life cycle management system attempting to capture downstream data for inclusion in engineering design decisions. However, the computer automated system was complex and lacking capabilities for capturing soft dimensions of experiences by downstream functions and customers. Subsequently additional steps were taken to better integrate the value stream. They added manufacturing engineers to the new development group to boost concurrent engagement in up-front design decisions. The bulk of employees responsible for services were relocated to a building across the street from the new development group to facilitate face-to-face exchanges at early development stages. The nascent transformation to relatively more concurrent development began to pay-in terms of reductions in late stage engineering changes and decreased disruptions to products in service.

(B) Services

A global bank focused on early collaborative team formation as an operational strategy for gaining a top position in syndicated banking. As soon as a potential opportunity was identified, a pre-concept team was formed. As a deal became eminent, a core team of collaborators was configured including representatives from all relevant functions required for overseeing execution and delivery. The top commitment of team members was to the project of designing and executing the syndicated financing instead of to their functional department heads. Many key players were collocated for the duration of the project. An agile matrix structure empowered cross-functional teams early-on to execute financial deals faster than competitors. The bank became so well regarded that it was among the very top choices globally for syndicated services.

2.2.2. IDC case examples

(A) Goods

The Stanley Works achieved a leadership position in its industry. A key practice was the formation of multi-functional core teams coupled with "discovery teams" tasked with visiting customer locations to observe how their products were used in actual practice. Based on observations by heterogeneous team members, as well as interview data, cross-functional product development groups designed new offerings to close gaps in observed customer needs. However, a structured process of continuous process improvement was needed for guiding exploitation of the wealth of up-front information garnered from the discovery teams. The Chief Technical Officer and the Global Product Development Director personally trained employees worldwide in a simple but flexible development process. Stanley complemented their people-centric approach with the discipline of flexible processes and analytical methods to achieve synergistic benefits from the composite model. Their prowess disrupted industry norms because their time to market decreased by nearly a third, sales from new product accelerated to over 10 percent per year, and margins increased by a quarter.[ii]

(B) Services

The benefit of structured processes has been well documented, particularly in financial enterprises where data is relatively objective and explicit. However, process may be even more important for development of intangible offerings because tacit knowledge is difficult to program and automate. Regardless, structured processes help developers define features using relatively more proven methods.

Employees in a world renowned financial services company underwent extensive training in development processes. Yet observation of a cross-functional team of nearly 50 people representing over 20 different functions revealed only modest observation of process discipline in developing a radically new customer offering. For example, a progressive proportion of meeting time was spent trying to get all participants on the same page, especially those who missed prior sessions. Their failure to deploy a structured process resulted in falling far behind schedule. To catchup, they belatedly adopted a technological quick fix to identify a solution. Unfortunately, the collective wisdom built up during prior team meetings was laid aside. Instead the corporation launched a technocratic offering which failed to be even remotely viable in the marketplace. Subsequent development projects salvaging facets of the original development project deployed flexible but disciplined processes to ensure that smaller but more focused cross-functional teams generated commercially viable options. Their ultimate achievement of most of the original projects objectives illustrates the potential synergies of ESI and IDC.

2.2.3. *CIT case examples*

(A) Goods

The wireless division of a major telecom corporation sought to devise a global process for coordinating design and manufacture across three continents. A multi-disciplinary team devised a global electronic development process termed WiSE (Wireless Simultaneous Engineering) which was made available on their intranet. Process coaches were employed by many development teams to ensure its proper utilization. Among a score of locations studied, however, one stood out well above the rest. One reason is because team members were encouraged to request adaptations to computerized process. Requests for improvement of the computerized development process were implemented almost immediately, often within two days. This strategic business unit rapidly evolved a somewhat customized version of the global standard termed PRIDE which was widely used by employees from design to manufacturing. By exploiting the adaptability of programs to continually improve processes, they achieved the highest rate of usability of any of the global locations due to synergies between CIT and IDC as well as with ESI. One reason is because they regarded PRIDE as an enabler of cross-functional teaming and continuously updated processes. By contrast, some other corporate business units attempted to force compliance with the standardized version of the process and monitor conformance. The business unit continually improving process based on team input developed product much faster and more profitably than any other in the global corporation.

(B) Services

A software provider, Intuit, is noted for customer empathy. This approach began when its founder, Steve Cook, followed customers home to observe how they used his software in actual practice. Today the corporation employs a bevy of researchers dedicated to understanding and improving customer experiences. Direct observation using anthropological field methods has been complemented by CIT. Examples include the use of sophisticated diagnostics of eye patterns from camera embedded in monitors to assess ease of customer use. Analysis of customer satisfaction data uses advanced modeling techniques. As a result, Intuit's customer centric value creation methods used by cross-functional teams up-front are credited for helping fuel consistent growth in revenues since its founding although increasingly augmented by structured processes and enabling tools/technologies.

2.2.4. *Composite model case illustrations*

(A) Goods

New management at a semiconductor manufacturer purposively implemented the composite model. Their initial goal was to reduce post-launch costs as well as develop new products. Prior to the adoption of concurrency, staff in the R&D lab created new kinds of machines which were usually purchased in advance of complete development because new features enticed early customers. The downside was that the rework required after initial shipment was often huge. The company got high marks from their customers for responsiveness, but at a significant cost post-launch. Often dozens of engineers and technical support staff went to the customer's fabrication site to get their machines up and running.

The enterprise pioneered concurrency during the development of a radically new product by collocating development and manufacturing from the outset. They engaged downstream functions up-front in *design for X* (e.g., manufacturability, serviceability, etc.) reviews. These review teams enabled many diverse functions to have input early in the development cycle, such as manufacturing, quality, install, service, and upgrade functions. The result was that the radical product developed in less than one half of the former time with relatively few defects.

Subsequently *design for X* scorecards were used ever further upstream at the research phase which resulted in 2/3rds reduction in cycle time, and in-process quality control so that most first builds were shipped with zero defects. They further disrupted their industry by leasing their new equipment with service support agreements at high margins.

> DFX helps employees focus on creating value throughout the development cycle so that everyone accepted collective responsibility for increasing customer value

Customer experiences in using the equipment in combination with its innovative technological advantages provided the corporation with an unprecedented competitive advantage because their equipment was designed from the outset to operate without breakdowns which enabled them to achieve high margins from follow-on services. The corporation exemplifies *design for value* which includes the total customer experience regardless of the mix of goods and/or services purchased.

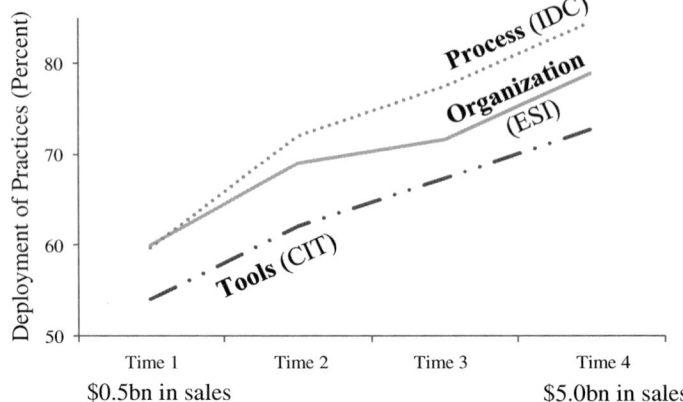

Figure 2.2. Deployment of Practices of the Composite Model (Semiconductor Manufacturer)

The deployment of the troika of practices dealing with Organization, Process, and Tools/Technologies was periodically benchmarked vs. Best-in-Class scores and systematically improved. Practices such as ESI, IDC, and CIT increased from a little over half the time to over three quarters of the time. This progressive increase in their use is shown in Figure 2.2.

As the percentage of time best practices were observed, synergistic benefits emerged among them. For example, a strong emphasis on a common development process was achieved because a cross-functional team drawn from the depth and breadth of the corporation was responsible for its development and continually improved it based on user input. Process was used to help bring disciplined cross-functional teaming at even the pre-concept phase in the research lab. Computer tools and technologies were regarded as enablers, not drivers of behavior. As a synergistic whole, the troika framework of concurrent practice provided specific actions for improvement orchestrated under an integrated umbrella of concurrent product development.

The enterprise introduced radically new product technologies, not only because they brainstormed for disruptive ideas in pre-concept meetings, but also because of their speed of development enabled them to make more rapid iterations. Profit margins from differentiated products were high and augmented by complementary service agreements because their equipment set new industry standards for reliability. A resulting indicator of performance gained from their transformation to a new business model based on concurrency is that organic growth resulted in doubling of capital value of the enterprise during a 5-year period from approximately half a billion dollars to reach a sale price of 5 billion.[iii]

> Systematic deployment of concurrent methods enabled the enterprise to rapidly innovate and raise industry standards in first build reliability

(B) Services

Chase retail bank benchmarked industrial firms to explore new ways of improving. They found that responsibility for product development was entrusted to specialists instead of diffused to those managing the businesses on a daily basis. They decided to emulate industrial practice and appointed a vice president (VP) for product development to head up a cross-functional group.

They explicitly adopted the composite model and had university faculty assist their cross-functional team develop a user friendly process to ensure a disciplined, but flexible approach to creating customer offerings. The creation of a formal process codified know-how that had formerly been implicit. This made product development more patent to all functions engaged in it, especially those outside of the group. Ultimately, the process was deployed on a shared drive with templates for customization.

The cross-functional group was relatively successful in building user friendly offerings for customers. However, they became even better after a failure to make tax filing information about a new product readily transparent to customers. Swamped telephone lines to customer services resulted in a spate of lost accounts. Afterwards, the VP of product development said she would never form another development team without including representation from the customer service department.

Chase also built capabilities for information technology and exploited them. They exploited various forms of knowledge technology to benchmark and analyze competitive trends. Sophisticated algorithms were developed for evaluating the cost/benefit of new offerings, etc. Communications among development team members was augmented by protocols and templates. Processes were distributed to all with opportunities for feedback and continual improvement. The deployment of the troika of building blocks of the composite model is summarized below.

The Evolution of New Service Development (NSD) at Chase Bank	
NSD Function	After benchmarking with industrial firms, Chase decided that the people developing new products should be different from those managing them on a daily basis. A VP of product development was appointed to ensure that no one function dominated, such as marketing over information technology, or vice versa.
Organization	Initially, the product development group comprised a handful of people. Over time, the composition of members on product development teams became increasingly cross-functional. Once the needs of development projects were known, the VP of product development recruited loaners from the required functions to populate the teams with appropriate representatives. The teams were a mix of full-time staff and part-timers. As operations matured, multifunctional involvement tended to occur at earlier stages. Key members were often physically collocated for important projects.
Process	The process of product development was initially an implicit one. Stages of development were generally understood by those in the development group, but were unwritten. Subsequently, the tacit knowledge of how to execute the process of product development was mapped. The new process included templates for customization with entry and exit criteria for each stage. It was made available to participants in all development teams on line.
Tools	Model product development templates were made available on a shared drive. The group increasingly used decision-support models and the web for information searches.

Once the New product development team was assembled, they generated a pipeline of new services, e.g., a revamped checking and savings line-up, online banking, debits cards, foreign currency innovations, and integrating mutual funds with their deposit offers. The bank subsequently enjoyed a reputation for generating attractive offerings as well as providing the best customer experiences in the New York area which was advertised by the tag line, "the right relationship is everything".

2.3. The Axiomatic Logic behind Concurrent Systems

Systems have emergent properties arising from interactions among its component parts. In integrated systems, benefits from the whole may exceed the sum of individual components. A "reciprocal" mode of interdependence enables systems to achieve relatively high levels of integration.[iv] The greater the level of reciprocal feedback among system components, the greater capabilities are likely to be for achieving synergies.

In concurrent development systems, synergistic capabilities emerge from reciprocal feedback among the trio of core practices comprising the composite model. Interactions among practices drawn from the domains of organization, process, and tools/technologies resonate with one another so as to optimize performance capabilities. The composite model is somewhat analogous to the molecular structure of a complex compound. As illustrated in case examples, mutually reinforcing relationships within the troika are capable of achieving high levels of multiple kinds of performance benefit simultaneously.

The notion of reciprocity is illustrated in concurrent systems by the mutual responsiveness of stakeholders to one another throughout the value stream. All stakeholders are simultaneously involved in product development decisions throughout the life cycle starting at the outset where opportunities for innovation are greatest. The entire value stream is reciprocally integrated — from idea to customer and back. Such cross-functional integration helps ensure that provisional decisions based on imperfect information at the concept phase are optimized as rapidly as possible during repeated cycles of collaboration. The system is agile and adaptive. Concurrency minimizes the downstream consequences of faulty decisions and compresses time to market, which reduces opportunity costs.

The logic behind the design of concurrent development systems is largely a rationale response to the benefit/costs from achieving greater levels of system integration. The logic behind concurrency is derived from a managerial wisdom built upon a wide variety of managerial experiences and

> The rationale driving the advantages of concurrent collaboration among diverse functions is compelling, easy to verbalize, but difficult to implement in bureaucratic hierarchies

analytical studies by academicians. Five axioms provide most of the logic underpinning concurrent systems. These axioms have broad applicability to managerial systems and are fairly widely known by practitioners of quality management, lean, and other kinds of managerial interventions to improve performance. Although easy to understand, these axioms are difficult to implement because cross-functional teaming is an unnatural act in large-scale bureaucratic corporations.

2.3.1. *Committed costs*

Concurrency places particular emphasis on up-front collaboration amongst multiple stakeholders along the value development stream. The gist of the first and most critical axiom is that early development decisions are inordinately more important than later ones.

Axiom #1
The bulk of financial and opportunity costs are typically committed at early steps of a development cycle even though not expended until later.

A kind of truism is that the more money being spent, the greater attention management pays to operations. Ironically, managerial attention after the conceptualization of development often yields only marginal utility. A key reason why concurrent practices are so predictive of performance is that relatively more of the best managers are engaged at the front-end where the great bulk of costs and options for innovative opportunities are determined. For example, 3M studied 54 projects and found that those with the greatest profitability were over managed at the front relative to the back-end of the development cycle and especially if attention was paid to the soft, tacit dimensions of knowledge that were difficult to quantify.

This axiom justifying up-front engagement is illustrated in Figure 2.3 for five stages of a typical development cycle: (1) Exploration; (2) Definition of the product concept; (3) Development and testing; (4) Test marketing and final release; (5) Ramp to volume sales. The bulk of costs are committed in many projects far prior to the commercial interface before much actual development begins. The area indicating committed costs under the inverse log curve at the left is much greater than on the right side.

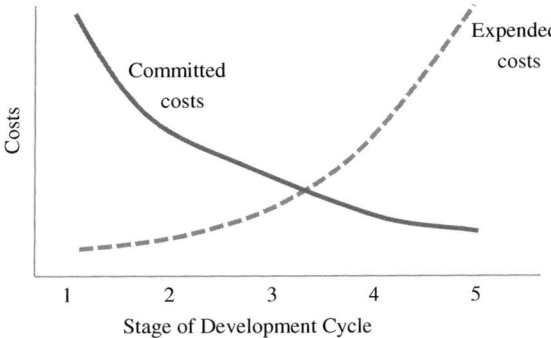

Figure 2.3.   Committed vs. Expended Costs

2.3.2. *Cost of change*

ESI, the cornerstone of the composite model, involves heterogeneous functions upstream to ensure ideas are cross-fertilized for optimizing product designs. One objective is to preclude late stage defects. Another is to generate the most innovative options prior to agreement on the design of the offering because once development commences the cost of change increases exponentially as cited in Axiom #2. The organized creativity of people, however, benefits from synergies with disciplined but flexible processes (i.e., IDC) as costs need to be calculated to the extent possible up-front because expenses rise rapidly over the life cycle. Tools and technologies (i.e., CIT) may be used to optimize designs, support asynchronous communications, and facilitate the use of dynamic processes in product development.

> **Axiom #2**
> The cost of fixing faulty upstream decisions at late stages is often exponentially greater than at earlier ones.

The downstream consequences of early decisions mean that serial deployment of role specialists along the value chain may miss upstream opportunities. Stakeholders at downstream stages need to be involved nearer the outset as their capability of preventing problems diminishes over the cycle. The drawback is that information is fuzzy at the front-end and definitive decisions are difficult to make. However, inserting the voice of the customer

> Proverbial saying: An ounce of prevention is worth a pound of cure

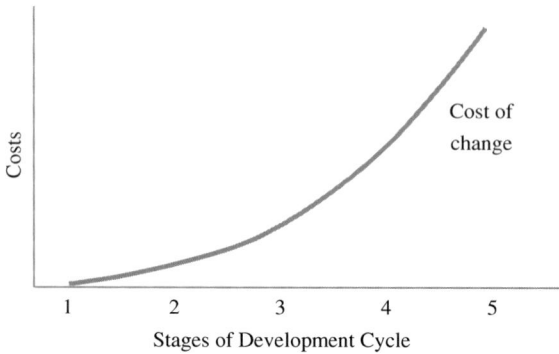

Figure 2.4.   **Rising Cost of Late Stage Changes**

into system-wide decisions at early steps is vital for minimizing late stage surprises. Over the cycle of development, heterogeneous specialists have a role. Only by systematically aligning their inputs from those dealing with customer needs can probabilities be increased that requirements will be met without late stage changes.

This axiom on the exponential rise in costs of downstream changes is illustrated in Figure 2.4. for five stages. The farther the product development cycles has progressed, the more expensive changes may become at an exponentially increasing rate. As suggested in Figure 2.4, preventing problems is far cheaper than fixing them.

To prevent problems from occurring, enterprises need to institutionalize continual learning. Processes for reusing knowledge from previous development projects for transfer to next generation initiatives reduces defects. Constant reviews of product development projects are necessary processes for capturing lessons learned. Continuous improvement occurs by building upon existing knowledge bases to reach ever-higher targets.

The cost of poor quality can be quite high even if difficult to quantify. However, calculations should include opportunity as well as actuarial costs of waste. Faulty upstream decision that necessitates changing commitments to customers is often risky.

The applicability of this axiom to services, varies across different businesses. Not all costs of change increase exponentially. The drawbacks of dealing with inventory pile-ups and reworking, common in goods industries, are less likely to occur in many services. For example, sometimes test marketing services may be attenuated or foregone, especially for intangible products. Unless the risk of losing customers is high, some services can simply be launched directly in the marketplace.

2.3.3. *Cross-functional teams*

The composite model is designed to develop fairly complex customer offerings at relatively low cost. A presumption underlying this axiom is that the development is not a simple standardized one amenable to serial, assembly-line methods. Heterogeneous input is needed at the front-end where the bulk of innovative opportunities and costs are determined. Cross-functional teams are commonly used in many enterprises. However, problems only arise if appropriate stakeholders are engaged at late instead of early phases of the development cycle.

Axiom #3

Cross-functional teams typically provide a better quality solution to complex, dynamic product development problems than solo individuals — especially at early phases of the development cycle.

This axiom is illustrated in Figure 2.5. for five stages. In early simultaneous product development, investment of time and money at the front-end pays off in cycles that are progressively speedier at end stages where cost and risks are high. By contrast, serial product development is often quick at the start, but snarled by many subsequent delays. Even

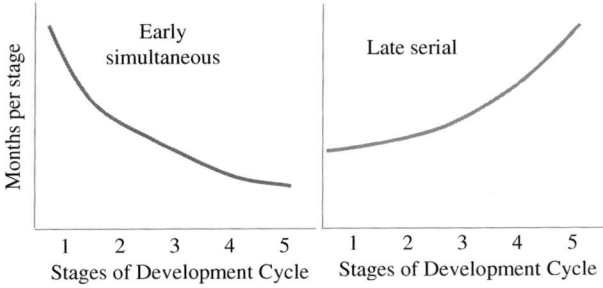

Figure 2.5.   Development Speed: Early vs. Late Influence

minor changes are best handled at the earliest stage, although the extent of teaming needed subsequently may be relatively low as the information for front-end decisions is relatively less complex. Regardless, the total area indicating time spent is smaller under the curve on the left rather than right side because concurrency is practiced. Importantly, the area on the right represents the latter phases of the development cycle when expended costs are comparatively greater than during earlier phases.

One reason the slope of involvement by latecomers is exponentially upward is because lack of early input may result in the addition of people to fix problems after suboptimal decisions were made. In many instances, dealing with faulty decisions up-front may precipitate an avalanche of problems which delay development and include significant extra expenses.

Postmortem analyses of real life projects show that time and money was almost invariably greater if the cross-functional team were formed late. For example, a quasi-experiment were conducted for executives at a conference on product development in San Diego sponsored by CALS, a US government organization to help promote the use of computers in industry. Participants from approximately 150 companies were asked to compare two projects in their direct line of experience. Project A was selected for successful outcomes, Project B unsuccessful outcomes. Respondents were asked to distribute the resources of people, time, and money for each project at three stages. The overwhelming majority of successful outcomes were resourced up-front rather than at later stages.

2.3.4. *Radicalness*

Axiom #4

Semi-autonomous cross-functional teams typically provide a better quality solution to complex, dynamic product development problems than solo individuals — especially under the contingency of radicalness.

The extent to which heterogeneous cross-functional teams are needed is partly a function of the extent to which the offering under development is complex with innovative features. The more radical the offering under

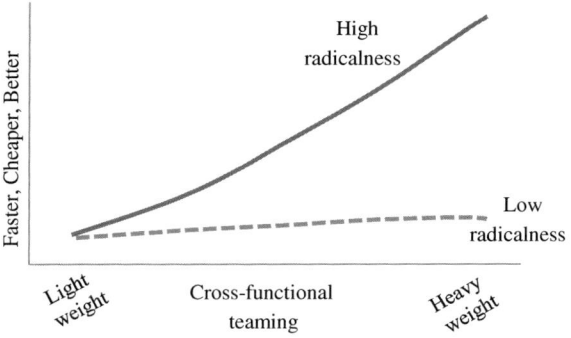

Figure 2.6. Level of Complexity/Radicalness

development, the more likely heterogeneous teams engaged up-front are needed for developing novel features.

This axiom is illustrated in Figure 2.6. To the extent development objectives involve radically new targets; cross-functional teams need to be relatively more heterogeneous and empowered. Visualizing this contrast is aided by comparing of two types of cross-functional teams. "Heavyweight" teams are empowered to make product development decisions and are led by relatively high level executives from the outset of the development project.[v] Heavyweight teams are best for novel, complex product development projects in contrast to "lightweight" teams where liaison staff can coordinate relatively minor improvements even though they have relatively low power over members from diverse departments.

If the offering under development is radical, the extent of crossfunctional teaming sharply boosts the upward slope indicating performance outcomes such as time compression, cost reduction, and quality. By contrast, the benefit of cross-functional teaming is less if the development involves little radicalness and does not require heavyweight team.

2.3.5. *Late to market*

Speed of development is associated with performance in some interesting ways. Some assume that the greater amount of time spent in development, the higher the level of innovation is likely to be. However, compressed schedules may actually stimulate innovation if heterogeneous teams are formed up-front as suggested in Axiom #4. For example, a study of a sample of 120 US R&D labs showed that the comparatively short development cycles were associated with a higher rate of issue of pioneering patents.[vi] Schedule is a constraint that may stimulate creativity in searching for solutions associated with what Jack Welch termed "time driven quality". Moreover, rapidly executed projects save money and free up resources for exploratory activities. For radical development, synergistically coupling collaborative teams up with disciplined but flexible processes that often helps achieve cost-effective innovation.

Axiom #5

The opportunity costs of being late to market are often very high, such as less market share and lower margins.

To achieve high levels of innovation, systems need to have communication channels open to all functions and ranks in the organization. Staff needs to be encouraged to engage in holistic, system-wide thinking as well as the pursuit of specialized knowledge. Knowledge must be viewed as a paramount competitive advantage to be gained from outside as well as inside the company.

This axiom is illustrated in Figure 2.7. It is based on studies of electronics industries. Followers in this market fight for a third of the remaining market. Moreover they have only one-sixth of the opportunity for profit margins. To achieve early market advantages, leaders must increasingly offer customers a portfolio of advantages, including both

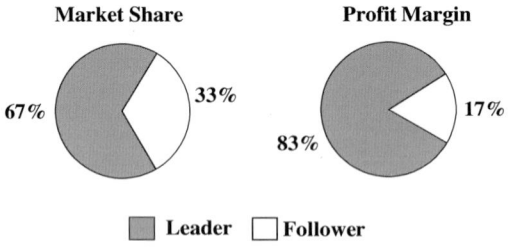

Figure 2.7.   Opportunity Costs of Being Late to Market

innovation and low cost. Moore's Law provides the foundation on which this axiom is based, twice the performance at half the cost every 1.5 years. This is a brutal combination of novelty, time, and cost.

Although this axiom is based on electronics, it is also applicable to several kinds of business beyond the chip industry. One reason is because revolutionary advances in computer technologies have stimulated many innovations in goods and services derived from the increasing speed and capabilities of chips at ever lower prices. Communications, e-transactions, electronic imaging, programmed trades are among the numerous applications built upon advances in the chip industry that cut across both goods and services.

The effects of electronics on service marketplaces are often indirect. For example, service delivery times have speeded up dramatically in many businesses. Because service innovations are often easy to copycat, making successive improvements may help sustain initial competitive advantages. This strategy is similar to that deployed by many electronics industries that maintain their prime mover advantage by successive innovations protected as trade secrets rather than by patents. Of course there are always situations in which a rapid follower strategy makes sense. But for many fast-paced service markets, rapidly evolving trends make followership less profitable an option.

First mover advantages are not unique to the chip industry. Consumer brand names such as Kleenex, Q-tips, Swiffer, and others have enjoyed long lasting market advantages from pioneering beachheads. Many companies have established new kinds of services that enjoy a halo effect which instills company loyalty, such as American Express, Vanguard Funds, Home Depot, etc.

2.4. Conclusions

These five axioms provide a springboard for thinking about the logical underpinnings of the business systems we design and operate to create value for customers. They provide a foundation for the TVD framework which comprises a myriad of

> Thinking axiomatically cuts the clutter and fosters creative thinking about how to design and exploit the advantages of an innovative business model

practices for capturing the benefits prescribed by the axioms. In the next chapter, images of concurrency systems in operation are provided which are derived from the logic embedded in these axioms.

Notes

[i]   Burns, T. and Stalker, G. M. 1961. *The Management of Innovation*, London: Tavistock.

[ii]   Hill, W. and Kardas, J. 2009. *Product Innovation Strategies*, Paper presented at the Society of Concurrent Product Development, Michigan State University: Michigan, June.

[iii] Rosen, G. 2013. *Transformation at Varian Semiconductor, Conference on Innovation & Productivity Pay-off from Enduring Best Practices of Concurrency*, NASA Ames: Mountain View, November 6–8.

[iv]   Thompson, J. 1967. *Organizations in Action*, McGraw-Hill: New York; Van de Ven, A. H. and Ferry, D. L. 1976. *Measuring and Assessing Organizations*, Wiley: New York.

[v]   Clark, K. B., Wheelwright, S. C. 1992. Organizing and Leading 'Heavyweight' Development Teams, *California Management Review*, 34, 3, 9–28.

[vi]   Hull, F. 1993. *Idea Generation and Commercialization in R&D Laboratory Organizations*, Stevens Institute of Technology: Hoboken.

CHAPTER THREE

ENVISIONING CONCURRENT DEVELOPMENT SYSTEMS

Overview

This chapter provides the reader with a vision of how high performance development systems operate in actual practice. This perspective of high performance development systems is built upon the axioms underlying the composite model and expands upon its core practices. Ten graphic images depict facets of concurrent systems in operation. Although holistic systems are difficult to depict, these images provide a suggestive collage, a pastiche of disparate perspectives of concurrent systems. Pictures are worth lots[j] of words and stimulate our imagination. The objective is to help envision concurrent product development as a "system" of interrelated practices. Readers are encouraged to apply the concept depicted in the image to their own enterprises. A list of ways of rethinking the development system of your enterprise is provided. This chapter is supplemented by a workbook enabling readers to benchmark development practices in their enterprise against Best-in-Class standards associated with each of the 10 images. These images of best practices may help in envisioning improved system capabilities for Total Value Development (TVD).

3.1. Envisioning a High-Performance System

This chapter provides the reader with a vision of how high performance concurrent NSD (New Service Development) systems operate. The approach is derived from Peter Senge's work on stimulating change through creative tension between "should be" vs. "as is" system states. Envisioning is the first step in transforming an enterprise to a higher level of capability. A good vision must be one which inspires people in an enterprise to strive to improve.

Total Value Development (TVD) relies on re-architecting new and existing features to generate distinctive value propositions. How development systems are operated affects the likelihood of generating compelling value propositions as well as capabilities for executing them. The crux of TVD is systems thinking from inputs to throughputs to outputs. Senge suggests several ways for jogging our thinking about how systems operate as well as ways of leading their

> Envisioning a better business model for creating value requires leaps in our imagination. This is fostered by heterogeneous stakeholders collaborating to design new systems transcending extant problems and achieving new capabilities

transformation. The following list may help stimulate thinking about innovative combinations of behavior and features in customer offerings as well as capabilities of development operations:

1. See leaps of abstraction.
2. Balance inquiry and advocacy.
3. Distinguish espoused theory from theory in use.
4. Recognize and defuse defensive routines.
5. See interrelationships, not things; processes, not snapshots.
6. Move beyond blame.
7. Distinguish detail complexity from dynamic complexity.
8. Focus on areas of high leverage.
9. Avoid symptomatic solutions.

3.2. Images of Concurrent Systems

Ten images are used to profile high-performance systems (see Figures 3.1–3.10). These images were initially intended to stimulate thinking about how to deploy concurrent engineering (CE) practices. They were co-created in collaboration with participants in concurrent product development user groups in industries formed to exploit learnings from the studies of goods enterprises reported herein. The goal was to profile how concurrent systems look in action. These images helped companies coalesce around a common framework for deploying best practices. Members of the group who helped draw the images vouched for their face validity. Follow-on studies provided additional validation of the associations between image and performance.

Two images are contrasted, the "do be" vs. the "don't be". One image depicts behavior practices positively associated with successful development; the other is an opposite contrast. The goal is to enhance TVD and stimulate our thinking about how to leverage such development system capabilities for business model innovation.

The facets of development systems depicted are sufficiently generic for application to the envelopment of new services even though created for the development of products. The images may be used as a kind of Rorschach exercise for stimulating our imagination about the design of development systems. Readers are encouraged to interpret the images and how they relate to systems in "as is" states with which they are familiar. The objective is to think about a "should be" state for your system capabilities that may enable your enterprises to achieve higher levels of performance capability.

> Because images only capture facets of reality, they are best exploited by using them as a springboard for imagining how to design more effective systems

Use the TVD framework to imagine new kinds of business possibilities for increasing the value your enterprise bring to customer offerings. Stakeholders from up and downstream functions may be better collaborators throughout the development stream. Holistic offerings integrating services and goods may be co-developed. Your development system will be more agile and able to deliver more innovative offerings faster and cheaper.

3.2.1. *Involve multiple functions throughout*

Downstream functions (e.g., manufacturing, service delivery, customer service) are involved at early steps without dominating the idea sandbox. Upstream functions, such as R&D, continue their involvement downstream.

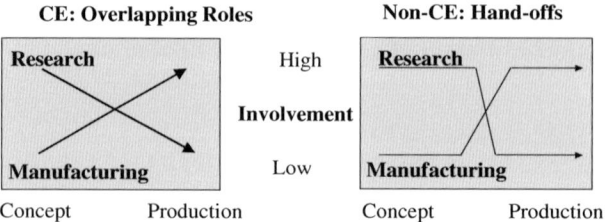

Figure 3.1.   Involve Multiple Functions Throughout

All functions are collectively responsible as a cross-functional team for total life cycle outcomes.

Concurrent:	Downstream functions participate in upstream design decisions. Upstream functions are involved with the downstream impact of decisions.
Non-Concurrent:	Product developers throw their new designs over the wall to those responsible for transforming them for delivery to customers. Developers disconnect to work on a new product, leaving others responsible for customer outcomes.

This diagram depicts the essence of concurrent methods for developing new products and services. Since most of the product design is committed early in the development cycle, it is essential to involve downstream functions from the outset. In goods industries, this typically is the manufacturing function. To wait to find out that the product design is difficult to manufacture until it is handed-off to production may entail expensive retooling and/or costly defects that are far more burdensome to fix at end rather than at beginning stages.

Upstream functions must also be involved at downstream stages to better understand the consequences of their design. In effect, both research and product development take on life cycle responsibilities for the product so that up and downstream functions are co-involved at all stages even though the proportion of responsibility shifts. By contrast, non-concurrent systems enact serial hand-offs among functions.

Black & Decker (B&D) adopted more concurrent product development practices after benchmarking against Panasonic. B&D was faster at the initial stage of development than Panasonic, but progressively slower at every subsequent one. The reason? Panasonic built holistic cross-functional teams from the outset of development. In response, B&D created "fusion cells", dedicated spaces for collocated cross-functional teams taking responsibility for the product design throughout its life cycle.

In services, the analog to the production function are people responsible for developing delivery processes and supporting the offering after sale, such as customer service staff. Chase retail bank always includes customer service staff on development projects starting at early stages. The consequences of failing to do so can be costly, such as selling a financial product that is difficult for customers to understand, especially at the time tax returns need to be filed.

3.2.2. *Balance portfolio of advantages*

Product designs fulfilling total customer requirements usually need to balance competing demands. Often innovative products are redesigned rapidly to achieve high quality standards at costs optimized for exactly fulfilling customer requirements.

Concurrent:	Concurrent strategy balances radicalness and cost reduction, achieving relatively high levels of both. Novelty and cost reductions are simultaneously achieved in conformance with customer requirements, often by rapid, reiterative improvements of existing products.
Non-Concurrent:	Performance features lack optimization if innovative features are are emphasized relative to other criteria, such as cost. This results in out of boundary conditions not only for meeting customer requirements, but also for sustaining competitive advantage.

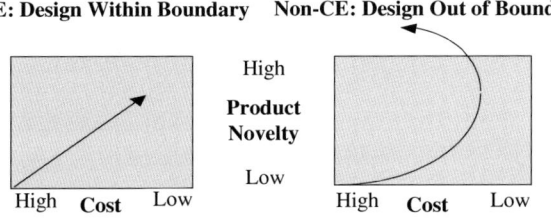

Figure 3.2.   Balanced Portfolio of Advantages

Two generic competitive advantages are cost and innovation. Yet, overengineering is common so that designers of services and goods often add features so that the costs spin out of bounds. A wide variety of products include features for which customers are unwilling to pay more to purchase, e.g., Motorola's high-end cell phones loaded with seldom-used capabilities, Ford models in early 2000 which included standard features for which customers were unwilling to pay more. Many service enterprises add features which add little value for customers and may even dilute the focus of the offering.

To compete under the conditions of Moore's law[ii] which cascades from computer chips to many kinds of business enterprise, both innovation and cost advantages must be developed simultaneously. The law also specifies time compression, a key benefit of concurrent systems which is not only a driver of cost reduction, but also associated with quality and innovation. Hewlett-Packard sums up the trade-off dilemma nicely. Quality is at the untouchable center of objectives. So, how to make trade-offs between time/cost on the one hand and innovation on the other hand has become all but impossible. Similarly, leading service companies, such as American Express, have increasingly found ways to offer their premium services at lower costs through cross-functional teaming, improved processes, and advanced computer information systems.

The need to achieve both competitive advantages simultaneously drives the melding of antithetically different types of system into synergistic hybrids. Hybrids are capable of achieving both kinds of generic performance advantages, innovation and low cost, simultaneously.[iii] The composite model explains the how refashioned practices, such as "process" instead of "standard operating procedures" and purposive cross-functional teams instead of "managers getting out of the way of creativity" have made hybrids possible. A growing body of evidence demonstrating interaction effects in multiple regression analysis shows that concurrent systems are much more likely to achieve both generic competitive advantages in cost and innovation simultaneously than known alternatives, not only in goods[iv] but also in services.[v]

3.2.3. *Focus on customer needs*

Customer requirements provide the focus for design activities. An authentic focus on customer needs resolves conflicts among competing performance criteria and political interests within the business and between its internal operations and external partners. Impersonal, non-political methods of identifying customer requirements and translating them into realizable specifications are employed routinely, e.g., Quality Function Deployment (QFD) by cross-functional teams.

Concurrent:	Customer requirements provide a unifying force for integrating diverse perspectives, e.g., managers and non-managers, upstream functions such as product design and downstream functions such as manufacturing engineering or customer service.
Non-Concurrent:	Customer requirements are identified, defined, and maintained by one power center to the relative exclusion of others. Developers define customer needs under the direction of top management without collaborating sufficiently with downstream functions, such as manufacturing, suppliers, customer service staff, and customer input.

The first maxim of quality management, the foundation upon which concurrency is built, is customer focus. Too often, managerial biases

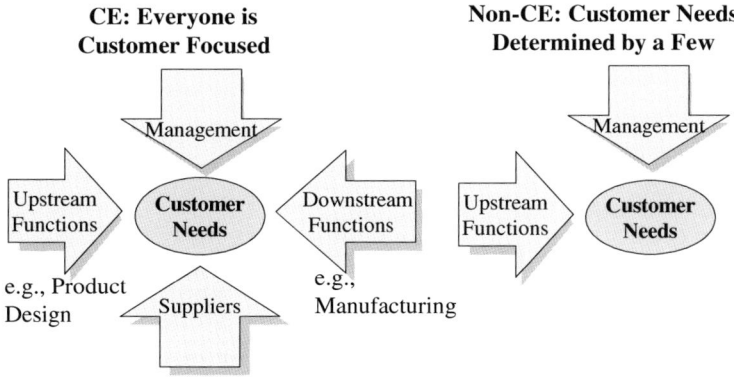

Figure 3.3.   Focus on Customer Needs

drown the voice of the customer. For example, a division of the Siemens Corporation lost a third of its market share in 5 weeks for failing to listen to the voice of the customer. What happened? With the permission of top management, the R&D group built a cross-functional team to conduct QFD for a new product. Management praised the team's presentation and process, but said somehow they had missed what the customer really wanted. So, they voted the new product proposal down. Within 2 months, their leading competitor launched a new product that closely matched features identified by the QFD.

Getting the voice of the customer right and focusing on meeting their needs requires input from external as well as internal functions. For example, in their heyday, Sun Microsystems and Chrysler were the benchmarks in their industries because they involved their suppliers early in the development process and sought their input on how to best meet customer needs from the outset of their development programs.

3.2.4. *Map processes and continuously improve*

Benchmarking of best of breed companies is done to set targets for improved performance and practice. Process maps are used to identify gaps between intended ways of work and how it is actually done. Realistic objectives are set for closing gaps. Once targets have been reached, lessons learned are collected for reuse. The process is repeated to achieve higher standards. Employees are encouraged to continually seek challenging opportunities so that improvement becomes institutionalized as a way of life.

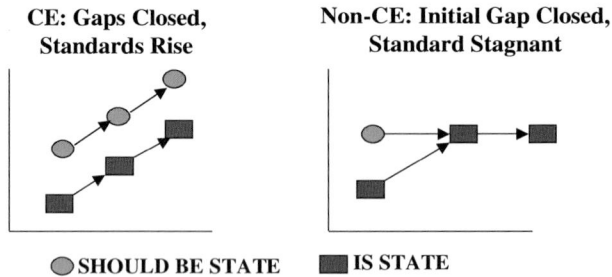

Figure 3.4.   Map Processes and Continuously Improve

Concurrent:	Process maps are used to identify gaps between AS IS and SHOULD BE states in development activities. Change is implemented to close gaps, lessons learned are collected for reuse and the process is repeated.
Non-Concurrent:	Once a gap is closed, the enterprise settles back into a complacent, steady state. Standards are not raised except in response to external threat so that improvement is discontinuous.

Complacency, if not arrogance, is the Achilles heel of successful companies. Books on business strategy abound with cases where market leaders fail to reconnoiter their environments and get unexpectedly whacked. External benchmarking and continuous improvement in product and services is increasingly a strategic necessity for survival in a growing number of markets. In the words of Rick Martin, a VP at Lockheed Martin, the goal of a strategy of rapid, continuous improvement is to never have to "play catch-up again".

To reach new heights, internal processes must also be benchmarked and continually improved. Process mapping is a key tool for reducing unnecessary hand-offs so that serial steps in product development are minimized. Mapping is a necessary, but insufficient cause of continuous improvement. The "reengineering" fad did almost as much damage as good. One reason is that external consultants wrote new processes for computerization in one-shot deals without engaging the people actually doing the work. Stakeholders in product development should not only do their own mapping, but also take responsibility for maintaining and continually improving the system.

When practices are too loose, introducing standardized processes generally improves performance initially. For example, Xerox mandated detailed procedures for development in restrained them from launching products lacking "technological readiness". However, projects vary and development processes can always be simplified and improved. Without a process for continually improving product development systems, people work-around the mandates and check boxes without due diligence either because the work was undone or because the requirement should not have been imposed in the first place. Often opportunities for innovative improvements in development systems are lost because team members are reluctant to reveal workaround practices they used to the next generation team, let alone the guardians of the product development system.

3.2.5. *Open communication channels*

Product design is determined through an open communication process, including external partners. The complete chain of activities necessary to generate ideas for product design and modify them is based on all channel feedback from the environment and incorporated into total life cycle decision-making.

Concurrent:	All channel communication within the organization and to a large extent with external organizations, such as suppliers and other partners.
Non-Concurrent:	Communications within the internal system are hierarchical and largely closed to influence by external organizations.

A familiar response to most business failures is, "Communications, we needed better communications!" But barriers to communications never go away permanently. The number of possible communicating pairs rises exponentially, from 1 for a single pair, to 4 for a trio, etc. The larger the size of the corporation, the greater the number of divisions and departments becomes. The upstream departments that originate work for those downstream tend to have relatively more closed doors. For example, the design group in Corporation X called their R&D lab to ask when the new product features would be specified. The response was true Hollywood, "don't call us, we'll call you".

So, communications need to be funneled by a strategic process that is focused on the customer. Processes should reduce the need for unnecessary face-to-face communications by helping manage routine information.

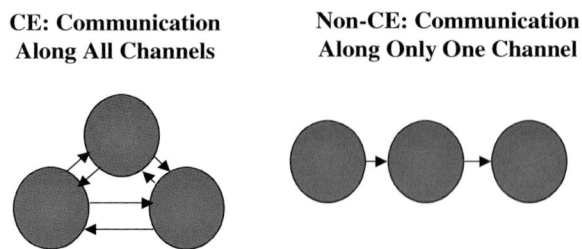

CE: Communication   **Non-CE: Communication**
Along All Channels   **Along Only One Channel**

Figure 3.5.   Open Communication Channels

Cross-functional teams need to be built before the conversations have to deal with problem-solving instead of problem-preventing and assessing new opportunities. Computer-based communications and telecommuting need to augment face-to-face contact, but never replace it entirely. The travel costs to bring people together to fix problems is so much easier for most development projects to justify that building interpersonal relationships in face-to-face meetings from the outset.

3.2.6. *Decide early, with reiterative feedback*

Cross-functional teams are responsible for making front-loaded, reiterative decisions in conjunction with other teams in the value chain. They base these decisions on the total product life cycle requirements for realizing customer satisfaction.

Concurrent:	Decision-making is dense and multi-functional up-front. Initial decisions are rapidly reiterated in narrowing feedback loops as the design progresses toward commercialization within boundary conditions.
Non-Concurrent:	Decision-making by fiat fails to adequately include diverse viewpoints, resulting in an inadequate design. The decision is not iterated until mid-or late-stage problems occur.

A conventional wisdom of the 1980s and early 1990s, when US firms began to address their lack of competitiveness, was that killing projects

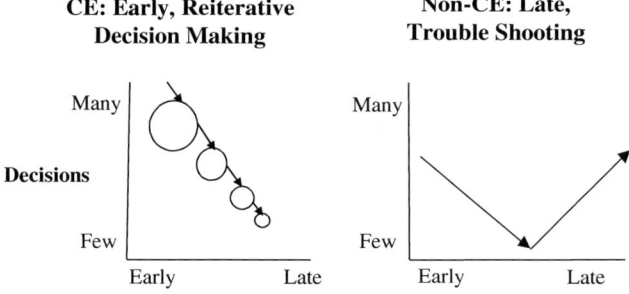

Figure 3.6. Decide Early, with Reiterative Feedback

is as important as starting them. Even today, almost all companies have too many projects in their pipeline, resulting in disconnects and urgent changes in assignment. Continual tracking of projects is a best practice. For example, Ford Alpha simultaneous engineering, which bet that most improvements to the Ford car could be made by improving development processes instead of focusing on designing car features, checked project costs weekly. Those over cost estimates without a solid recovery plan were discontinued, especially if the gaps against budget were not narrowing.

Tracking at the outset of projects is especially critical in companies with tall silos. For example, the head of a large R&D lab proudly said, "When we get something really good, we keep it secret as long as we can and back it with as many resources as we can afford so that it can fight back when it shows up on the radar screen". Approaches to ramming products through the gauntlet help explain the contrasting patterns in Figure 3.6. Companies practicing serial development often encounter delays at the middle point of cycles. Companies practicing concurrency spend a lot of time up-front building cross-functional consensus, and then accelerate progressively faster at subsequent phases.

Project tracking needs to be enabled by a concurrent design review process that involves not only top management, but also other stakeholders from the outset. For project tracking to work properly, all stakeholders must also own the product development process and its continual improvement. Otherwise, the development team hides or downplays adverse information and sometimes even falsifies it. This is especially true for stage-gate approaches that review every project with equal rigor at every phase. This hinders rather than enhances what should be an enabling process.

An alternative way of visualizing this process is as a so-called "golden gate bridge". Project teams face high hurdlers to get the concept approved at the tower before the main body of the suspension. But then they are semi-autonomously empowered to race to the other suspension tower for another high-hurdle review. What is the logic behind this? Most costs are committed before reaching the main span of the suspension while the cost of correcting defects is greatest after exiting the far-side tower.

3.2.7. *Hire and develop ambidextrous capabilities*

Specialists are trained to work not only in depth within their subject matter expertise, but also as generalists able to integrate and balance disparate kinds of thinking e.g., creative fuzzy logic vs. sequential logic. Hiring decisions and team staffing are based on diverse criteria to foster ambidextrous capabilities.

Concurrent:	In-depth specialists are often trained to think simultaneously in generalist, holistic terms and/or are teamed to work with those providing these complementary capabilities.
Non-Concurrent:	Functional specialists make serial decisions, step-by-step, which are inadequately framed by holistic requirements of the strategic business system. A typical problem is that the specialists make decisions piecemeal without general context.

Specialization has been the key factor in achieving the productivity gains large-scale machine bureaucracies achieved over earlier craft organization. For example, in 1776, Adam Smith's *Wealth of Nations* argued that specialization of labor in factories resulted in a 40-fold increase in productivity in pin making. Fredrick Taylor's scientific management and Ford's assembly lines raised productivity levels even higher. But with the growth in knowledge complexity and accelerating rate of change, products are no longer as simple as pins or even model T automobiles. A specialist often

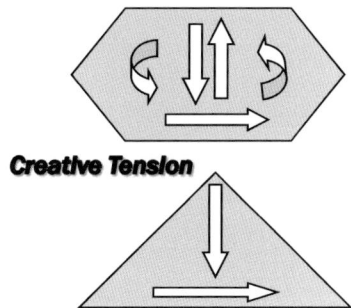

Creative Tension

Figure 3.7.   Hire and Develop Ambidextrous Capabilities

cannot know all and must team with others to search for optimal rather than perfect solutions, especially under the conditions of time-based market competition. The business purpose of knowledge is sometimes as important, or more important, than the technical details. Thus, even if employees do their specialized jobs well, the enterprise may fail.

An example of the value of generalists as well as specialists is AT&T's development of a new digital transmission product, Model A. The customer, NTT, required a faster development cycle and higher quality standards than the serial approach typical of AT&T Bell Lab operations made possible. So, they configured their first empowered, cross-functional team in 1990. The result was a smashing success. A follow on survey showed that those making the greatest contribution were managers lending a technical hand and engineers helping with management, the ambidextrous ones.

Technical specialization may be a barrier to innovative thinking. For example, Canon made a breakthrough in photocopying by capturing blue ink almost as well as black ink. The way they did it was to have the chemical engineers report to an electronics engineer and vice versa. The "five whys" approach was used until nobody could think of "why not". Then, they found a way to make possible the previously impossible task — copying blue ink.

3.2.8. *Pull rather than push designs to the customer*

Semi-autonomous, cross-functional teams pull knowledge into their group as requisite for realizing customer requirements. A strategic framework set

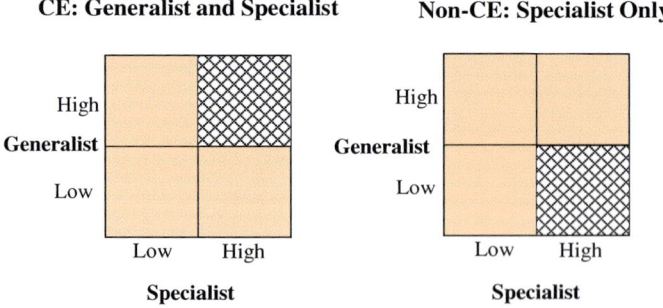

Figure 3.8.   Pull Rather than Push Designs to the Customer

jointly with managers, who also serve as coaches and resource personnel, bounds their activities.

Concurrent:	Downstream functions reach upstream to pull work and enabling processes toward them.
Non-Concurrent:	Managers and product designers push work downstream and impose inflexible rules.

Cellular manufacturing is a model for concurrent product development. Everyone is cross-trained, at least to some degree. Once a component is picked up, typically from a Kanban, it never rests until inserted into the product. Each action is far less efficient than an assembly-line operation. Although the direct costs are relatively high, the indirect costs are relatively low. Moreover, the capability of dealing with complexity and change is great, which results in the opportunity of realizing greater margins than typical for mass produced commodities.

An example of an effective cellular operation was the Siemens Business Communications operation in Cherry Hill, New Jersey. Everyone was highly skilled and cross-trained. The hierarchy was flat with essentially two levels. Innovation in process as well as product was encouraged. If someone asked a manager if they could do something a different way, the response was, "Is it a good idea?" If yes, "Why ask me? Just do it". So the company motto became, "Did it".

The facility tried to involve their design group in the cellular approach. Prototypes were built from designs far from release. This enabled final designs to be produced in volume in only a quarter of the former time. This competitive advantage more than paid back the cost of scrapped prototypes.

3.2.9. *Acquire external and internal knowledge base*

Knowledge is gathered, systematized, analyzed, and made accessible to all stakeholders with translations as necessary. Knowledge is regarded as a competitive advantage for business to which all contribute. Knowledge is not to be wasted, so that the rate of reuse of knowledge is high, from both external and internal sources. Training is intensive, both long-term and Just-In-Time (JIT).

CE: Feedback from Outcomes, External Knowledge Used

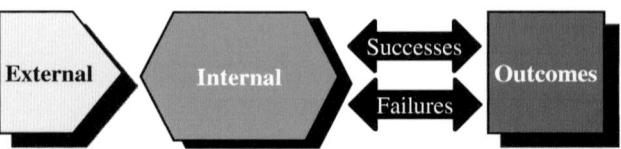

Non-CE: Internally Focused, e.g., Not Invented Here Syndrome

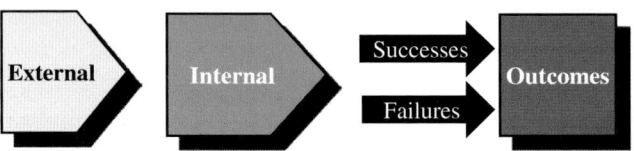

Figure 3.9.   Acquire External and Internal Knowledge Base

Concurrent:	Knowledge reuse is high from both external and internal sources, including both successes and failures.
Non-Concurrent:	External knowledge is undervalued and internal knowledge is overvalued. The "not invented here" syndrome hampers decision-making and little effort is made to learn from failures.

The tendency to overengineer is difficult to resist. An example of success is Motorola's "bandit pager". Their idea was to benchmark competitor products and design a new pager without inventing anything. It was a great triumph even though a few inventions were patented anyway.

The *not invented here* syndrome may also be overcome by garnering information from customers. An example is the lead customer involvement process used by 3M.[vii] They ask customers what they have to do that is outside of their core competencies. If it is within 3M competencies, they co-develop or do the development entirely. This captures the customer's prior investment in knowledge as well as locking in initial sales.

Not invented here may also be overcome by involving suppliers as partners. In a marketplace of increased speed and technical complexity, innovations from suppliers are becoming increasingly important for competitiveness. For example, GM had a huge technical center in Warren, Michigan that was far larger than that of Toyota. But Toyota had a win–win partnership with their leading suppliers and derived a large proportion of its inventions from them.

3.2.10. *Build flexible, reciprocal adjustments in processes*

Rapid responsiveness to environmental changes is built into operations because of openness and the common stake all players have in satisfying the customer. Everyone linked in the value-added chain, from product design idea to end of product life, is busy anticipating what may be needed upstream and investing in their flexible capacity to adapt in advance of actual demand. An example is design for manufacture by product designers and flexible manufacturing systems by manufacturing engineers.[viii]

Concurrent:	Mutual responsiveness along the value-added chain includes pro-actively anticipating the needs of others, resulting in reciprocities that keep the system constantly adjusted.
Non-Concurrent:	One-Way, inflexible flows. Product designs are thrown over the wall.

Before the advent of CE as a discipline, product development was more likely to be serial than simultaneous. Company X was a core business within a conglomerate ranking in the top 25 of the Fortune 500. Its product development process included numerous steps that required sign-offs by a minimum of 21 functions. The company hired product managers to run the gauntlet. However, the company was divided into competing fiefdoms, such as marketing and manufacturing. Product managers were almost never able to get the required sign-offs. The conflicts had to be settled by horse-trading in the executive suite before halting progress was possible.

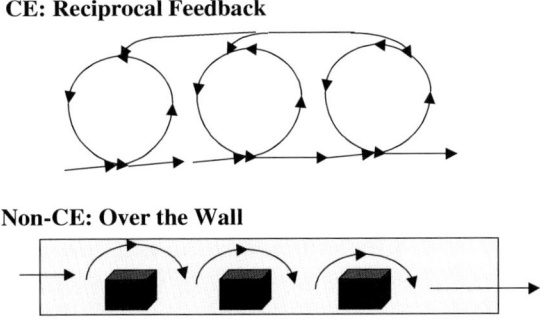

CE: Reciprocal Feedback

Non-CE: Over the Wall

Figure 3.10.   Build Flexible, Reciprocal Adjustments in Processes

The drawback of a serial development process in a silo organization was dramatically illustrated at a meeting on new products touted as the largest of its kind in the world. The VP of R&D prepared for weeks and brought his key staff to world headquarters to make a scheduled presentation. The marketing VP sitting to the right of the president ran the meeting. As the meeting dragged on, the time slot for R&D to present new products dwindled. The VP of R&D was finally allowed to present with 5 minutes left in the meeting schedule. Interruptions were frequent, so the presentation was essentially aborted. The VP appealed to people to stay, but resorted to following key marketing people out into the corridor as they left.

The company was quite profitable. Its revenues came from cash cows developed two decades earlier before the development system was devised. In 20 years, only one new product had achieved a moderately successful launch. Others were incremental line extensions. Not surprisingly, the turnover rate among product managers was far higher than typical for the industry.

3.3. Concurrent Practices as a Pathway for Success

Do the images of concurrent vs. non-concurrent systems connect with reality? Each of the 10 images depicted in this chapter has a survey question in the services data analyzed herein that at least loosely if not exactly corresponds with it. Respondents were asked to rate the extent each practice occurred in their organization. An index summed up these practices. Respondents also rated the performance of their enterprise in terms of product differentiation.

The scatterplot depicted in Figure 3.11 shows an approximate alignment between measures indicative of the images with performance. The scatterplot between practice and performance clusters along an

> The images of systems we hold in our imagination have real world consequences for performance

upward slope. The correlation for an index summing these practices with performance is far from perfect, but explains almost 40 percent of the variation in the level of product differentiation performance. Correlation is not causation. But the associations between the practices depicted with performance suggest a reasonable association.

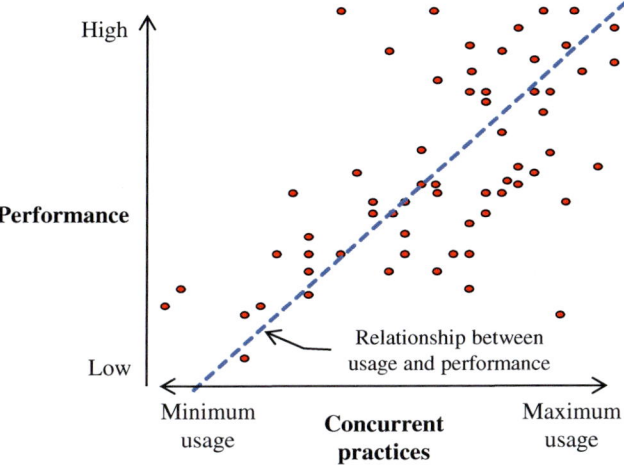

Figure 3.11.   Scatterplot for 10 Practices with Performance in Service Data

Research Note: Association between Images and Performance in Goods
The relationship between questions indicative of these 10 images has been reconfirmed in a recent study of goods industries that follows up on the initial industrial research that stimulated the parallel study of services analyzed herein. In this recent goods data, the correlation between questions indicative of the 10 images with performance is 0.72 which explains over 50 percent of the variation in performance.

One of the leading enterprises in the data depicted in the scatterplot above ranked at the 94th on indicators for the 10 images. However, this enterprise, which also participated in the recent goods study, ranked at the 75th percentile compared with industrial standards. This single comparison does not necessarily mean that services are less advanced in their deployment of best practices for development than goods, but it raises the possibility.

Many enterprises in services, in contrast to counterparts in goods, lack a formal function dedicated to the development of new customer offerings. As described in later chapters, less than half of the enterprises in the service sample had a formal function responsible for NSD. To the extent the contrast exists between goods and services, opportunities for applying concurrency in services offer promise.

3.4. Summary and Follow-up Exercises

This book argues that similar practices provide parallel results in both sectors. The promise of new business models is not only to beef up the deployment of proven best practices, but also to integrate operations for creating value regardless of sector. To the extent enterprises in both sectors deploy proven practices, holistic offerings integrating goods and services may be achieved to optimize TVD. Thus, the TVD framework may be potentially valuable not only within each sector, but also for enterprises creating new integrative business models.

> A system has throughput operations for transforming inputs into outputs which applies to the creation of value regardless of sector

As a follow-up to this chapter, readers are encouraged to look at each of the 10 figures and try to decide whether a development system of their choice is more concurrent or non-concurrent in its operation. For a more rigorous analysis, see *Workbook A: Benchmarking "As Is" Development Systems vs. Best-in-Class*. Readers may answer questions pertinent to each of the 10 images and rank themselves on a bar chart showing proximity to Best-in-Class scores at the top. This exercise uses questions extracted from the analysis of the 70 service enterprises reported herein. Similar questions are also available from a recent study of goods enterprises so that that trans-sector assessment is feasible. The purpose is to show that images of concurrent systems have similar benefits for performance in both sectors. These images may stimulate ideas for application in services and/or goods enterprises to optimizing TVD in deploying a new business model.

Notes

[i]   Senge, P. 1990. *The Fifth Discipline: The Art & Practice of the Learning Organization*, Century Business: London.

[ii]   Moore, G. E. 1965. Cramming More Components onto Integrated Circuits. *Electronics Magazine*, 86(1), 4.

[iii]   Daft, R. L. 1978. A Dual-Core Model of Organizational Innovation, *Academy of Management Journal*, 24, 68–82; Leonard-Barton, D. 1992. Core Capabilities and Core Rigidities: A Paradox of Managing New Product Development, *Sloan Management Review*, 13, 111–125.

[iv] Hull, F. M., Collins, P. D., and Liker, J. K. 1996. Composite Forms of Organization as a Strategy for Concurrent Engineering Effectiveness, *IEEE Transactions on Engineering Management*, 43(2), 133–142.

[v] Hull, F. 2004. Innovation Strategy and the Impact of a Composite Model of Service Product Development on Performance, *Journal of Service Research*, 7(4), 167–181.

[vi] Adler, P. S and Borys, B. 1996. Two Types of Bureaucracy: Enabling and Coercive, *Administrative Science Quarterly*, 41(1), 61–89.

[vii] von Hippel, E. 1988. Lead User Analyses for the Development of New Industrial Products, *Management Science*, 34(5), 569–582.

[viii] Liker, J., Collins, P., and Hull, F. 1999. Flexibility and Standardization: Test of a Contingency Model of Product Design-Manufacturing Integration, *Journal of Product Innovation Management*, 16, 248–267.

SECTION B

EVIDENCE FOR ADVANTAGES OF A COMPOSITE MODEL

CHAPTER FOUR

CONCURRENT TVD: THE EVOLUTION OF A COMPOSITE MODEL

Overview

This chapter chronicles the evolution of high-performance systems for developing new kinds of customer offerings. An organic alternative to the rigidity of mechanistic bureaucracies emerged in the post World War II era along with the advent of electronics, which were too complex and dynamic to manage with rigid procedures and hierarchical controls. While organic development systems generated inventive features pleasing customers, costs were often high. Therefore, academic researchers and progressive managers sought to design development systems that could simultaneously deliver both cost and innovation. Concurrent engineering, which fosters collaboration among diverse functions from the outset of the development cycle, focused principles of quality management on integrating the development value stream by organizing people disciplined by processes and enabled by tools/technologies. The synergistic capabilities of a composite system of development evolved which is robust enough to generate holistic offerings integrating goods and services to optimize customer experiences.

4.1. Introduction

This composite model is a generic system for creating and delivering valued customer offerings. A systems perspective on value development is critical because many solutions to customer needs require the coordination of input from diverse functional specialists typically employed in large-scale organizations and/or distributed networks. Large organizations encounter barriers to innovation because bureaucratic structuring typically increases with growth in size whether in goods or services.[i] As an antidote, Burns and Stalker[ii] proposed "organic" organization design as more conducive for innovation than "mechanistic" bureaucracies. But they did not specify how to infuse organic elements into mechanistic bureaucracies. To close this gap in theory and practice, this book puts forward a "composite" model profiling how large-scale systems can achieve cost-effective innovation in large-scale enterprises regardless of sector. The composite model synergistically melds the efficiency of mechanistic practices characteristic of bureaucratic forms of organizational efficiency with organic practices fostering innovation. A composite system is a synergistic combination of elements which drive a portfolio of performance advantages that are critical for success in an increasingly global market environment:

- Time compression.
- Cost reduction.
- Quality improvement.
- Innovation.

The "composite" model is derived from the discipline of concurrent engineering (CE), a methodology of proven effectiveness in goods industries. This book extends the application of concurrency and the composite model to New Service Development (NSD). From a systems perspective, inputs (whether physical components and/or knowledge) are transformed into outputs regardless of sector.

Goods and services have become increasingly bundled. On the one hand, many goods companies offer follow-on services. For example, some aerospace companies make more revenue from selling services than jet engines, e.g., GE speedily gets planes back on wing and Rolls-Royce profitably sells "power by the hour". On the other hand, many services provide their customers with physical accoutrements to fulfill complementary needs. Thus, a goods–services business model is increasingly needed that focuses on the value proposition offered to customers regardless of sector. From a systems perspective, development operations for creating value for customers have generic similarities regardless of sector.

4.2. Systems Thinking

A systems approach to developing valued customer offerings is needed in both goods and services. However, the literature in goods is relatively more explicit and mature. A growing body of knowledge about formal development processes in goods industries has been in the making for over half a century partly because the creation of new physical entities entails greater tangibility. By contrast, knowledge about how to go about NSD has often remained tacit and lacking in definition and process.

A systems approach potentially addresses gaps in our understanding of managing new service development. Literature on services marketing is strong in identifying customer needs, but relatively neglectful on how to manage operating system capabilities required for transforming targeted inputs to outputs. In many service enterprises, a single departmental function decides on features of customer offerings and leaves others in the company to scramble to somehow get it delivered. This over-the-wall approach leaves many necessary steps to be performed by other functions inside as well as outside the company lacking in planning and coordination from a systems perspective.[iii] The integration of inputs by multiple functions into a coherent value proposition is often poorly executed. This approach relegates systems thinking to a kind of "black box" status. Yet the creation of new products and services is typically the most complex business process within any large corporation because of the number of diverse functions that need to contribute to the development and delivery of the customer offering. A systems approach to understanding the value creation process of the

> Systems thinking is valuable for developing customer offerings, but requires design of throughput operations for transforming inputs into outputs in services as well as goods enterprises

enterprise enables us to better understand how to manage businesses effectively regardless of sector.

Concurrent systems achieve synergies by regulating interactions among components so that they are in a constant state of mutual adjustment. In this way the components are mutually reinforcing so as to maximize performance outcomes. A cornerstone practice is a simultaneous involvement by all stakeholders in product development decisions from the outset and throughout the life cycle so that the entire value stream is reciprocally integrated — from idea to customer and back. Processes and tools help achieve this collaborative integration effectively and efficiently.

Mutual adjustment among stakeholders in the value stream is required for system-wide optimization of reciprocal integration capabilities.[iv] Collaborative reciprocity enhances the capability of the product development systems because each player is more proactively responsive to the needs of the other than in serial modes of integration. Concurrent product development systems are characterized by a numerous reciprocities, particularly those that align resources so as to rapidly respond to customer needs.

Concurrent development systems exemplify generic principles of best practices. In practice, however, system configurations are partially contingent upon the types of output development targeted, which moderates optional characteristics. Even though configurational differences occur both within and between sectors, our systems framework for creating value propositions for customers attempts to transcend the goods vs. services debate.

4.3. Concurrent Development

Leading service corporations increasingly seek new business models for improving their performance. The promise of concurrency is the development and delivery of faster, cheaper, and more innovative customer offerings. Historically, companies made strategic trade-offs between two generic performance advantages, either innovative product differentiation or cost leadership.[v] The model of concurrency espoused herein is a "composite" of practices that synergistically enables systems to deliver both types of competitive advantage simultaneously, which is a huge competitive advantage.

Concurrency simply means simultaneity in communications and actions built upon a foundation of Total Quality Management (TQM) which is customer focused. The essence of concurrency is the reiterative involvement of multiple functions in development cycles from the earliest stages using structured processes and enabling tools to create a systematic approach for launching new products and/or improving existing ones.

Early literature on concurrency focused on how different engineering disciplines could collaborate more effectively as members of a cross-functional team. The people who designed products and those who manufactured them were segregated from one another by hierarchical walls within bureaucratic structures and lacked a common set of integrative processes and tools.[vi] Integrated product and process development was adopted by US government agencies to drive concurrent practices in their supplier base.[vii]

Recent proponents of concurrency, however, have expanded its scope because creating new products and services requires many non-engineering functions, such as marketing, purchasing, finance, strategy, etc. Professional societies promulgating its practices are more likely to use more inclusive terms such as "concurrent product development" or "concurrent enterprising".[viii]

Regardless of labels, the principles of concurrency are generic and may be applied to almost any system wherein multiple actors with stage-based skills transform inputs into outputs. A bare-bones definition of concurrent product development follows below:

> Simultaneous influence by all stakeholders throughout the cycle of product development and delivery using disciplined, but flexible processes and enabling tools/technologies in rapidly pursuing collaboratively set strategic targets.

In serial development systems, practices are activated step-by-step. In concurrent systems, these practices are activated simultaneously instead of serially so that collaborative exchanges may occur among multiple functions. The simultaneous

> Simultaneous rather than serial development operations are necessary for generating highly valued outputs cost-effectively

approach was initially touted as a time saver, which also reduced costs. The reasoning was simple. Not only does time translate to money and opportunity costs, but collaborative decision-making up-front enables potentially expensive downstream problems to be anticipated and prevented.

Recently correlations have been observed between concurrent practices and innovation in addition to associations with time compression, cost reduction, and quality improvement. This association is not surprising as the cornerstone of concurrency, early cross-functional collaboration, is quite similar to the well-established finding that innovation is driven by the cross-fertilization of ideas. Thus, the concurrent practice of early cross-functional collaboration is a capability which enables product creation systems to offer customers rich value propositions in terms of multiple simultaneous advantages. This duality of benefit has been established not only in two statistical studies of goods industries,[ix] but also in the services data analyzed herein.

4.4. Evolution of Concurrent Systems

Beginning with the industrial revolution, many businesses evolved from traditional craft-types of organization to large-scale mechanistic bureaucracies. Mechanistic organizations were higher performers for standardized goods in mature technologies. Adam Smith[x] chronicled how the division of labor enabled a pin factory to be 40 times more productive than medieval craft guilds. The scientific management of Fredric Taylor and the assembly-line of Henry Ford ensconced assembly-line methods in large-scale operations. Mechanistic organizations came to increasingly dominate by crushing craft organizations. Economies of scale and learning curve drove cost efficiencies that could be readily charted in inverse log curves between inputs and outputs.

Mechanistic bureaucracies triumphed over traditional productions systems, such as craft guilds and small family businesses because of its division of labor, learning curve advantages, and economies of scale in operations. Max Weber, a sociologist and economist, detailed seven reasons for the bureaucratic advantage.[xi] Employees in bureaucracies do the best job because (1) the division of labor among specialists focuses on expertise, thereby providing learning curve advantages, and because (2) hiring/promotion is done on the basis of merit instead of family ties. Bureaucratic coordination is superior to alternative because of a (3) hierarchical chain of command and the (4) standardization of operating procedures as rules are universally administered. The rationality of the mechanistic bureaucracy is ensured by (5) contractual relationships specifying task performance and remuneration, so activities are rationally predictable, ensured by (6) norms of impersonality, e.g., salute the uniform, not the person. Strategy and operations are stratified so that (7) roles are vertically differentiated into policy makers, functionaries responsible for translating strategy into operations, and workers for executing them. The characteristics of mechanistic bureaucracy efficiency relative to guilds and family businesses are:

- Best Job   Division of Labor; Hires based on Merit
- Control   Hierarchy; Rules & SOP
- Rationality   Contracts; Impersonal Norms
- Direction   Policy makers direct functionaries

The division of labor and ability to hire on the basis of merit instead of nepotistic family and their connections enabled mechanistic bureaucracies to produce the best work. Bureaucracies achieve coordination across huge numbers of people distributed across distance, such as armies, navies, and railroads[xii] by hierarchical controls and standardized operating procedures. The rationality of the enterprise was enhanced by contracts whereby employees exchanged their work for pay under pre-set norms of impersonality. For example, in the military the norm is to salute the uniform, not the person. Importantly, the middle managers and workers are directed in their activities by policy makers who set the organizational goals and the operational requirements for functionaries to achieve them. This separation of policy from administration dismembers the ends targeted by the organization from the means of achieving it epitomized by the phrase, "ours is not to reason why, ours is to do or die".

Mechanistic bureaucracies are best for performing uniform, standardized tasks and continue to be optimal in many competitive environments where products are relatively non-complex and standardized. Their reliability and predictability provides the backbone of advanced economies. However, they lack capabilities for innovation and adaptation. Bureaucratization means that employees perform narrowly defined roles in prescribed ways that limit creativity. The leadership style is typically type X, one that presumes that employees are lazy self-seekers.

In the scientific and technology boom era after World War II, an "organic" alternative to mechanistic bureaucracy evolved to facilitate innovation in such complex, dynamic product markets as electronics. The knowledge required to develop complex products meant that behaviors were covert instead of overt, such as were highly visible on an assembly-line. The directors of policy lacked critical knowledge held by people creating the products. Strategies could no longer be effectively dictated by policy makers as the people on the journey of product creation encountered unanticipated obstacles and opportunities. Rules and standard operating procedures could preclude the adaptive behaviors required to rapidly solve problems and exploit new discoveries. Thus, operating decisions, and to lesser extent strategic decisions, were decentralized so that the ends and means of the organization were re-coupled.

4.5. Seesawing Organizations

Many early studies documented the efficiency of the mechanistic, bureaucratic design.[xiii] Later studies focused on the benefits of non-bureaucratic forms for innovation.[xiv] Burns and Stalker advocated the advantages of organic forms of organization design for product differentiation; the mechanistic for cost-efficiencies.[xv] Many enterprises have the capability for achieving either cost efficiencies or innovation advantages, but not both simultaneously. Consequently many enterprises seesaw between mechanistic and organic forms of organization trying to achieve some kind of balanced performance.

The two types of organization initially defined by Burns and Stalker qualitative study were viewed as opposites at polar ends of a continuum. Each offered alternative kinds of performance advantage. The mechanistic was best for cost efficiencies, the organic for innovative product differentiation.[xv] Companies often seesaw between these two extremes, depending on

> The predictability of bureaucratic operations provides structural foundations upon which innovation options may be deployed despite resistance

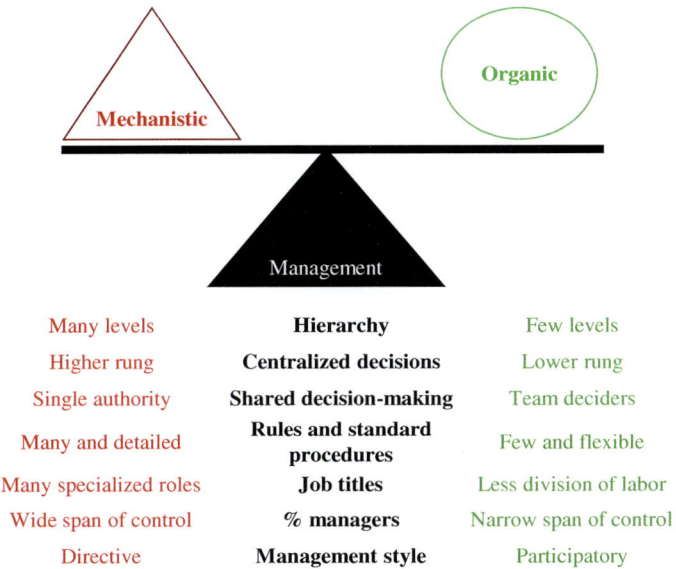

Mechanistic	Management	Organic
Many levels	**Hierarchy**	Few levels
Higher rung	**Centralized decisions**	Lower rung
Single authority	**Shared decision-making**	Team deciders
Many and detailed	**Rules and standard procedures**	Few and flexible
Many specialized roles	**Job titles**	Less division of labor
Wide span of control	**% managers**	Narrow span of control
Directive	**Management style**	Participatory

Figure 4.1.   Seesawing between Mechanistic vs. Organic System Designs

management and competitive contingencies with which they deal in the market environment, e.g., the need for cost vs. differentiation advantages. Sometimes managers seek to control tightly. Other times, especially during relative periods of prosperity, they explore new alternatives in a looser, less tightly controlled structure as depicted in Figure 4.1. Characteristics of these two types are contrasted at opposite ends of the continuum.

The pervasiveness of the seesaw dilemma is illustrated by a talk at Columbia University School of Engineering by the number two ranking executive at McKenzie. As an alumnus, he let his audience in on a little secret of the consulting business from 30,000 feet. He said we go to a company and see if they are structured too loose or too tight. If they are too loose, we tell them some things to do to tighten up and send them a bill. If they are too tight, we tell them some ways to loosen up and send them a bill. This seems to be a profitable consulting business, but is it a necessary one?

The perennial problem of an unbalanced seesaw needs a resolution that managers can design with little or no aid from consultants. According to theories advocated in this book, the reason the seesaw is so often wiggly is because the mechanistic and organic types of organization are two antithetically opposite kinds of system that are antagonistic. To the extent this is so, the competitive advantages of the company are invariably compromised to some extent by conflicting objectives and modes of operation. As the pendulum of management styles swings, one group will emphasize centralized control while a following group will offer incentives for participatory decision-making to foster the loyalty of partisan groups.

4.5.1. *Mechanistic organization*

The swing of the pendulum of organization design historically defaults to mechanistic bureaucracy, the default form or organization in industrial societies.

In mechanistic systems performing relatively standardized kinds of work, roles are delimited and specific to phases of an assembly-line sequence so that those responsible for delivery, such as manufacturing and/or customer service are engaged only at the back-end. The dominant mode of communication is top-down command through a relatively tall hierarchy. Decisions are centralized and typically crystalized within the authority of a single position, rather than distributed among a team of people. Rules and standard procedures are profuse and typically detail-specific actions to be followed. Labor is often finely divided with roles delimited so that each designated job is responsible for performing a specialized task.

Managerial style is directive for the most part as subordinate tasks are typically prescribed in detail. Because work is often routinely predictable, managers may often oversee a wide span of subordinates. According to Weber, the bureaucratic type of organization is like a social machine in which people perform almost as predictably as mechanical cogs.

The competitive advantage of mechanistic bureaucracies is the efficient production of standardized outputs at relatively low cost. The downside is its lack of innovative capability. Mechanistic systems are often very internally focused and sometimes die because of a lack of timely adaptation to changes in their external environment.

4.5.2. *Organic organization*

The organic type of organization is often viewed simply as that of antithesis mechanistic bureaucracy. At one extreme, its ethos is contrarian with regard to authority. Its *modus operandi* is focusing the diversity of human creativity on the solution of problems. The need for the exercise of human judgment is partly a function of the complexity of knowledge required for designing and developing solutions to customer needs especially if they are ill-defined and/or changing due to environmental conditions. The more dynamic and novel the developmental challenge, the relatively more suited organic organization is for providing an innovation than a mechanistic bureaucracy.

To bring decision-making closer to the operating level for creative input, hierarchies are relatively short. Decentralization not only enables lower ranks to participate in decisions, but also fosters diversity of input. Often cross-functional teams share power for making several kinds of decisions. Rules are largely ad hoc and often emerge from team consensus.

Management style is consultative and relies heavily on influence. One reason is because the professional and technical knowledge required to develop innovative new products is covert in contrast to the overt behavior of operatives working on physical objects on an assembly-line. Therefore, leadership is often consultative rather than directive. Spans of control are narrow because managers need to deal with subordinates more individually depending upon the extent to which the problem is complex, the knowledge heterogeneous, and the dynamics of the developmental situation fluid.

The competitive advantage of the organic organization is creativity and innovation, but not cost. The downside is its lack of integrative discipline focused on defined objectives that may be achieved cost-effectively. People in organic systems often engage in very discursive interactions that may reach for blue sky, but are sometimes impractical from a grounded perspective.

Early deployment of the organic type treated it as the absence of mechanistic bureaucracy. This approach failed to specify activities constituting organic practices. This notion was too simplistic and impractical. For example, many managers in the 1990s viewed the solution to achieving higher performance as simply cutting out the bureaucracy and "getting out of the way".

> The benefit of organic approaches to managing development operations is suboptimal if a disciplined focus is lacking

Their approach placed heroic confidence in a theory Y approach to leadership, which presumes people are self-actualized in seeking to accomplish challenging tasks. While a great many discoveries in R&D laboratories were achieved with this approach, the rate at which inventions were commercialized was often limited. Moreover, attempts at breakthrough innovations sometimes hit, but more often missed. Many inventions were just impractical and much effort was wasted. For example, skunk works were pioneered in the early 1970s with some notable successes. However, failures of these empowered multifunctional groups were common although seldom chronicled. Moreover, such emergency efforts sometimes burnt out the organization, as happened at Data General.[xvi]

Cross-functional teaming emerged as an alternative approach for managing relationships among people in the organization, especially in the late 1980s and early 1990s. However, teaming became so popular that the word was overused and lacked specificity. Some teams were merely nominal, others were highly empowered. Regardless, a common problem was a lack of discipline in the conduct of project teams which often wandered off in unproductive directions. Therefore, this book defines and operationalizes the concept of cross-functional teams in specific ways as a friendly amendment to the pioneering concept of the organic type by Burns and Stalker.

4.5.3. *Organic team structure*

To infuse organic practices into large-scale mechanistic structures is usually difficult. Economies of scale and the division of labor favor a vertical vector of power which is exerted downward and inhibits horizontal communications. Organic Team Structure OTS is a general approach to horizontal integration of the value stream that cross-hatches hierarchical lines of authority. Efforts to weave reciprocal relationships among employees along the workflow are often met with something akin to organizational antibodies. The result of the face-off is the extent to which a pivotal shift occurs between the vertical vector of mechanistic organization and the horizontal vector of organization. The more horizontal slope of the convergent angle, the greater the proportion of resources in terms of people, time, and money allocated to project teams instead of specialized functions reporting up a bureaucratic hierarchy. The inclusion of functions from all departments and points on the value chain helps cross-fertilize ideas so that more innovative customer solutions are designed.

OTS explicitly integrates the work of specialized functions, including line and staff. OTS serves as a wedge for horizontally integrating work across the base of the hierarchy. It infuses organic practices into mechanistic bureaucracies. OTS realigns the organization to focus on project-based organization where employees work as cross-functional team members cutting across the horizontal breadth of the firm. Sometimes these team members are physically collocated and rewarded as a group to reinforce collaboration. OTS includes a variety of practices that attempt to integrate the value realization cycle from concept to delivery. The most prominent three are: (1) cross-functional teams, (2) collocations, and (3) group rewards transcending individual incentives controlled by hierarchical authorities. Cross-functional teams are the principal battering ram because they cut across functional lines of authority. Collocation reinforces the influence of project managers relative to line managers. Group rewards provide incentives for employees to work to add value to the development along its flow to the customer relative to work on specialized knowledge domiciles in hierarchical silos. The notion of OTS, however, transcends practices *per se* and represents a mindset focused on the creation of value by integrating horizontally organized knowledge and resources within the framework of a larger hierarchical organization. OTS is the precondition for the establishment of hybrid forms of development systems. A troika of elements of the composite model operates upon the horizontal platform OTS creates within the hierarchical structure of mechanistic bureaucracies.

> Organic linkages provide diverse people with opportunities to perform work collectively instead of just individually

4.6. Hybrid Systems

Customers have increasingly resisted being pigeonholed by providers in categories such as low cost or luxurious features. Global competition is constantly exerting pressure on prices. Technological capabilities are growing exponentially for developing new features. The challenge is epitomized by exponential improvements in computer capabilities price, and capabilities consistent with Moore's law:

"Twice the performance at half the cost every 1.5 years".[xvii]

Although Moore's law was formulated to track technological progress in semiconductors, its drumbeat is felt in an increasing number of segments of economies where over a third of the value of autos are in electronics and financial services are ever more sophisticated in computer automation.

Product development systems have attempted to respond to the challenges of offering customers solutions to needs that are low cost as well as innovative. Mixing mechanistic and organic systems dates at least to the early 20th century when large manufacturers created R&D laboratories so that professional knowledge could be focused on innovative opportunities of the future, rather than the production issues of the day. However, this segregation of staff with professional knowledge from line operations creates conflicts.[xviii] The line organization typically seeks advantages from economies of scale and learning curves to contain costs. Professional staff typically seeks to innovate, which takes investment, undermines economies of scale, and reduces the efficiency of routine operations. These conflicting strategies mean that synergies between mechanistic and organic practices are difficult to realize in mixed systems.

A hybrid development system is proposed to enable enterprises to simultaneously compete on the basis of both cost and innovation. In theory, hybrids have the capacity for achieving both kinds of generic performance advantages, innovation and low cost, simultaneously[xix] as illustrated in Figure 4.2.

Melding relatively organic practices of provisional team organizations with relatively mechanistic ones, such as product development procedures, can create hybrid systems at least temporarily. However, attempts in mixing mechanistic and organic development systems often have the stability of oil and water and seesaw between alternative designs. Unfortunately, theorists postulating a mixture of the two types provided little specificity about the nuts and bolts of how development systems with such incompatible elements could actually be put into harmonious operation. For

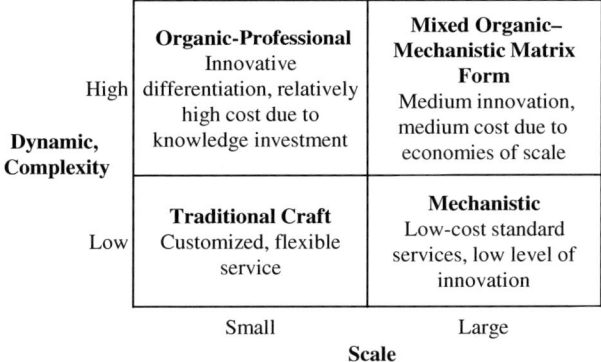

Figure 4.2. Hybrid Systems

example, matrix management, whereby employees had two bosses, one in a functional department and one in a professional–technical discipline, has remained a source of confusion. Matrix forms of organization do not entirely resolve split loyalties in the mixed organic–mechanistic type. Because the theoretical base used for these integrative notions were derived from polar opposite types, how to mix oil and water has remained poorly understood. The theory of hybrid organization lacks operational specificity for real-world implementation.

4.6.1. *Concurrency as a catalytic agent for hybridization*

Concurrency offers an integrative solution for the stand-off between mechanistic and organic practices. Concurrency maleates each type into forms offering the potential for interconnectivity to meld these otherwise incompatible practices together in a synergistic whole. Concurrency succeeded by weaving reciprocal links across specialized functions at the horizontal base of the organizational pyramid to integrate work along the value stream. Establishing "organic" relationships based on reciprocity among people supported richer and more frequent communication regardless of rank or position in the value chain that occurred in mechanistic bureaucracies.[xx]

Horizontal cross-hatching reduces the constraints of bureaucratic structures by infusing relationships among people with reciprocal obligations focused along the workflow toward customers as well as vertically up to higher. In organic organizations, hierarchies are flatter, decisions are decentralized, rules are less rigid, and roles include general as well as specialized responsibilities. The organic infusion creates hybrid forms of development systems that are better suited for hyper-competitive markets because of their capacity for achieving multiple kinds of performance outcomes simultaneously, such as product innovation and low cost.[xxi]

> Hybrids of organic and mechanistic development systems have the capabilities of providing customers with both kinds of competitive advantages simultaneously, innovation and low cost

The notion of a hybrid value development system is an emergent property meaning that the whole is greater than the sum of its component elements. Concurrent systems are highly integrated because of the "reciprocal" interdependence among its component elements.[xxii] Alternative ways of achieving system integration are: Reciprocal team, feedback, serial, and pooled (see Figure 4.3).[xxiii] The reciprocal team approach is the operational mode as shown in the upper-right quadrant of Figure 1.1.[xxiv]

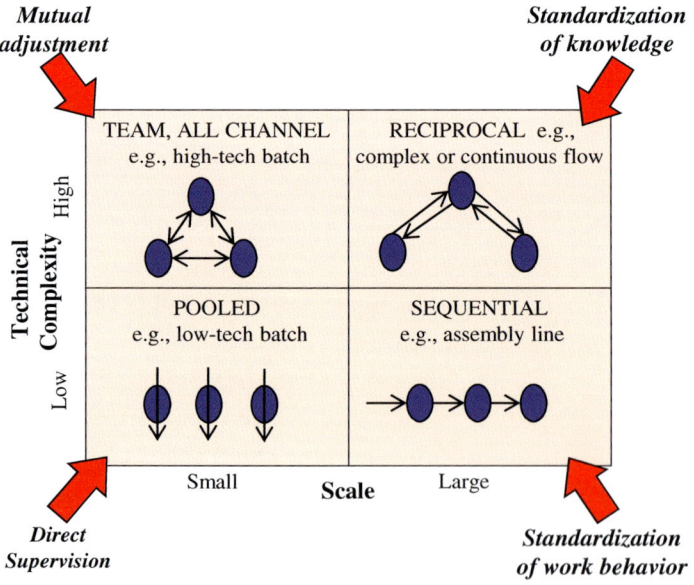

Figure 4.3.   Modes of System Integration
Source: Adapted from Van den Ven and Ferry, 1980

The diagram for the reciprocal team mode of coordination is iconic of concurrent development systems. It corresponds with the mixed model in Figure 4.3. The vertical relationships recognize that hierarchical coordination is necessary in large-scale development systems. The horizontal relationships integrate people as reciprocal stakeholders in collaborative actions along the value stream. Hybrid organizations are honeycombed by small groups of people united reciprocally as stakeholders in attempting to serve the interests of the enterprise and its customers. It is in such small groups that the vertical vector of mechanistic bureaucracy meets the horizontal vector of organic relationships.

By contrast, coordination in traditional craft organizations is largely lacking. Often work is pooled from separate batches. However, some batch operations are high-tech and require professional–technical expertise. In such enterprises, all-channel communications are relatively more frequent for integrative coordination. In sequential workflows, coordination is via one-way flows as on an assembly-line directed by hierarchical authorities.

4.7. Concurrent Systems

A solution to the dilemma of simultaneously integrating the benefits of mechanistic and organization design elements has been identified in recent research on a "composite" model. This composite uses the concepts from each of the two types, but recasts each in ways making synergies between them possible.

At the operating core of the composite model is a troika of elements dealing with *organization, process,* and *tools.* Each of the components serves a general purpose. Organization provides coordination of people, Process provides control, and Tools provide transformation capabilities as well as enhancing the capabilities of people to communicate electronically and structure their activities. The constructs of the troika are defined in simple terms below:

- *Organization* — Early Simultaneous Influence (ESI) means that diverse specialists, including downstream functions, collaborate as a team in developing products and services starting at the conceptual outset of the development cycle. ESI includes the early formation of cross-functional participants from the entire value chain. Simultaneity of participation is particularly important because some cross-functional teams do not include all relevant stakeholders required for successful development.

- *Process* — In-process Design Control (IDC) provides flexibility, enabling guidance to team members working on development projects outside of their functional homes. This is a more adaptive, and flexible alternative to control by rigid rules and standard operating procedures of mechanistic bureaucracy.
- *Tools* — Computer Information Technology (CIT) helps transform inputs into outputs, supports communications among team members regardless of time or location, and enables continuous updating of processes.

Many of the advantages of concurrent systems are due to synergistic bonds among a troika of constructs at the operating core of the composite model. Research on goods companies has shown that these constructs bond together as a "composite".[xxv] As shown in Figure 4.4, each component of the operating core synergistically interacts with the others as suggested by the two-way arrows. The effectiveness of the operating core is limited without the correct foundations delivered by OTS.

Concurrent methods hybridize organic and mechanistic practices. Each of the practices in the framework must be refashioned so that their properties at either extreme are softened. This enables them to be harmoniously integrated into a synergistic whole. How each of the

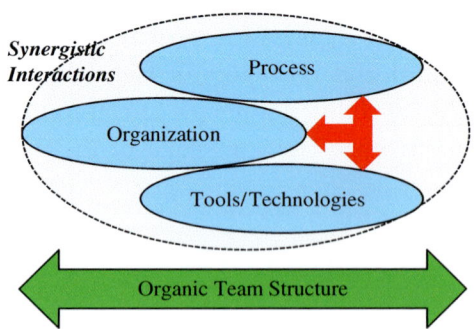

Figure 4.4.   Operating Core of the Composite Model on a Platform of OTS

Table 4.1.　Concurrent vs. Mechanistic and Organic Modes

	Concurrent mode	(M) Mechanistic & (O) Organic mode
Organization	Project-based organizations for disciplined, cross-functional teaming.	(M) Functional hierarchies with specialized roles. (O) Open, unstructured communication channels.
Process Controls	Enabling product development, e.g., model product development templates and standards customizable for specific applications.	(M) Bureaucracy and coercive, rigid rules. (O) Lax rule enforcement.
Tools, Technology, and Information Management	Project and product management software for transforming physical objects and/or symbols, including communicating, coordinating, reusing knowledge, etc. Soft, programmable automation, e.g., project plans and designs via distributed networks.	(M) Hard automation, fixed capital sunk in assembly lines, hard copy, read-only files. (O) Knowledge intensive technologies that are highly creative and customized.

constructs is refashioned in the concurrent mode, in contrast with mechanistic and organic modes, is illustrated in Table 4.1. In the right column, mechanistic vs. organic modes are provided. The concurrent mode typically falls in between the two extremes and is described in the left column.

4.7.1. *ESI*

Early input by all functions is needed because the bulk of the product design is committed at initial stages even though the actual costs are expended much later. Correcting faulty decisions at late stages is far more expensive than getting it right up-front. The essence of concurrency is that spending the time and energy at the fuzzy front end pays back in faster and more cost-effective realization of better products at the back end. ESI is a specific form of cross-functional teaming that ensures downstream participation at the front-end which is impossible without a foundation of

OTS which infuses the creative capabilities of people along the value creation chain which otherwise would be hierarchically controlled.

4.7.2. *IDC*

The "P" in the troika refashions the controls of mechanistic bureaucracies so as to provide flexible and adaptive guidance to product development teams instead of rigid rules and inviolate standard operating procedures. A lack of discipline in the conduct of project teams sometimes proved to be a problem. As members were working outside of their functional homes, many of the intra-department rules were inapplicable. Over time, a process for managing development projects evolved, including charters, model plans, stage-gates with exit and entry criteria, product review criteria, etc. Partly because the team members were semi-empowered and because projects varied, control by process proved to be much more flexible and enabling relative to the rigid constraints typical of mechanistic bureaucracies.[xxvi] Whereas organic teaming and inflexible bureaucratic rules were antithetical; process offered an alternative method of control that guided rather than stifled. This concurrent process seeks to retain some of the considerable advantages of the mechanistic form of organization design.[xxvii]

Process provides a synergistic complement to the creativity stimulated by cross-functional interchange because the development is framed and kept within boundaries for meeting market opportunities. Previously, organic firms had loose control systems, which permitted novel creations to emerge, but seldom in a timely and cost-effective manner. Ironically, the flexible constraints of IDC provide boundaries that reduce the risk of project teams wandering around fruitlessly. Recent literature on the theory of constraints suggests that some degree of boundary conditions may actually foster creativity as compared to a blue-sky approach. Leadership styles need to combine task and people's approaches, challenging people to do their best while at the same time guiding their activities.

4.7.3. *CIT*

CIT may range in its position along the mechanistic vs. organic continuum. Prior to the advent of programmable automation, most tools and technologies were coercive and were more congruent with the mechanistic type. Today many tools that were once hard to change and difficult to share are now soft, flexible, and easily distributed via electronic networks. Computer-based tools have capabilities that help product developers model how to transform inputs into outputs. Continually updated processes and instant exchanges among cross-functional team members — regardless of distance — foster reciprocal integration. The mechanistic constraint of tools is thereby softened by the greater flexibility it permits in controls and increased frequency of communications.

CIT is hypothesized as having a positive impact on system integration because of the speed and scope of data distribution. The lower cost of data transmittal and greater reliability are hypothesized as improving performance. However, data is not information. IT is presumed to be more effective to the extent that it supports mature processes and cross-functional organization.[xxviii]

4.7.4. *Evolutionary trends in work*

The rise of organic team structures reflects a revolutionary change in the nature of work in the modern organization. The competitive advantage Fredrick Taylor described as "scientific management" was based on time and motion studies of overt behaviors. The span of control of factory managers could be quite wide to the extent work performed by subordinates was standardized. However, automation has replaced an increasing proportion of physical work. The balance has shifted from physical toward more cognitive, less observable work.

Knowledge has increased exponentially. Over 90 percent of the scientists who have ever lived are alive today. The explosion of knowledge has been augmented by the conversion of the written word into digital form which enables electronic sharing. The pace of growth in knowledge is so rapid that subordinates increasingly know more about the nature of their work than their super-ordinates, which narrows the span of control. Enterprises failing to invest in human capital rather than capital equipment are increasingly at risk of failure.

The covert nature of mental work has reduced the relative power of managers over employees. Of necessity, leadership styles have undergone a parallel transformation from directive to consultative. Organic team structures reflect the need to decentralize decisions closer to the knowledge of the doers at the base of the organization. OTS helps foster the interconnections that need to be made along the value stream from concept to customer.

However desirable, the prospect of a flat organization without a hierarchy remains a challenge. The height of hierarchical forms of organization has been diminished, but not eliminated. The problem is that communication of all with all is risks chaos even when abetted by electronic exchanges. The number of relationships increases exponentially in organizations with growth in size. $N(N–1)/2$ is the formula for calculating the number of communication channels where N = the number of people. Large-scale organizations will of necessity impose some degree of hierarchical ordering on communications. OTS is an antidote that ameliorates but not fully cure the overwhelming complexity of communication channels.

The virtue of organic structures is that human judgment may be exercised building interpersonal relationships that cross-hatch with those in the hierarchy. The wisdom of people in cross-functional teams is a partial antidote to the bureaucratic structures that provides the backbone of industrial economies. OTS is essential for keeping opportunities for integration and innovation open that are beyond the capabilities of managers and computer programs to purposively control.

4.8. Strengths of Concurrent Systems

The evolution of the composite model represents a considerable advance in the capability of development systems. Historically many trade-offs were accepted in designing customer offerings, such as between cost and quality. As knowledge has become ever more essential for developing differentiated offerings, investment in human capital has risen sharply. However, brainpower needs to be managed differently than manual exertion. Organic practices emerged to capitalize on the covert capabilities of humans. But issues of control surfaced as creative inventions were often impractical and cost prohibitive. Mechanistic controls common in bureaucracies overseeing over behaviors needed to be adapted in ways that guided human creativity without stifling it. The transformation of inviolate standard procedures into flexible processes was a breakthrough which made the synergistic axis of the composite model possible, a hybrid between the organic organizations of human creativity with disciplined focus. This axis is reinforced by the growing capabilities of CIT, which facilitate electronic communications among people and allow procedures to be rapidly rendered into guidelines appropriate for focused discipline instead of blind conformance.

The advantage of the troika, of practices comprising the composite model, is that each makes a vital contribution to performance separately and in synergistic interaction:

- Organic organization helps professional–technical people to cross-fertilize ideas to achieve high levels of creativity. By integrating human capital from concept to delivery, innovative opportunities may be captured up-front and downstream problems precluded.
- Disciplined control by flexible processes helps ensure that creative ideas get commercialized instead of left wandering in outer space or squashed by bureaucratic constraints. Processes that are guided by strategic foci help creative people identify opportunities consistent with core competencies so that knowledge is reused as well as newly created in rapidly repeated development cycles.
- Enabling tools for computer-based product development and project management provide synergistic support for team organization and processes for managing concurrent product development.

The composite model offers synergies enabling development systems to be capable of generating innovative customer offerings that are not only of high quality, but also competitively priced. However, this hybrid competitive advantage is perennially at risk from either those in the bureaucratic hierarchy who want to assert control over their subordinates within each function or project managers that stray from strategic objectives and the core competencies of the enterprise. The previous seesaw image illustrates double-edged threats to hybrids which are inherently fragile.

Notes

[i] Blau, P., Falbe, M., McKinley, C., and Phelps, W. T. 1976. Technology and Organization in Manufacturing, *Administrative Science Quarterly*, 21, 20–40.

ii　Burns, T. and Stalker, G. M. 1961. *The Management of Innovation*, Tavistock: London.

iii　Shaw, R. and Kotler, P. 2009. Rethinking the Chain, *Marketing Management*, 18(4), 18–23.

iv　Liker, J., Collins, P., and Hull, F. 1999. Flexibility and Standardization: Test of a Contingency Model of Product Design-Manufacturing Integration, *Journal of Product Innovation Management*, 16, 248–267.

v　Porter, M. E. 1980. *Competitive Strategies: Techniques for Analyzing Industries*, Free Press: New York.

vi　Hartley, J. R. 1992. *Concurrent Engineering: Shortening Lead Times, Raising Quality, and Lowering Costs*, Productivity Press: Cambridge; Susman, G. I. and Dean, J. W. Jr. 1992. Development of a Model for Predicting Design for Manufacturability Effectiveness, In Susman, G. I. (Eds.), *Integrating Design and Manufacturing for Competitive Advantage*, Oxford University Press: New York, pp. 207–227.

vii　Magrab, E. 1997. *Integrated Product and Process Design and Development: The Product Realization Process*, CRC Press: Boca Raton.

viii　Examples include the Society for Concurrent Product Development, http://scpdnet.org/ and "Concurrent Enterprising," http://www.esoce.net/.

ix　Collins, P. and Hull, F. M. 2002. Early Simultaneous Influence Across Stages of the Product Development Cycle: Impact on Time and Cost, *International Journal of Innovation Management*, 6(1), 1–24.

x　Smith, A. 1776. *Wealth of Nations*, W. Strahan and T. Cadell: London.

xi　Weber, M. 1947. *The Theory of Social and Economic Organization*, Free Press: New York.

xii　Chandler, A. 1977. *The Visible Hand*, Harvard University Press: Massachusetts.

xiii　Blau, P. M. and Schooenheer, R. A. 1971. *The Structure of Organizations*, Basic Books: New York; Pugh, D. S., Hickson, D. J., Hinings, C. R., and Turner, C. 1968. Dimensions of Organization Structure, *Administrative Science Quarterly*, 13(1), 65–105.

xiv　Damanpour, F. 1991. Organizational Innovation: A Meta-Analysis of Effects of Determinants and Moderators, *Academy of Management Journal*, 34(3), 555–590.

xv　Hage, J. 1980. *Theories of Organizations: Form, Process, and Transformation*, Wiley: New York.

xvi　Kidder, T. 1981. *The Soul of a New Machine*, Little, Brown & Co: New York.

xvii　Moore, G. E. 1965. Cramming more Components onto Integrated Circuits, *Electronics Magazine*, 86(1), 4.

[xviii] Mintzberg, H. and Quinn, B. (1996). *Strategy Process*, Prentice-Hall: Englewood Cliffs.

[xix] Daft, R. L. and Lengel, R. H. 1986. Organisational Information Requirements, Media Richness and Structural Design, *Management Science*, 32(5), 554–571; Duncan, R. B. 1976. The Ambidextrous Organization: Designing Dual Structures for Innovation, In Kilmann, R. H., Pondy, L. R., and Slevin, D. (Eds.), *The Management of Organization Design: Strategies and Implementation*, North Holland: New York, pp. 167–188; Hage. 1980. *Op. cit.*

[xx] Burns and Stalker. 1961. *Op cit.*; Damanpour. 1991. *Op. cit*; Hull, F. and Hage, J. 1982. Organizing for Innovation: Beyond Burns and Stalkers Organic Type, *Sociology*, 16, 546–547.

[xxi] Duncan. 1976. *Op. cit.*; Hull, F. M., Collins, P. D., and Liker, J. K. 1996. Composite Forms of Organization as a Strategy for Concurrent Engineering Effectiveness, *IEEE Transactions on Engineering Management*, 43(2), 133–142; Susman and Dean. 1992. *Op. cit.*

[xxii] Thompson, J. 1967. *Organizations in Action*, McGraw-Hill: New York.

[xxiii] Adapted from van den Ven, A. and Ferry, D. 1976. *Measuring and Assessing Organizations*, Wiley: New York.

[xxiv] Tidd, J. and Hull, F. 2003. *Service Innovation: Organizational Responses to Technological Opportunities & Market Imperatives*, Imperial College Press: London, see Figure 1.1, page 6.

[xxv] Hull *et al.* 1996. *Op. cit.*

[xxvi] Adler, P. S. and Borys, B. 1996. Two Types of Bureaucracy: Enabling and Coercive, *Administrative Science Quarterly*, 41(1), 61–89.

[xxvii] Liker, J., Collins, P., and Hull, F. 1999. Flexibility and Standardization: Test of a Contingency Model of Product Design-Manufacturing Integration, *Journal of Product Innovation Management*, 16, 248–267; Susman and Dean. 1992. *Op. cit.*

[xxviii] Mitchell, V. L. and Zmud, R. W. 1999. The Effects of Coupling IT and Work Process Strategies in Redesign Projects, *Organization Science*, 10(4), 424–438.

CHAPTER FIVE

EVIDENCE FOR THE COMPOSITE MODEL

Overview

Research evidence on the composite model is needed for assessing the extent to which its adoption may improve performance capabilities. To the extent the composite model is statistically correlated with development performance, readers may have added confidence in applying its principles and practices. Measures of development behaviors predict cost-effective innovation of two parallel samples, one of goods and one of services. Evidence from analyses of parallel surveys of enterprises in goods and services samples is described as well as research from other studies that buttress the results. The benefits of the composite model of value development are explored using quantitative data from a database of 70 services enterprises and compared to a database of 100 goods enterprises. Data from goods and services samples are juxtaposed which is helpful because much of the literature on development is segregated by sector. Comparative analyses of the two databases test the extent to which the building blocks of the model transcend sector differences in predicting performance. The robust capability of the model for developing both goods and/or services offers enterprises opportunities for enterprises for integrating tangible and intangible assets in holistic offerings.

5.1. Justification of the Composite Model

The composite model comprises a trio of building blocks of value development systems well established in the literature on organization design. These building blocks are sets of behavioral practices dealing with *organization, process,* and *tools/technologies.* Composite development systems integrate development from concept to customer, not only through the collaboration and influence of diverse stakeholders (especially early in the innovation process), but also by flexible discipline enabled by tools and technologies. Composite systems organize cross-functional teams to generate creative options early-on with costs bounded by the flexible discipline of process. Tools and technologies not only provide design options, but also support cross-functional communications. The composite model maleates the antithetical practices of the mechanistic vs. organic types so that synergistic bonds are forged. Organic Team Structure (OTS) synergistically moderates the coercive effects of mechanistic bureaucracy on creativity and innovation.

The cornerstone of the composite model is Early Simultaneous Influence (ESI). This is an operationally focused practice that epitomizes the essence of the broader concept of OTS. ESI is an operational practice focused on the organization of reciprocal relationships along the horizontal workflow at the base of the pyramid. ESI specifies that downstream functions responsible for the realization and delivery of customer offerings are engaged at the up-front concept phase of decision-making. ESI specifically bridges the divide between up and downstream functions by up-front engagement of those responsible for activities at late phases of the development cycle.

The axis of the composite model is a synergistic bond between organic bonds organizing integration among functions along the work stream (*organization*) and the procedural controls hierarchically imposed on their activities (*process*). The organization building block may be measured either as a variety of practices which may be subsumed under the general concept of OTS or the relatively specific practice of ESI. The controlling procedures of mechanistic bureaucracy are conceptualized as In-Process Design Control (IDC). The term process, which connotes malleability, is preferred to procedures which tend to be rigidly inviolate.

Processes may be adapted by those responsible for integrating work along the value stream which makes synergies between *organization* and *process* possible.

Tools and technologies are conceptualized as Computer Information Technology (CIT). They are useful means for creating valued offerings. Moreover, information technology (IT) enables people from diverse functions to collaborate and processes to be continually adapted and updated to preclude mechanistic rigidity.

5.1.1. *Evidence for the composite model in research literature*

The trio of building blocks of value development systems at the core of the composite model is well established in the research literature on organization design: *organization, process,* and *tools*. For example, descriptions of the Toyota product development system focus on this triad of practices[i] as did a national survey of US industries.[ii] These building blocks have also been used in the service literature. For example, Meyer and DeTore[iii] argued for deployment of practices similar to those used in goods industries based on "three key elements: multidisciplinary teams, very specific processes, and computer systems technology". A statistical analysis of measures of these same concepts in a sample of 175 service companies found that all three concepts were significantly correlated with performance.[iv] Other studies have found that one or more of these three sets of practices are predictive of performance in services.[v] Such parallel studies of goods and services suggest that the fundamental building blocks of systems design transforming inputs into value added outputs are basically similar regardless of whether the system entails physical objects, data, people, or some combination thereof.[vi]

Synergies among the troika of the operating components of the composite model enable designers of new business models to consider the option of leveraging development operations sufficiently robust to provide multiple competitive advantages in both goods and services. The molecular structure of the composite model and synergies amongst its components may also provide a schema for use in designing innovative business models. Synergies among the troika are illustrated by the two-way arrows in Figure 5.1.

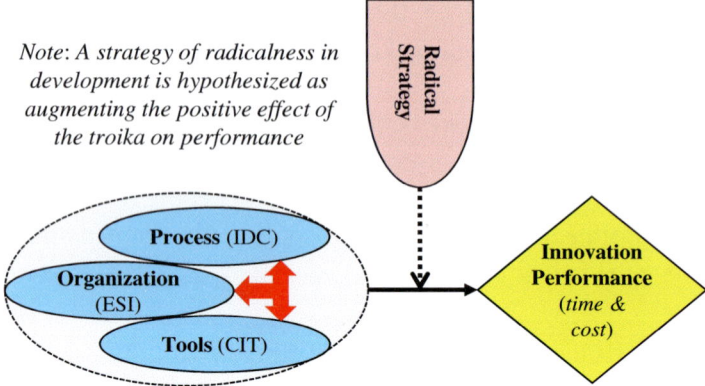

Figure 5.1.   A Composite Model of Development Systems: Including the Moderating Effect of Strategy

5.1.2. *Radicalness as a moderating contingency*

According to contingency theory, high performers adjust their structures to be more congruent with the task undertaken. Companies vary in the extent to which they attempt to offer new and differentiated services. It has been shown that the strategic intent has an influence on both the approaches firms take in developing new products and services and the success of those approaches.[vii] The more radical the customer offering development strategy, the greater the level of uncertainty encountered. This should require greater levels of integration to achieve synergies among the elements at the operating core of the composite model. In other words, the more novel the work to be undertaken, the greater the benefit from deploying relatively more organic than mechanistic practices should be. This hypothesized moderating effect on the troika is depicted by a dotted line between deployment of a strategy of development of radical offerings, such as those that are new instead of modifications of existing ones, and the impact of the troika on performance.

5.2. Collecting the Data

5.2.1. *Sample*

Evidence for the benefits of a composite model of value development is explored using quantitative data from a database of 70 service enterprises.

Data from these service enterprises are juxtaposed with a parallel dataset in manufacturing organizations.[viii] Comparative analyses of the two databases test the extent to which the building blocks of the model transcend sector differences in predicting performance.

Large companies were targeted because growth in size increases bureaucratic structuring and other barriers to innovation. The largest service companies in terms of employment were identified from Crain's New York Directory of the top 100 firms. Smaller service businesses ranking in the top 25th percentile of their category were also selected to capture the diversity of enterprises within the region. Phone calls were made to identify the most appropriate respondents. Respondents were people with specific responsibility for product or business development, total quality management (TQM), business process reengineering (BPR), or productivity improvement.

Respondents from 70 businesses completed questionnaires, a response rate of 31 percent. The largest industry category was financial services. Most major categories in the service sector were represented except advertising. With this exception, survey respondents appear to be reasonably representative of large service companies in the New York area as detailed in the Appendix. The enterprises were almost entirely businesses within large corporations. Of the 12 largest corporations in New York, 11 were represented. Only four companies employed less than 500 people.

A user group of leading service enterprises met every 60 days to share best practices. Case study information was collected during visits hosted by each of participating company. Development practices shared in benchmarking exchanges, follow-on interviews, and supporting documents was codified by category of behavior and logged. The Appendix on methods of research and analysis provides additional detail about the composition of the sample and analysis.

5.2.2. *Comparable goods data*

The initial study was conducted on large-scale manufacturing corporations. The measures used in the goods survey, as detailed in the Appendix, were adapted for used in service enterprises survey. Additional case study information was gained from survey respondents and participants in user group workshops. Dozens of leading companies from goods industries were selected to share best practices for product development for two decades from 1993.

The parallel studies allow comparisons for the first time to assess ways in which relationships are like or unlike across sectors. The two studies were designed to assess the extent similar practices predict performance outcomes within each sector.

5.2.3. *Measures*

The measures employed in the model were a compendium of best product development practices derived from the literature and from a user group of leading New York service companies. These companies helped adapt concepts of best practice to services by recasting measures in more abstract terms to better accommodate the diversity of establishments under study. They also added new measures focusing on the organization of the service function and service delivery. The bulk of the questions asked the respondent to rate the extent of deployment of practices dealing with organization, computer tools, and processes during the past 5 years. Ratings of the extent of deployment of practices were rated by respondents on four point scales ranging from "Not at all" to "A great deal". Each construct is defined over the following pages. The precise variables measured are shown in the Appendix.

(A) ESI

ESI measured the extent to which downstream functions, such as customer service, were involved at each stage of the development process, including the concept phase. In the services study, three stages were assessed: product concept, final release, and after sale. In the services study, involvement was measured using a dummy variable for 10 functions (*Note*: only 62 of the 70 enterprises supplied this amount of detail). Four of these were used in an ESI index: marketing, process development, finance, and customer service. In the goods data ESI was measured in six stages, the second one being product concept, which is used for comparison with services. The influence of manufacturing engineering was taken as an indicator of the extent to which a function typically involved only at late stages in serial development was engaged from the outset.

(B) IDC

IDC was measured as a scale dealing with process controls and continuous improvements. In constructing the survey for services, additional questions were added including benchmarking against best-in-class companies, Quality Function Deployment, and continuous process improvement. In the goods study, IDC was measured as behaviors that had the potential of aiding knowledge reuse, such as design standards, documentation, and product reviews with broad-based participation. The intent was to capture enabling processes instead of bureaucratic constraints.

(C) Computer information technology

Nine items are summed up to measure CIT. All questions were unified by the theme of computer tools supporting information management in general and project management pertinent to electronic exchanges along the value chain. User group participants suggested additional practices dealing with software and analytical tools. Seven of the items dealt with the internal deployment of computer information tools and general measures of computer utilization, such as solid modeling. Two items dealt with electronic linkages with external customers and partners. In the goods study, CIT was measured as an index of database usage and the deployment of Computer Automated Design /Manufacturing (CAD/CAM).

(D) Performance (the dependent variable)

Initial comparisons use the same signature benchmarks of development performance effectiveness. Time compression in development cycles is associated with advantages of speed to market and what Jack Welch of GE refers to as "time driven quality". Cost reduction indicates efficiencies due to better management of development operations.

5.3. Analysis and Findings

Correlations between the composite model element and innovation performance for both the services and goods data are shown in Table 5.1. The parallels in the two correlation matrixes are quite strong. Each of the

Table 5.1.   Correlations in Goods/Services[ix]

Measure		Perf.	ESI	IDC	CIT
Performance (Time & Cost)	Perf	—			
Organization	ESI	0.47**/0.51**	—		
Process	IDC	0.45**/0.52**	0.80**/0.45**	—	
Tools	CIT	0.40**/0.36**	0.50**/0.19	0.53**/0.33**	—
Reliability (α)		0.79/0.87	0.85/0.58	0.78/0.82	0.80/0.88

** = 0.01 level of significance (p)

Table 5.2.   Excerpts from Regression Analyses on Performance[x]

	Goods	Services
Direct Effects		
ESI	0.27*	0.26*
IDC	0.15	0.17
CIT	0.23*	0.16+
Interaction Effects		
ESI × IDC — Organization & Process	0.36*	1.43*/0.96*[1]
ESI × CIT — Organization & Tools	0.21*	n.s./0.74*
IDC × CIT — Process & Tools	0.50*	n.s./0.66*

1. Results of two-way interaction/Results of three-way models with radicalness (i.e., offerings more novel than major or minor modifications to existing ones).
   * = 0.05 level of significance; (p) + = 0.10 significance (p); n.s. = not significant.

troika of practices in each dataset is significantly correlated with performance. All inter-correlations are statistically significant except for the relationship between ESI and CIT in services. However, among services adopting a strategy of radical innovation, an association exists as explained further below.

To understand how the troika drives innovation performance regression analysis was employed. The results of moderated regression analyses from the goods and services studies are summarized at the top of Table 5.2.

Only the beta coefficients showing the strength of the direct and interaction effects of the components of the composite model are shown for parsimony. The direct effects are significant for ESI and CIT in both datasets. However, the interaction effects of IDC are significant as detailed in moderated regression analyses of interaction effects shown at the bottom of the Table.

5.3.1. *ESI and performance*

The cornerstone of the composite model is the reorganization of work to foster collaboration among functions at early phases of the development cycle, especially those traditionally engaged only downstream after most of the creative decisions have already been made. The level of upstream influence of downstream functions is measured for manufacturing engineering in the goods data and service staff in the service data. The correlation of ESI with performance is 0.51 ($p = 0.05$) in the goods sample and 0.47 ($p = 0.05$) in the service sample. In services, ESI has significant correlations with all other practices although its relationship with CIT is less than significant. However, this generally parallel result for product development cycles at the product concept stage is somewhat more complex if simultaneous influence is also examined after the outset. In goods, ESI has consistently strong correlations with all other practices. The regression of ESI with performance is 0.27 ($p = 0.05$) and 0.26 ($p = 0.05$) respectively for goods and services. This result confirms that the concept of ESI is pivotal for the deployment of value creation because input from downstream functions at the concept phase precludes subsequent defects costing time and money in both sectors.

5.3.2. *IDC and performance*

Flexible processes *in lieu* of rigid procedures are important for guiding development so that best known methods are used. The correlation of similar measures of IDC with performance is 0.55 ($p = 0.01$) in the goods sample and 0.45 ($p = 0.01$) in the service sample. This result is consistent with the presumption that the practice of IDC provides competitive advantage in both sectors. However, the impact of IDC on performance is less than significant in the regression analysis of the troika, 0.15 (*n.s.*) in the goods sample and 0.17 (*n.s.*) in the service sample. Yet IDC has an effect on performance in moderated regression analyses. The implication is that the solo value of process is limited. Instead its contribution is mostly made by providing flexible discipline guiding development in combination with other components of the troika. This result is consistent with the notion that procedures *per se* are best deployed in combination with human judgment, which is embodied by ESI, and enabled by tools and technologies as measured by CIT.

5.3.3. *CIT and performance*

IT helps with the design and development of customer offerings as well as the transformation of inputs to outputs. Measures of CIT have similar correlations with performance, 0.41 ($p = 0.01$) in the goods sample and 0.40 ($p = 0.01$) in the service sample. In goods, CIT has consistently strong correlations with all other practices. In services, there is a lack of significant correlation with ESI. The contrast in these correlations of CIT is one of the relatively few differences in the services and goods data. The regression of CIT with performance are 0.23 ($p = 0.05$) and 0.16 ($p = 0.10$) respectively. This result is consistent with the presumption that the practice of CIT provides competitive advantage in both sectors by helping design offerings, fostering electronic interconnectivity, and continually updating processes.

5.3.4. *The composite model and performance*

Moderated regression analyses showed an interaction between ESI and IDC on performance in both datasets at the 0.05 level of confidence. ESI fosters collaboration among diverse functions so that downstream problems in value creation are precluded. IDC provides flexible discipline for collaborative work among diverse functions guiding their effective execution of project objectives. Synergies observed between the axis of the composite model, ESI and IDC support the notion of a hybrid bond melding adaptations of mechanistic and organic design elements. Synergy between the creativity of people and processes for exploiting knowledge, the axis of the composite model, is robustly applicable across both sectors for the design of high performance value development systems.

Cross-functional organization is enabled by electronic communications. Especially in large corporations, the capability of diverse functions to communicate asynchronously up-front and throughout the value realization stream is a valuable capability. In the goods dataset, the interactions of ESI and CIT are statistically significant ($p = 0.05$). In the service dataset, however, the interaction is significant only if moderated by the deployment of a strategy of developing radical offerings.

The discipline of flexible process is enabled by computer-based information systems that permit adaptions to be made and shared globally. In the goods dataset, the interactions of IDC and CIT are statistically significant ($p = 0.05$). In the service dataset, as before, this occurs only with high radicalness.

5.3.5. *Radicalness as a contingency factor*

A strategy of developing radical offerings is often a vital method for gaining competitive advantage. However, the more complex the development, which is often associated with radical innovation, the greater the need for human capital of all kinds, the greater the benefits from the composite model because of the cross-fertilization of ideas among heterogeneous functions. The radicalness of the innovation strategy was measured by the extent to which the firm develops novel services/products. The extent to which the firm develops major and minor modifications was also measured.

Novelty is a critical contingency synergistically augmenting the positive impact of ESI on performance in both the goods and services datasets data (not shown in Tables). In the goods data, the interaction effect between ESI and a strategy of radicalness is significant only at the two earliest phases of the development cycle: (1) research and (2) concept.[xi] This result is consistent with other research showing that organic practices have their greatest impact in goods industries early in the development cycle.[xii] However, interactions of IDC and CIT with a strategy of radicalness were insignificant.

ESI also has a significant interaction with the strategy of radicalness in the services dataset (not shown in Tables). Importantly, this effect is significant for the engagement of key functions only at the concept phase and not at later phases as discussed in subsequent chapters.

Analysis of data from both sectors confirms the synergistic benefit from interaction between the axis of the composite model, organization (ESI) and process (IDC). However, the absence of two-way interactions between CIT with ESI and IDC noted above is interesting especially because this effect is only triggered under the contingency of radicalness.

One reason for this is because of the relatively recent rise in formal New Service Development (NSD) activities in services. Whilst all industrial corporations in the goods data had formal groups focused on innovation, most of the enterprises in the service sample were functionally organized and relied on one or two departments, such

> The more radical developments targeted by service enterprises, the greater the likelihood of deploying the composite model and achieving its performance benefits

as marketing or IT, for generating innovative offerings. However, service enterprises with a formal NSD function are more likely to deploy the trio of practice-sets measuring the composite model and to innovate.[xiii] Perhaps, this contrast accounts for the fact that interactions for CIT in the services dataset were only significant under the condition that the enterprise strategically targeted novel ways of creating value. Presumably, a strategy of radicalness in NSD is a trigger for investment in CIT and/or its integration with other practices in creating valued customer offerings in service enterprises. With this proviso, the composite model holds across both sectors.

5.4. Differentiation and Delivery Performance for Services

There is a need for a wider measure of innovation performance in services. Many relationships between providers and customers in goods industries terminate at point of sale. By contrast, the intangibility of some services provides opportunities to augment offerings post-launch. Although the principal focus of the research design was on service development, for many types of services its delivery processes are tantamount to the product itself.[xiv] Sometimes the features of the service offering are intertwined with its delivery and may entail continued exchanges between provider and customer. Exchanges which are based on tacit knowledge, such as automated bank transactions, delimit opportunities for innovation. However, interpersonal exchanges between provider and customers may provide rich opportunities for innovation in delivery as well as novel features augmenting the initial offering.

Table 5.3.   Measures of Performance in the Service Dataset

A. **Differentiation Performance** — *To what extent have your service products changed during the past 5 years?*

- Reduced cost;
- Higher quality;
- Upgraded features;
- New features;
- Shorter time from concept to test market of service product;
- Shorter time from test market to full-scale delivery of the service product;
- Reduced cost of development.

B. **Delivery Performance** — *To what extent has your service delivery changed during the past 5 years?*

- Shorter response time to order for existing service products;
- Shorter time for adjustments to complaints;
- Better after sales support services;
- Higher quality of delivery process, e.g., fewer customer complaints;
- Conformance with service product development process and procedures.

Overall Innovation Performance — Differentiation and Delivery Performance: Reliability (α) = 0.94 for all 12 items.

Therefore, measures of performance in the services dataset captured not only differentiation, but also delivery performance measured as time, cost, and quality (see Table 5.3 for full list of the measures). In addition the development performance index was widened to create a service differentiation index. This was needed as it includes both innovation and time/cost measures which enables a test of the composite model as a hybrid capable of providing both kinds of performance advantage simultaneously. Overall innovation performance combines the two dimensions.

These two dimensions of service performance are significantly correlated with one another ($r = 0.60$), but not so strongly as to preclude the analysis of ways in which practices predicting variation are like and unlike. One reason is that some services are more likely than others to augment their offerings post-launch.

Table 5.4. Correlation of Composite Model with Innovation Performance (Services)

	Differentiation performance	Delivery performance
Organization (ESI)	0.49**	0.31**
Process (IDC)	0.60**	0.45**
Tools (CIT)	0.45**	0.26**

** = 0.01 level of significance

The components of the composite model were found to have strong associations with both performance dimensions (see Table 5.4).

5.5. Discussion

Overall, the results of the two studies are roughly parallel and consistent with the model. This parallelism argues for the robustness of the model. Although the similarities in results from the two sectors are striking, differences were also observed.

First, a subject matter discipline for concurrent methods of product development seems to be lacking in services. Doubtlessly much training in new service development includes components that are analogous to those of *concurrent engineering*. Common themes sometimes include strategic goals of improving time to market, reducing costs, and developing novel products, as well as a growing emphasis on cross-functional teaming and the use of disciplined processes.

Second, simultaneous influence by multiple functions in product development is of benefit for services after initial sale in services. This is particularly true for services involving intangible personal exchanges and transactions. By contrast, involvement after sale in goods companies often means expensive correction of defects in the physical product.

Third, the role of CIT seems to be somewhat different in services than goods. Visualization of intangible services is more difficult than for physical goods. But in both sectors CIT can help support the organization of cross-functional teams and sustain dynamic, flexible processes. If the service enterprise targets the development of radical new products as a strategy, CIT has similar interactions with organization and process as in goods.

Qualitative studies observed contrasts in the formalization of the product development function in goods and services.[xv] All of the goods enterprises had a defined role for product development. By contrast, often the same people managing services

> The recognition of a need for formally organizing development functions in services is more recent than in goods industries

also took responsibility for developing them on the side. To focus on innovation, several large service enterprises created a formal product development function. Typically this involved redefining their offering in terms of "products". They created dedicated jobs and departments for this activity. For example, several major firms such as American Express and Chase Bank consolidated formal responsibility for new service development in an executive with responsibility for integrating activities across function departments. One may speculate that the creation of a formal product development function was in response to increased competitiveness in services stimulated by new technologies, globalization, and deregulation.

The largely parallel results observed in goods and services suggest that product development systems characterized by concurrent practices are more likely to outperform other systems. A generic model may be helpful for managers in both sectors — especially to the extent goods and services are bundled. In applying concurrency to services, however, some contextual contrasts between the two sectors need to be noted. While the term concurrency is used in industry, service firms are more likely to use general phrases to mean some of the same things, such as "time to market". However, this phrase does not have the subject matter underpinnings of the discipline of concurrent engineering. Therefore, the adoption of concurrent practices in services has been eclectic and diverse. Often, service firms view the discipline of engineering as largely inapplicable. In addition, the notion of a service as a product is relatively new. For example, leading service companies in the US have created new positions for product development only recently. But those that do create this function are higher performers. The results of these parallel studies show that a generic model of concurrency appears to have benefits for performance largely regardless of sector.

Notes

[i]   Morgan, J. and Liker, J. 2006. *The Toyota Product Development System: Integrating People, Process and Technology*, Productivity Press: Boca Raton.

[ii]   Hull, F. M., Collins, P. D., and Liker, J. K. 1996. Composite Forms of Organization as a Strategy for Concurrent Engineering Effectiveness, *IEEE Transactions on Engineering Management*, 43(2), 133–142.

[iii]   Meyer, M. H. and DeTore, A. 1999. Product Development for Services, *Academy of Management Executive*, 13(3), 64–76.

[iv]   Froehle, C. M., Roth, A. V., Chase, R. B., and Voss, C. A. 2000. Antecedents of New Service Development Effectiveness: An Exploratory Examination of Strategic Operations Choices, *Journal of Service Research*, 3(3), 3–17.

[v]   For example, Avlonitis, G. J., Papastahopoulou, P. G., and Gounaris, S. P. 2001. An Empirically-Based Typology of Product Innovativeness for New Financial Services: Success and Failure Scenarios, *Journal of Product Innovation Management*, 18(5), 24–342; Cooper, R. G. and Edgett, S. 1999. *Service Product Development*, Perseus: Cambridge.

[vi]   Collins, P., Hage, J., and Hull, F. 1988. Technical Systems: A Framework for Analysis, in *Research in the Sociology of Organizations*, Bacharach, S. and DiTomaso, N. (Eds.), JAI Press: Greenwich, Vol. 6, pp. 81–100.

[vii]   Avlonitis *et al.* 2001. *Op. cit.*

[viii]   For the goods industry study see Hull *et al.* 1996. *Op. cit.* For the service industry study see Hull, F. 2004. Innovation Strategy and the Impact of a Composite Model of Service Product Development on Performance, *Journal of Service Research*, 7(4), 167–181.

[ix]   For the goods data see Hull *et al.* 1996. *Op. cit.* Table 1, p. 136; For the services data see Hull. 2004. *Op. cit.* Table 1, p. 174.

[x]   For the goods date see Hull *et al.* 1996. *Op. cit.* Table 3, p. 138; For the services data see Hull. 2004. *Op. cit.* Tables 2 and 3, p. 175.

[xi]   Collins, P. and Hull, F. M. 2002. Early Simultaneous Influence across Stages of the Product Development Cycle: Impact on Time and Cost, *International Journal of Innovation Management*, 6(1), 1–24.

[xii]   Olson, E. M., Walker, O. C., and Ruekert, R. W. 1995. Organizing for Effective New Product Development: The Moderating Role of Product Innovativeness, *Journal of Marketing*, 59, 48–62.

[xiii]   Tidd and Hull. 2003. *Op. cit.*

[xiv]   Storey, C. and Easingwood, C. 1998. The Augmented Servicing Offering, *Journal of Product Innovation Management*, 15, 335–351.

[xv]   Tidd and Hull. 2003. *Op. cit.*

SECTION C

THE SYNERGISTIC ELEMENTS OF THE COMPOSITE MODEL

CHAPTER SIX

EARLY INFLUENCE: THE CORNERSTONE OF INNOVATION

Overview

The primary purpose of this chapter is to explain the importance Early Simultaneous Influence (ESI) and its effects on performance in both goods and services. ESI represents an operationally specific subset of organic teaming practices focused like a laser rifle on the integration key stakeholders in the value stream from concept to customer experiences. A defining characteristic of ESI is its inclusion of the outset of development of functions typically involved only at late phases of the value stream, such as manufacturing and service. Development operations in mechanistic bureaucracies is serial so that specialized functions performs prescribed roles at points as though working on an assembly-line. In concurrent development systems, all functions in the value creation stream are engaged in decision-making up-front where the bulk of costs are committed and opportunities for innovation are greatest. Engaging downstream functions, such as those in manufacturing and service only after key decisions have been made, means that their contribution are of marginal utility for realizing total value for customers. So much has already been determined at early phases of the development cycle that subsequent changes may be so expensive that innovative options at late stages are limited in both sectors, especially goods.

6.1. Benefits of Early Simultaneous Influence

Large-scale corporations in goods industries typically segregate specialized functions along the value stream into many different departments or divisions. The three most common divisions are research and technology, product development, and manufacturing. Rank and pay degrade along the value stream from research to manufacturing which is typically segregated in operational sites distant from headquarters locations. The initial focus of concurrent engineering was to improve integration of manufacturing with upstream functions. Over time, concurrent product development has grown to including collaboration among all functions in the value creation stream within enterprises including marketing, business development, etc.

ESI is hypothesized as benefiting performance for several reasons. First, up-front decision-making by all relevant functions reduces total cycle time and money for maintaining project teams. ESI may require somewhat more time at initial stages, but progressively less so at subsequent ones. Second, the bulk of costs are committed at early steps of a development cycle even though not expended until later. Third, the cost of fixing faulty upstream decisions at late stages is exponentially greater than earlier ones.[i] Collaboration at early stages saves money at the back-end because costly late stage changes are reduced. Fourth, non-value added activities are minimized because of rich direct, immediate communications instead of serial hand-offs. Fifth, the opportunity costs of being late to market are often enormous. Sixth, heterogeneous input in decision-making typically provides a better quality solution to complex, dynamic product development problems than solo individuals.[ii] Seventh, heterogeneous input stimulates creative ideas for improving not only products, but also the process of developing and servicing them.

ESI is important for overcoming barriers to innovation such as differentiation driven by scale and complexity. ESI helps transform mechanistic bureaucracies by infusing organic practices into their structures. Open communication channels enable team members to collaborate horizontally as well as vertically which may result in a kind of hybrid development system melding the advantages of organic and mechanistic capabilities.

Analogies to the game of rugby have proved useful for conceptualizing the value of ESI. A rugby scrum analogy is helpful for thinking about concurrent development because of the holistic effort of players to progress the ball downfield as a swarm of bees rather than specialists handing off a baton in a relay race.[iii] The relay race epitomizes the development approach typical for mechanistic bureaucracies where people enact roles that are serially enacted on a specific segment of

> Simultaneous engagement by diverse functions fosters agility enabling development operations to adaptively overcome obstacles and seize emergent opportunities

the field. A rugby scrum engages players as a whole team regardless of specific function which is analogous to the relatively unfettered development roles people play in organic organizations. A concurrent approach to development melds the advantages of both, but can only do so if the players are engaged at the start. ESI and concurrent methods are illustrated by agile scrum methods of software development have become increasingly deployed in goods and service industries. Agile scrum and concurrency rely on collaborative and reiterative development where ESI is a cornerstone of practice.

6.2. Results from the Data and Cases

6.2.1. *ESI in goods industries*

The extent to which the manufacturing engineering function is engaged in decisions by stage and how much influence they exerted was measured in the initial goods study for six phases. Unsurprisingly, their influence was relatively low at early stages relative to later ones as products approached production operations. But the more influence manufacturing exerted at early stages, the higher the level of performance.

One may speculate that ESI should work at least to some extent in both directions. Upstream functions should also exert some degree of influence in downstream. Analysis of the goods data contains a hint supporting this notion. High manufacturing influence over operations has a negative relationship with performance that is modestly significant. The implication is that just as downstream functions need to be allowed to play in the idea sandbox, correlatively, upstream functions need to take responsibility for the realization of their designs. This is consistent with analysis of 120 R&D labs showing that those commercializing a high percentage of their patented inventions for businesses served continued the involvement of their scientists and engineers at downstream stages of testing and production readiness.[iv]

Case studies show the benefit of cross-fertilization of influence along the entire value stream. An exemplar is Hewlett-Packard where product development/design engineers and manufacturing engineers often worked together under a common report and were paid similarly. After HP split-off its original core business as Agilent Technologies, some of these same traditions of collaborative influence among designers and makers persisted.

Micro-Electronics Development at Agilent Technologies

Responsibility for developing new microelectronics products is a collective responsibility at the Santa Rosa lab in California. Physicists are responsible not only for creation and development, but also for collaborating with test and manufacturing in bringing the product to realization. Co-involvement begins at the concept phase and continues throughout until manufacturing capability is relatively assured.

ESI stimulates inventions by cross-fertilizing ideas and helping them into new products. Horizontal collaboration across the base of the pyramid where work is done to add value to customer offerings is a key for innovation. On the one hand, it might seem that downstream functions such as manufacturing and customer service might

> ESI enables downstream functions, which usually have less organizational influence than upstream functions, to have a say at the outset of the development cycle

know relatively little about new value creation headed up by subject matter experts such as physicists and chemists in goods or econometricians and financial analysts in services. However, Axiom #4 suggests that ESI may be even more vital to the extent enterprises target a strategy of developing novel products because downstream function not only precludes designs that are difficult to realize, but also contribute creative ideas beyond their sphere of functional competence.

In the goods data, ESI has a positive correlation with performance as indicated by time compression and cost reduction. But if the enterprise targets radical customer offerings, the impact of ESI on performance is even stronger as illustrated in Figure 6.1 for the *concept phase* of the development cycle.[v]

The slope of the line between early manufacturing influence and performance is more sharply upward under the condition of radicalness.

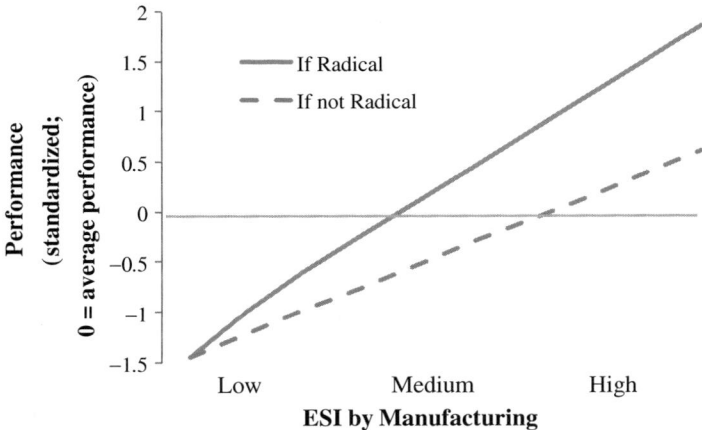

Figure 6.1. **Synergistic Impact of ESI at Concept Phase of Radical Strategy (Goods Industries)**

The more novel the offering, the greater the contribution of ESI to performance as stated in Axiom #4. Surprisingly, the advantages of manufacturing influence for time and cost under the condition of radicalness even extends as far upstream as the *research phase.*

> The more radical the product under development, the greater the benefit of early influence by downstream functions such as manufacturing and customer service

If early input by downstream manufacturing only boosted time to market and lower costs by precluding innovative options that were difficult to make, product innovation would suffer. However, these results suggest that the cross-fertilization of ideas along the length of the value stream is associated with increases in innovative features as well as time compression and cost reduction. Paradoxically, overcoming real world constraints actually stimulates as well as inhibits innovation.[vi]

Productization Centers at Westinghouse

Product development engineering was joined with manufacturing at the hip at one time at Westinghouse. The vice president (VP) of either function could sign-off on purchase authorizations for the other. This collaboration was taken into integrated teams for creating new products. The newer the product, the greater the number of diverse engineering and manufacturing functions collocated in a productivity center to rapidly develop manufactured solutions.[vii]

6.2.2. *ESI in services*

Does ESI also hold in services as well as goods? To test this notion, the after-sale customer service function was selected as reasonably analogous to manufacturing in the goods data for comparison. The contrasts between high vs. low performers for goods and services are juxtaposed as shown in Figure 6.2. at the concept phase. Because influence was measured using different scales in the two studies, the comparisons are shown in standard deviations from the mean.

In both Goods and Services data, high performing enterprises were those in which a key function representative of downstream operations had relatively high influence at the concept stage vs. low performers.

> Upstream engagement by downstream functions is a driver of performance in both services and goods

Although the contrast is slightly greater in goods than services, these results provide support for the notion that engaging downstream functions upstream at the concept phase is beneficial for performance in both sectors.

The example of collaborative engagement in value creation at Agilent Technologies has parallel in-service enterprises. For example, some finance businesses are increasingly able to access diverse information sources and use algorithms to rapidly provide customers with offerings that take their

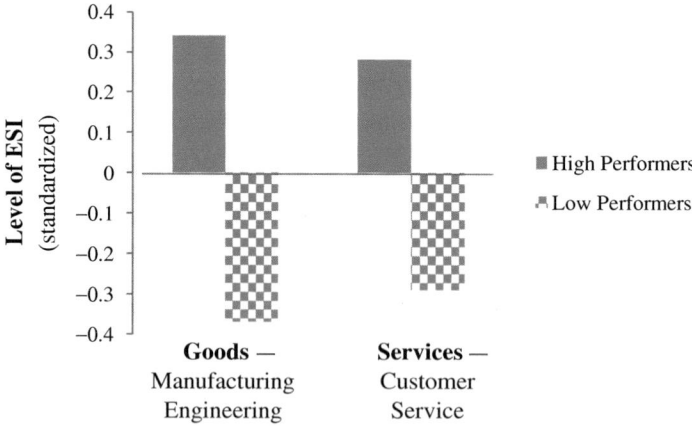

Figure 6.2.   Extent of Influence at the Development Concept Stage for High vs. Low Performers

total circumstances into account. An example of this capability is provided by activities at Chase syndicated banking.

> **System at Chase Syndicated Banking**
>
> Chase has a strong reputation in syndicated banking. Its competitiveness was achieved not only by its economies of scale, but by building a system that supports integrated solutions. After building a highly capable delivery processes, they decided to compete with a strategy of rapidly developing numerous varieties of their basic service. Up and downstream functions were reorganized into semi-autonomous project teams. These teams were responsible for product development and service delivery, from start to finish. The latest tools and technologies were used to manage development, update processes, and speed service delivery. Their value chain sequence was reciprocally integrated and rapidly adjustable, from opportunity to customer delivery.

Influence by downstream functions, such as customer service, at the concept phase is also important for the development of novel customer offerings. A case study illustrates the contributions of downstream functions not only for post-launch support, but also for concept development. The case of CNY bank (pseudonym) underscores the importance of ESI in services, but it also serves as an alert to the role service plays post launch in the delivery process.

> **Investment Product at CNY Bank**
>
> An innovative financial product was offered to customers at a major bank and attracted many customers. However, the rules and requirements for filing tax returns were not detailed in a user-friendly way at the time of sale. When customers began attempting to file their returns, they were confused by unclearly written guidelines and called the customer service number by the tens of thousands which swamped the phone lines. The high level of customer dissatisfaction with this and related financial products cost the bank a large number of customers estimated at over 10,000. As a corrective, representatives from the service function were always included at the outset when of subsequent development teams were formed. The VP remarked that the inclusion of customer service was not only necessary to prevent defects in the offering, but to help improve the conceptualization of features of offering as well.

In the services dataset, ESI is measured as an index of four functions engaged at the concept phase: marketing, process development, finance, and customer service. The more radical the development, the more likely diverse functions are to be engaged at the concept phase. Analysis of engagement of diverse functions at the concept phase not only supports the benefit of ESI, but is also consistent with Axiom #4 that early collaboration is more necessary for achieving novel offerings. This measure of ESU has a significant correlation with performance measured as time compression and cost reduction $(0.51, p < 0.01)$ and also with the development of radically new products $(0.37, p < 0.01)$.

A strategy of radicalness plays a broader role in the services data than goods data where novelty is a moderator only for ESI. A strategy of radicalness in the services data not only moderates the impact of ESI on performance, but also the impacts of In-process Design Controls (IDC) and Computer Information Technology (CIT). A strategy of radicalness has statistically significant interaction effects with each of the troika. This trio of synergistic interaction effects in the services data are indicated by dotted lines in Figure 6.3. The three-way interaction adds 7 percent to variance explained in time and cost and 5 percent to innovative product differentiation.

Synergies between ESI and IDC, the axis of the composite model, are substantially stronger with performance if the enterprise strategy targets the development of radically new offerings. One reason may be that the discipline of process helps focus ideas cross-fertilized through ESI so that higher yields of development concepts are realized as customer offerings. The interaction between ESI and IDC, the axis of the composite model,

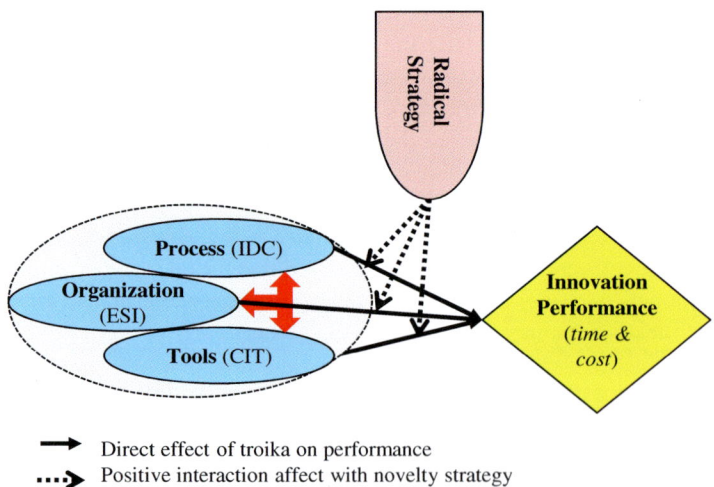

Direct effect of troika on performance
Positive interaction affect with novelty strategy

Figure 6.3.   Impact of the Composite Model on Performance Moderated by Radicalness

suggests the benefits of a hybrid bond between organic and mechanistic practices.

CIT only has interaction effects with ESI and IDC under the contingency that a strategy of radical product introductions is pursued by the service enterprise. One reason is because many services provide traditional offerings with little or no modifications. However, those services affected by environmental changes were much more likely to adopt computer technologies to enhance their competitive capabilities. The need to innovate seems to have been a contingency

> Strategic intent to develop radically new customer offerings triggers the deployment of the composite model in service enterprises

driving the formation of the NSD function and the deployment of the troika of practices in the composite model.

6.3. Post-Launch Collaboration in Goods and Services

As already noted in Figure 6.2, high performers in both goods and services are similar in that both are far more likely to engage a key downstream function at the concept phase than low performers. The importance of ESI is somewhat greater in goods than services partly because of the physical nature of the offering. Modification after sale is difficult for manufacturers of a physical object as the product must either be returned for rework or field technicians sent out to the customer site. Even rapid cycle goods companies, like leading computer manufactures, usually take about a year and a half to incorporate modifications into the next generation of products based on initial customer experiences.

In goods industries, involvement by manufacturing engineers trends slightly upward from concept to pre-launch. The rationale is the confluence of up and downstream functions is highest just prior to launch because of the exponentially higher costs of corrections afterwards consistent with Axiom #2. At this cross-roads of up and downstream development activities, many functions must be simultaneously engaged prior to launch to avoid costly rework.

Many services, especially intangible ones, may be comparatively easier to modify post-launch than most goods. Therefore, cross-functional

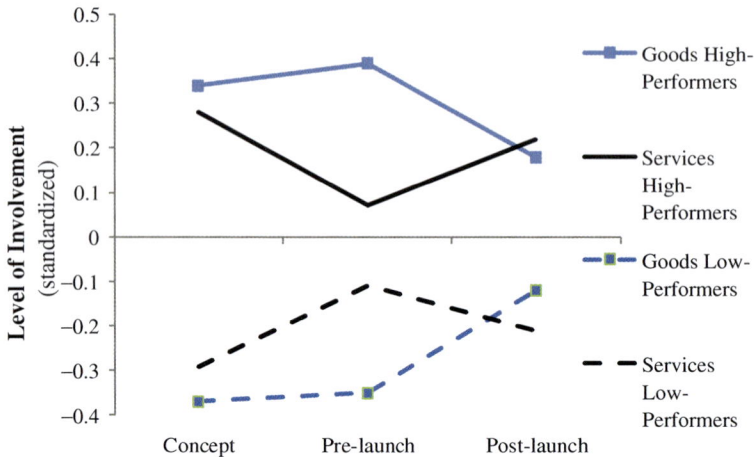

Figure 6.4.   Influence of Manufacturing Engineering (in Goods) and Customer Support (in Services) over the Development Cycle

collaboration for manufacturing and customer service staff is compared not only at the concept phase, but also the pre- and post-launch phases in Figure 6.4. What is strikingly different is the post-launch pattern. High performance goods slope downwards while high performing services trend upwards. Diminished engagement by manufacturing engineering post-sale is presumably a positive indicator that defects were precluded by their early involvement at the concept phase.

Why does the customer service function increase its involvement post-launch despite engagement in concept decisions? One explanation is that post-launch engagement by customer service shows an uptick to fix whatever problems may arise. Another is that many service offerings are amenable to augmentation of value post-launch. Service offerings are more likely to provide opportunities for augmentation to the extent they are intangible and/or involve ongoing exchanges with customers.[viii]

Low performers in services, however, have a much sharper uptick from concept to pre-launch. On interpretation is that these low performing service enterprises did not form dedicated groups responsible for NSD which is associated with ESI. A likely scenario is that the new launch was initiated pretty much by a single function with only belated efforts to engage others.

Early engagement has parallel effects on performance in goods and services. However, an important difference between goods and services is the extent to which the knowledge adding value to the offering is embedded within it. In goods industries customer offerings are delivered with much of the knowledge contributing to its value embodied within it such as designed features, programs, automatic mechanisms, etc. This usually means the delivery of a physical object from a store or distribution center to customers terminates the transaction.

> Many services are more amenable to post-launch augmentation than goods so that late stage influence may add value especially to the extent that interpersonal transactions are entailed in delivery

Many opportunities for servicing goods post-launch arise during the interval from delivery to end of life. In some instances relationships between producer of goods and customer continue during the lifetime of product use. Instead of terminating after sale, many goods companies offer service contracts, upgrades, and guarantee sustainability until end of life disposal. Some organizations servicing physical products are divisions within the manufacturing corporation producing the original product. More often, goods companies affiliate with service companies via alliances, partnerships, or long-term subcontractual relationships to support customers purchasing their products. Some corporations such as Xerox make a significant proportion of their profits by operating their equipment as a copy center service inside customer locations. This represents vertical integration toward customers via services.

> Opportunities for business model innovation by developing holistic offerings integrating goods and services may be greatest where augmentation occurs after initial sale

Some service offerings are dependent in varying degrees on physical goods. The gap between the sale of goods and life-time sustainability is often filled by stand-alone service enterprises. Independent enterprises may focus on specific kinds of products or components manufactured by conglomerates providing a myriad of supporting services. Often tacit knowledge is associated with the use of physical products which sometimes seem to have a mind of their own and need the exercise of human judgment in controlling them. The rise of companies developing applications for electronics products represents a kind of knowledge-based service. In some cases, service providers provide or even operate physical equipment made by others for owners in-house or on location. For example, so called "fractionals" provide a variety of independent services for aircraft that eat away at profit opportunities of the manufactures.

Other service enterprises provide offerings in which tacit knowledge is delivered mostly as a free standing value even though physical accoutrements may play a supporting role. Tacit knowledge may be delivered to the customer in a single transaction. In other instances the transfer of tacit knowledge involves recurring exchanges. Recurring delivery of offerings are valued because tacit knowledge offers opportunities for improvement after initial sale. Modification of intangible services post-launch may occur relatively rapidly in some instances, especially those involving personal interchanges. Service providers may often improve their delivery processes based on customer reactions by modifying behaviors instead of physical objects. This allows for augmenting the service offering and provides opportunities for innovation that are more difficult to achieve in goods industries after sale.

6.4. Conclusions

In conclusion, this chapter shows that goods and services benefit from the cornerstone of concurrent practice, ESI. However, our comparative analysis across the two sectors shows opportunities for post-launch collaboration, especially in services that entail tacit knowledge and continuing exchanges.

Notes

[i]   Clausing, D. P. 1994. *Total Quality Development*, ASME Press: New York.
[ii]   Gerwin, D. and Susman, G. I. (Eds.), 1996. Special Issue on Concurrent Engineering, *IEEE Transactions on Engineering Management*, 43(2), 118–123.
[iii]   Wang, X. 2013. *Agile and Lean Service-oriented Development: Foundations, Theory, and Practice*, Information Science Reference: Hershey; Nonaka, I. 1994. A Dynamic Theory of Organisational Knowledge Creation, *Organization Science*, 5(1), 14–37.

iv   Hull, F. 1993. The Impact of Knowledge on the Survival of America's Manufacturing Plants, *Social Forces*, 223–246.

v   Collins, P. and Hull, F. M. 2002. Early Simultaneous Influence across Stages of the Product Development Cycle: Impact on Time and Cost, *International Journal of Innovation Management*, 6(1), 1–24.

vi   Goldratt, E. M. 1984. *The Goal: A Process of Ongoing Improvement*, Quality Press: Milwaukee.

vii   Westinghouse Electronic Systems: Integrated Product Development," with John W. Kamauff, Jr. and Larry G. Richards, in *Cross-Functional Management of Technology Cases and Readings*, M. Dayne Aldridge (Ed.), Paul M. Swamidass, Richard D. Irwin, 1996.

viii   Storey, C. and Easingwood, C. 1998. The Augmented Servicing Offering, *Journal of Product Innovation Management*, 15, 335–351.

CHAPTER SEVEN

ORGANIC TEAM STRUCTURE: INTEGRATING HORIZONTAL WORKFLOWS

Overview

Organic organization is a horizontal vector fostering interfunctional relationships necessary for the transformation of mechanistic bureaucracies into concurrent development systems. Organic organizations relax hierarchical structures on communications and observance of strict procedures. Structuring teams with the mission of developing customer offerings frames and focused communications and work activities. Organic Team Structure (OTS) integrates the work of people along the development stream who are segregated from one another by hierarchical lines of authority. OTS is broad concept encompassing many practices, such as cross-functional teaming, collocation, and group rewards. Benefits of OTS include enhanced utilization of human capital though the creative opportunities are offered by cross-skilling and the exchange of ideas. OTS provides a collaborative platform for early simultaneous influence, an operationally specific version of teaming whereby downstream functions are engaged in development up-front. Parallel results from the goods and services data show that OTS is positively correlated with performance in both sectors.

7.1. Organic Team Structure (OTS)

Early simultaneous influence by diverse functions at the front-end of development cycles is contingent upon the infusion of organic practices in bureaucratic structures. OTS inserts an inclusive swath of practices to facilitate collaboration among up and downstream functions. In mechanistic bureaucracies, communication channels are vertically channeled so that a person in one silo of a hierarchy needs to push communications up to a common report who relays messages downward to those in other silos in order to communicate horizontally. By contrast, leapfrog communications in organic organizations sometimes enable employees to communicate directly with their boss's boss. Barriers to horizontal communications are semi-porous in an organic environment. The notion of all-channel communications contrasts greatly with serial information flows in mechanistic bureaucracies where work is transferred along a one-way, serial flow analogous to a factory assembly-line. OTS enables reciprocal collaboration among people along the base of the pyramid where purposive development work is done.

A primary factor in the development of successful new offerings is the creation of an innovative environment where ideas and open communications are encouraged by supportive management.[i] Organic organization enables collaboration among diverse functions. Structuring teams in an organic environment provides a specific context framing and focusing communications on the development of customer offerings. People from diverse functions are empowered to execute specific development projects. Research in the service sector stresses the importance of involving and empowering front-line staff throughout the development process.[ii] This allows constructive ideas to improve not only the service, but also the processes of developing and delivering them. Cross-fertilization of ideas among diverse functions is especially needed at the outset of the development process where the opportunity for innovation is the greatest.[iii] Cross-functional communication also builds commitment for the project and reduces the amount of risk and uncertainty surrounding it.[iv]

7.2. A Trio of Key OTS Practices

OTS horizontally integrates the work of specialists at various points along the value stream. Team members with some degree of autonomy within

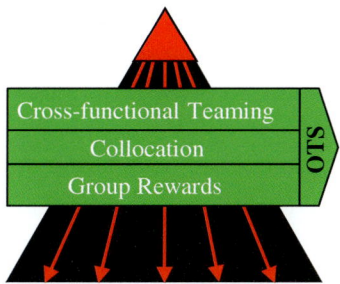

Figure 7.1.   Organic Team Structure and Vertical Communications

the larger hierarchical structure are better able to focus on serving customer needs regardless of functional constraints. OTS is a multifaceted concept with several component practices including (1) cross-functional teaming, (2) collocation, and (3) group or team rewards. How these three sets of practices infuse organic behaviors into the bowels of mechanistic bureaucracies is illustrated in Figure 7.1.

The trio of OTS practices cuts across the vertical hierarchy to provide opportunities for collaboration along the horizontal workflow of the enterprise. Communications become cross-hatched so that horizontal collaboration may occur among teams members who have vertical reporting relationships to higher level authorities responsible for assuring their capability for functional purpose. Collaboration among diverse functions along the development stream enables reciprocal feedback to occur so that communication flows are two-way instead of serially unidirectional.

7.2.1. *Cross-functional teaming*

Cross-functional teaming entails the formation of groups representing a diversity of stakeholders from appropriate functional hierarchies. Achieving cross-functional integration is a necessary step for concurrent enterprising. It is a more proactive implementation of organic organization design than the traditional approach of removing

> One of the most difficult challenges in deploying concurrency is to have the project team leader exercise greater say over the roles played by members from diverse functions than their the authorities in their home departments

bureaucratic constraints to permit unstructured communications and ad hoc encounters. Cross-functional teaming brings varied disciplines together and charters them with a common task. This means that a significant proportion of time is spent outside of functional departments. Implicit in this definition is the notion of some degree of empowerment in terms of staffing and budget so that the team bounded delimited autonomy in making decisions relative to functional departments.

Teaming fosters communication among heterogeneous functions to cross-fertilize ideas so that superior knowledge is applied to developing products and/or services. Communication among people from various divisions helps development of the project by reducing uncertainties about customer requirements, competitive threats, emerging technologies, and business strategies.[v] Too much functional homogeneity and groupthink amongst team members can constrain the inflow of new knowledge and limit the search for knowledge outside the team. One of the biggest challenges for enterprises developing new offerings, especially in services, is building diverse teams and preserving heterogeneity. Cross-functional co-operation among team members improves their support for the project and helps stimulate innovation as well as reduce project risk.[vi]

Cross-functional teaming may be even more needed in developing services than in goods especially when the delivery process is tantamount to the customer offering itself. Customer offerings involving interpersonal interactions entail intangibilities which are hard to define, tricky to cost, and difficult to standardize.[vii] To the extent a significant proportion of value is added during delivery, failure to engage downstream functions in early development decisions can result in high costs at the back-end, such as swamped customer service lines, faulty computer programming, and misdirected advertising campaigns.

The literature on cross-functional teaming is lengthy. Teaming enables people to be relatively more creative in the face of new and uncertain tasks.[viii] Cross-functional teaming is easy to conceive, but difficult to implement and sustain. Nominal teams are far more frequent than authentic collaborators, who take collective responsibility for achieving a commonly agreed upon task. But even when teaming is genuine, it may be hard to sustain institutionally.

Teaming as a Way of Life at Motorola

Motorola leads the American response to the Japanese challenge in quality which was due in large part to teamwork. Employees were expected to be team players or counseled out of the corporation. The norm was reinforced by Frank Arkell, chief software architect, who repeatedly said: "teaming is an unnatural act, so we've got to do it". Motorola built such a strong commitment to teaming that most employees formed problem-solving teams on their own initiative just to "make things better". During its heyday, cross-functional teams were the bedrock of Motorola's operations. Unfortunately, the Iridium debacle resulted in the adoption of complex and detailed procedures for new product development that eroded team empowerment and demotivated creative initiatives.

Cross-functional teaming is not only hard to maintain, it is sometime hard to get started. The follow case illustrates difficulties at a private banking service.

Financial Services at Blackwater Bank

Wealthy clients were assigned to a highly touted service "team". The so-called team was charged with helping manage their client's wealth as a portfolio. Each team member was a functional specialist responsible for a segment of the million or more dollars of a given customer's money. However, the team as a whole lacked collective responsibility for collaboratively managing the portfolio as a holistic asset. Each team member performed functionally specific tasks with little collaboration with others. An external assessment of roles found that members of wealth management teams spent almost 40 percent of their time leaving messages for one another. As a result, wealthy customers sometimes had to make as many as five or six phone calls to receive information about their various accounts, e.g., checking, savings, bonds, stocks, insurance, etc. Changes were proposed to reorganize private bankers as a genuine team collectively responsible for the total portfolio. Although some changes were initiated, overall implementation has occurred in fits and starts largely because senior executives in tall hierarchies controlled each of the functions and had little incentives to share their turf with others.

Despite difficulties, genuine cross-functional development teams have spread in goods and services. AT&T was a global leader that somewhat serendipitously discovered the power of cross-functional teaming.[ix] Their first cross-functional team was so successful that the practice rapidly spread to its most profitable divisions as well as others.[x]

The default in many services as well as goods companies is for each function to serve their own interests first and the offering under development for customers second. At Morgan Stanley, managers of client

---

Cross-Functional Teaming: Bell Labs and AT&T

An innovative new product at Bell Labs was developed and a prime customer, NTT in Japan, wanted it. However, NTT insisted on faster delivery time and far fewer defects as well further improved features. The corporate development approach was quite serial and involved hand-offs across eight divisions with specialized expertise. Recognizing that there was no way they could meet customer expectations within the existing mechanistic hierarchy, representatives from various departments pooled their discretionary funds to form a large-scale cross-functional team. Stakeholders collaborated on a charter which all signed to indicate acceptance for collective responsibility. Whatever it took to speed the project toward success was everyone's job. Managers did hands-on work, bench engineers made managerial decisions. A survey found that the most innovative members identified in a survey were those who took personal responsibility for project outcome regardless of their individual job assignment. The upshot was that the project was completed earlier than scheduled, with significantly fewer defects than mandated and exceeded customer expectations.

---

relationships would develop new offerings to make their customers pleased to gain commissions with little regard for corporate profit. Each group responsible for various client sectors competed with one another for resources. Only by forming a centralized team they termed a user group where customer and customer interests simultaneously served.

OTS at Morgan Stanley

At Morgan Stanley's global custody business, new products were originated by a variety of players. Most of these new products required resources from the Information Technology department. The competition for these resources was sometimes intense. Therefore, the firm appointed a vice president for new product development whose responsibilities included convening cross-functional "user groups" to prioritize projects for resource allocations. The user group integrated product development activities and made resource decisions more strategically focused around collective priorities. The advantage of this cross-functional integration across and within groups was rapid development of services tailored to customer needs that were also profitable for the firm.

The benefits of cross-functional teaming within the framework of OTS are well documented in a wide variety of studies and settings, including non-profits and even social service organizations. For example, cross-functional teams have proved effective in holistic medical care where diverse specialists simultaneously assess patient needs up-front instead of relying upon a general care physical to relay them out serially for pre-specified segments of care. Similarly, a National Center for Special Need Adoption Services in Michigan deployed principles of concurrency, including cross-functional teaming to reduce the waiting time for permanent adoption from nearly 41 to 19 months.[xi]

7.2.2. *Collocation*

Interpersonal communication can be either one-to-one or many-to-many and may occur via formal meetings or informal exchange via hallway interactions and after-work socialization. Face-to-face interchanges provide the richest forms of communication. Such interaction allows verbal, para-verbal (tone, inflection, volume), and non-verbal (facial clues, body language) information to be shared. Some estimates are that as much as 80 percent of content communicated in face-to-face exchanges is non-verbal.[xii] For sharing provisional ideas in the upstream stages of service development, subtle cues like body language and other messages may affect the amount of trust others feel. Rich communication fosters trust and other relational characteristics that are important enablers for sharing knowledge in organizations.[xiii] Therefore, physical collocation may augment the capabilities of cross-functional teams to collaborate effectively especially to the extent information is provisional at early phases of the development cycle.

Bringing project team members together in a shared space creates opportunities for exchanging conjectures and hypotheses via face-to-face contact. To facilitate personal exchanges, many companies house product development teams in dedicated area. However, recent research shows that rich communication has pervasive effects throughout the life cycle and especially in services where interpersonal exchanges involve the exploitation of tacit knowledge.[xiv] Recently many companies have emphasized on virtual communication. However, others have relied on physical collocation. For example, Black & Decker (B&D) has regarded eye contact among team members as essential as stated by a norm: "If have to pick up the phone, you are too far away." However, collocation is very helpful only if collaborative activities are structured. Just sitting in proximity with one another is insufficient as the following case illustrates.

Fusion Cells at Black & Decker
B&D was falling behind their Japanese competitors in the power tool business. They took a benchmarking trip to understand why. The key reason was a lack of cross-functional integration in development. In response, B&D configured all key functions in a single room with a community table at the center. Although everyone's workstation faced the surrounding walls, the reduction of privacy enabled anyone interested in a conversation to wheel around and join in. The fusion cell was a great success. New products were developed far faster and less expensively than before with inventions generated that were unanticipated at the outset. Although collocation was a huge success factor, it was augmented by up-front team training in project planning and collective adoption of common strategic objectives.[xv]

Some of the most progressive service enterprises in the services sample adopted collocation as a tactic for improving new service development (NSD). Chase bank formed a product development function by housing participants from various departments in one corner of an office. Their collocated space also included visitor desks for representatives on temporary assignment to the cross-functional development team.

Collocation at Chase Bank
A core team of representatives from diverse functions responsible for NSD were collocated in a convenient corner of the building. The core members were able to exchange development plans easily. Other functions knew a central meeting they could go to for the latest information on NSD projects relevant to their work.

Physical collocation of teams is an enabler of collaborative development, but an insufficient cause of it. For example, employees representing different functions may sit next to one another. But if their principal allegiances are to their hierarchical bosses instead of their common project leader, opportunities for authentic collaboration are compromised. Without organically structuring collaborative commitment to achieve shared objectives, the benefits of physical collaboration is often close to nil.

> Collocation without shared objectives and common processes is unlikely to be effective

7.2.3. *Group rewards*

By integrating the input of diverse people, organic team structure achieves more output per person than organizations reliant upon lone geniuses.

Seldom is a good idea generated by a single person and transformed into a realized customer offering by solo effort. This reality is recognized by a common saying that innovation is a team sport.

Group rewards help teams achieve innovation partly because it is difficult to trace an idea to a single individual as a notion by one gets modified by many as it progresses from concept to reality. Although mechanistic bureaucracies reward individuals, enterprises deploying OTS also reward groups. The more innovative the development challenge, the more important it is to foster exchanges among team members to generate creative ideas. The collective wisdom of heterogeneous team members is more likely to generate good ideas, but to devise innovative paths for their development.

Analysis of a following-on study of goods industries shows that team rewards have only a negligible effect on overall performance and product innovation. However, team rewards have a very strong interaction effect on both overall performance and product innovation if the strategy of the enterprise targets new product development. Similarly, rewarding teams has a large synergy bonus if the enterprise strategy targets the development of new process technologies. The results are consistent with the notion that innovation is a collaborative endeavor and management is advantaged by rewarding it.

A conversion from individual to collective responsibility is required for achieving the advantages of concurrency. However, most performance evaluations are based on the performance of individually defined jobs. Performance appraisals in mechanistic bureaucracies provide little or no incentive

> Innovation requires group rewards, rather than individualistic incentives, because cross-fertilization of ideas is the principle driver of creativity

for collaborative endeavor. The contribution of the collectivity needs to be rewarded as well as that of individuals. Group rewards incent collaboration among diverse functions because everyone shares a stake in outcomes. A rule of thumb for assessing the extent to which OTS is viable is the answer to the question, "we accept personal responsibility for project outcomes regardless of our individual job function".

Group rewards may be financial and/or social. Examples of financial rewards include team bonuses. More indirectly, 360-degree performance evaluation systems use ratings of how both up- and downstream functions rate each another as well as super and subordinates. However, the results of 360-degree ratings only affect individual pay. Because 360-degree performance evaluations can become bureaucratically complex, some corporations have inserted evaluations of teaming performance on individual performance evaluations. However, it is difficult for functional managers to know directly how well someone from their department actually behaved in actual practice as a teammate.

Social rewards for team performance are far more common and less contentious. Examples include various kinds of recognition such as plaques, awards, group dinners, etc. But social rewards are only so good as the extent to which team members value the good esteem of their mates. Thus, a prerequisite for the effectiveness of social rewards is structuring collaborative responsibility for the outcome of development projects regardless of individual function.

Initial efforts to reward groups are usually resisted by entrenched bureaucrats. However, rewarding groups is a problematic issue not only because of the context of mechanistic bureaucracy, but also because seldom do all team members make equivalent contributions. As a concurrent approach to development matures, a hybrid reward system typically emerges blending group with individual rewards.

Group Rewards at Lockheed Martin

An example of a successful reward system is a mixed approach to incentives at Lockheed Martin, where every team member receives the same and bonus based on grades through customer ratings. However, individuals are also compensated separately by administrators who allocate each individual a share of the overall corporate bonus based on their rank on a totem pole. Performance achievement was quite high partly because of dual incentives for individual and collective endeavor.

A classic study was important because it provides some of the earliest documentation for the value of social rewards based on the esteem of peers. Groups wiring telephone banks were paid based on individual piece rates. Surprisingly, groups were more productive if they had a common performance norm so that the collective target was met even though faster workers underreported their completed pieces at the expense of their own pay so that slower workers could avoid managerial penalties. The value of the norm was that "rate busters", who put more in their pockets by high achievement, were eschewed so that management could not raise the performance bar to get more than what the group regarded as a fair standard.[xvi] The advantage of group responsibility, as opposed to solely individual incentives, is underscored by a well-known study comparing two groups in a social service organization.

Group Rewards at Job Placement Agency[xvii]
A comparison of two groups of employees at a job placement agency showed that Group A, the members of which received rewards based on individual performance, had several star achievers. Group B, the members of which shared rewards collectively, had no super achievers. But the average productivity was higher for Group B than Group A because they collaborated in making placements instead of hiding information about jobs for their own personal gain.

The benefits of group reward therefore apply in a wide variety of settings, social services, as well as private enterprises. However, structuring team activities with group norms is a precondition for benefits.

7.2.4. *Comparison of OTS in goods and services*

OTS practices used in the goods data focus on the integration of upstream design engineers and downstream manufacturing engineers. Indicators include the extent to which they are on the same development team, collocated at the same site, and share group rewards. The focus was similar in the service data as shown in Table 7.1.

In the goods data, measures of OTS practice are correlated with performance measured as time and cost (cross-functional teams, 0.37; collocation, 0.21, group rewards, 0.30). In the services data, the correlations are somewhat more strongly significant (cross-functional teams, 0.44; collocation, 0.58; group rewards, 0.39). All are statistically significant at the 0.01 level of confidence except for collocation in goods.

One reason the correlations are somewhat stronger in the services data may be that the cross-functional integration of functions in goods industries has been established as a best practice since the late 1980s. By contrast, the notion of cross-functional integration of NSD groups in services is much more recent. Many service enterprises lacked a formal NSD group deploying OTS practices despite the fact that those that do are

Table 7.1.   Organic Team Structure

Goods

Cross-functional teaming

- Extent ME assigned to cross-functional product design team on a full-time basis.
- Increase use of cross-functional teams in last 5 years.

Collocation

- Collocation of design and manufacturing engineers at same site.
- Increased collocation during the past 5 years.

Group rewards

- Extent to which groups vs. individuals rewarded for new designs, and design implementation.

Services

Cross-functional teaming

- Using cross-functional teams.
- Cross-training specialists.
- Reorganizing jobs to reduce hand-offs.

Collocation

- Collocating complementary functions.

Group rewards

- Rewarding project teams/groups.

more likely to be high performers. Regarding the contrast in physical collocation, however, the tangible aspects of goods may make face-to-face exchanges relatively less necessary than in many services. For example, CAD/CAM may be used to exchange quantitative data between up and downstream functions.

7.3. Benefits of OTS

Among the several benefits of organic team structuring, two are particularly important: (1) cross-skilling, and (2) cross-fertilization of creative ideas. However, benefits from organic organization principles are contingent upon the type of work performed. Mechanistic organizations are highly efficient for producing standardized products if the work is stable that it can be broken down into specialized segments. This mechanistic approach pioneered by Fredrick Taylor was successfully deployed in mass production assembly-lines. Ford, a mechanistic assembly-line became the default paradigm for how to organize operations in goods and services, including development.

7.3.1. *Cross-skilling*

Mechanistic systems degrade skills because role enactment is prescribed in advance to preclude human judgment. By contrast, OTS raises the potential value of human capital instead of reducing the need for human skills. A huge advantage of cross-functional skilling is that people play roles that lie outside the boundaries of their traditional specialization. In the early phases of projects these people often have different knowledge bases and lack a shared understanding of their work mission. Interpersonal communication helps development personnel build common mental models, unify their work by cross-functional understandings, and integrate diverse knowledge in new and different ways to create shared meanings.[xviii] So-called T-people form bridges across different functional specialists because of their general understanding of system level-requirements.

> Generalists are needed to help integrate the work of diverse specialists to ensure systemic solutions to customer needs

In organically structured organizations, teams are committed to achieving project outcomes regardless of specific role specializations. In a cross-functional setting, diverse specialists learn by on-the-job training how others perform their roles. But some degree of formal cross-training also helps the team pull together as collective units where everyone understands each other's roles and can help out in balancing and covering shortfalls. In dynamic environments where new products are introduced, the capability of employees to not only understand, but also execute multiple kinds of tasks is quite valuable for ensuring project success. After all, it is relatively easy for each employee to execute their individual role properly, yet the project may fail nevertheless because of lack of timely integration of diverse contributions. Generalists as well as specialists are required to integrate collaborative work. A certain degree of ambidexterity is required of at least a few integrators who understand the general requirements of the project and its link to the fulfillment of customer needs.

As technological complexity and the tastes of customers have become more dynamic and individualistic, however, advantages have increased for employing multi-skilled people who can perform a variety of tasks. The overhead costs of administering the division of labor in mechanistic bureaucracies can be a significant proportion of revenues, such as 40 percent or more because administrators devise prescribed roles scripting behaviors to preclude the exercise of human judgment. However, the exercise of judgment by cross-trained employees can be quite valuable for performing complex, variable work.

Cellular Manufacturing at Siemens PBX

For making assemblies of complex PBX telecom systems, a cellular manufacturing approach was used. A large central table was surrounded by Kanban trays for easy reach and place. All of the dozen cell members were cross-trained to perform any job. Once a part was picked up, it never rested until properly installed. Everyone was responsible for the collective product and ensuring its quality. Upon completion of the assembly, the product was boxed, addressed to the customer, placed on a platform near the door for pick-up by a freight handler. When the customer opened the box, the toll free number to call for any assistance rang at one end of the table. Of course, the cost of the direct labor was relatively higher than that for employees performing similar but repetitive tasks in assembly-line work. But the cellular operation was largely self-managed. The reduction in overhead costs, which was below 20 percent of sales, as well as higher quality, more than compensated for higher direct labor costs.

In many services delivery processes supporting new products after development is also important. Cross-skilling can be an important method for pooling the organizing work so that bits don't have to be started and stopped as a solo individual waits for information and/or materials to complete a specific task.

Problems in Fin Delivery of Card Services at American Express

American Express was once was plagued by a high error rate in processing applications from customers for a new credit card product. Customers received needless repeat calls, conflicting information, and inconsistent assessments of their creditworthiness. Change was initiated by reorganizing an assembly line into cells of cross-functional team members. Instead of multi-step hand-offs and fumbles, a "one touch" process was developed that resulted in higher quality service delivery.

7.3.2. *Cross-fertilization of creative ideas*

OTS is a project-level application of the principles of "organic" organization design that increases the generation of ideas. People are the wellspring of product creation. The lone genius or maverick cowboy is usually less important for successful innovations in established corporations than team players, especially in hyper-competitive markets. Even though many scientists and engineers may say they are more creative working on their own, leading companies have increasingly organized them in cross-functional teams because data show teaming increases invention rates. Comparison of R&D laboratory organizations demonstrates that invention as well as innovation is a team sport. For example, the least inventive R&D staff were those who either spent a little time in teams, 0–2 days per week, or too many, 5 days a week. Those with a moderately high level of teaming behavior were by far the most inventive presumably because of the cross-fertilization of creative ideas.[xix] Cross-fertilization of ideas among team members results in greater cumulative innovation than if individuals worked solo and their individual output was pooled post hoc.

The advantages of organic vs. mechanistic forms of system design for creative inventions is illustrated by a study contrasting how mechanistic vs. organic designs are more conducive for innovation than mechanistic ones. An organic organization design was found to moderate innovative payoff from investment in R&D. A sample of 110 manufacturing business units were divided into the most and least bureaucratic according to the following design criteria:

- Tall hierarchy;
- Centralized decisions;
- Few team decisions;
- Many rule;
- Many job titles;
- Low % managers;
- Directive management style.

The innovative effectiveness of the organic vs. mechanistic types was tested by correlating the percentage of R&D expenditure with inventions per employee as shown in Figure 7.2.[xx]

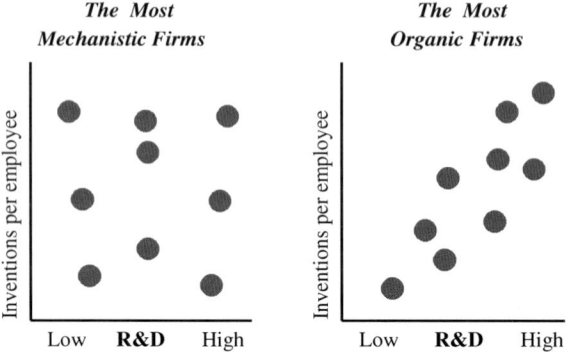

Figure 7.2.   Inventive Payback from R&D in Mechanistic vs. Organic Establishments
Source: Hull, 1988.

The correlations between R&D input and inventive payoff are not statistically significant for the 55 most bureaucratic firms with scatter-plots fairly random. By contrast, the correlations are statistically significant between input and inventive output for the 55 less mechanistic. The

> Mechanistic bureaucracies stifle human creativity because functional roles are delimited by rigid procedures for the execution of specialized tasks

implication is that the design of the product creation system matters because the subsample with organic practices has significant correlations with inventions measured as patent applications per employee.

But many product creation systems need to offer customers solutions that are low cost as well as innovative. How have goods industries resolved this dilemma? Attempts to mix mechanistic and organic systems date at least from the early 20th century, when large manufacturers created R&D laboratories so that professional knowledge could be focused on innovative opportunities of the future, rather than the production issues of the day. However, this segregation of staff with professional knowledge from line operations created conflicts.[xxi] The line organization typically seeks advantages from economies of scale and learning curves to contain costs. Professional staff typically seek to innovate, which takes investment, undermines economies of scale, and reduces the efficiency of routine operations. These conflicting strategies mean that synergies between mechanistic and organic practices are difficult to realize in mixed systems.

Organic organizations are designed to bring a diverse group of specialists together with a common focus regardless of their reporting relationships in a bureaucratic hierarchy. The essential requirement of OTS is that the diverse functional specialists bond together so that their commitment to project on which they are working to deliver customer value equals or exceeds their conformance with hierarchical lines of reporting. Solidarity around a customer-focused mission is critical for the success of the composite approach to Total Value Development (TVD). According to participants in a concurrent engineering user group in the US, a rule of thumb is that practicing concurrency is feasible only if at least 60 percent of resources are allocated up-front to project teams instead of departmental functions. However, up-front resource allocation is a necessary but insufficient cause of organizational effectiveness.

7.4. Conclusions

Successful cross-functional integration in product development is the exception rather than the rule despite all the talk about teaming. Single managers, temporary teams, or groups without an explicit product focus, such as quality departments, undertook much of the product development and process improvement initiatives observed in the studies of both goods and services. Even when cross-functional teams were formed to develop products and processes, they were seldom either chartered or rewarded for achieving objectives. Moreover, tall hierarchies in many of the large service businesses made horizontal integration of work by cross-functional teams difficult.

Almost all goods industries had an explicit product development group headed by managers with multifunctional experience. Such groups are responsible for coordinating and advising development activities in various businesses rather than directly managing the creation of value. By contrast, less than half of the service enterprises had a formally dedicated NSD group. But those that did were higher performers.

Notes

[i]　de Brentani, U. 1993. The New Product Process in Financial Services: Strategy for Success, *International Journal of Bank Marketing*, 11(3), 15–22.

[ii]　Storey, C. and Easingwood, C. 1998. The Augmented Servicing Offering, *Journal of Product Innovation Management*, 15, 335–351.

[iii]　Goffin, K. 1988. Evaluating Customer Support During New Product Development An Exploratory Study, *Journal of Product Innovation Management*, 15(1), 42–57; Hull, F. 2003. Simultaneous Involvement in Service Product Development: A Strategic Contingency Approach, *International Journal of Innovation Management*, 7(3), 1–32.

[iv]　Lievens, A., de Ruyter, K. and Lemmink, J. 1999. Learning During New Banking Service Development: A Communication Network Approach to Marketing Departments, *Journal of Service Research*, 2(2), 145–164.

[v]　Lievens, A. and Moenaert, R. K. 2000. Project Team Communication in Financial Service Innovation, *Journal of Management Studies*, 37(5), 733–766.

[vi]　Lievens *et al*. 1999. *Op cit*.

[vii]　Grönroos, C. 1990. *Service Management and Marketing: Managing the Moments of Truth in Service Competition*, Lexington Books: Lexington; Reichheld, F. F. Sasser, Jr., W. E. 1990. Zero Defections: Quality Comes to Services, *Harvard Business Review*, 68(5), 105–111; Storey and Easingwood. 1998. *Op. cit.*

[viii]　Damanpour, F. 1991. Organizational Innovation: A Meta-Analysis of Effects of Determinants and Moderators, *Academy of Management Journal*, 34(3), 555–590.

[ix]　Katzenbach, J. R., and Smith, D. K. 1993. The Discipline of Teams, *Harvard Business Review*, 71(2), 111–120.

[x]　Gatenby, D. Lee, P. Howard, R., Hushyar, K, Weaner, J. 1994. Concurrent Engineering: An Enabler for Fast, High-Quality Product Realization, *AT&T Technical Journal*, 73(1), 34–47.

[xi]　McKenzie, J. 2003. *Spaulding for Children, Inc., National Resource Center for Special Needs Adoption*, Southfield: Michigan.

[xii]　Knapp M. L. and Hall, J. A. 2006. *Nonverbal Communication in Human Interaction*, Thomson Learning: Stamford.

[xiii]　Daft, R. L. and Lengel, R. H. 1986. Organisational Information Requirements, Media Richness and Structural Design, *Management Science*, 32(5), 554–571; Szulanski, G. 1996. Exploring Internal Stickiness: Impediments to the Transfer of Best Practice within the Firm, *Strategic Management Journal*, 17(Special Issue), 27–43.

xiv   Storey, C. and Hull, F. 2010. A Value Contingent Model of Service Product Development, *Journal of the Service Industries*, 21(2), 140–161.

xv   Smith, P. 1994. *New Products in Half the Time*, John Wiley: Hoboken.

xvi   Roethlisberger, F. J. and Dickson, W. J. 1939. *Management and the Worker: An Account of a Research Program Conducted by the Western Electric Company, Hawthorne Works, Chicago*, Harvard University Press: Cambridge.

xvii   Blau, P. 1958. *Dynamics of Bureaucracy*, Chicago University Press: Chicago.

xviii   Nonaka, I. 1994. A Dynamic Theory of Organisational Knowledge Creation, *Organization Science*, 5(1), 14–37.

xix   Hull, F. 1993. *Idea Generation and Commercialization in R&D Laboratory Organizations*, Stevens Institute of Technology: Hoboken.

xx   Hull, F. 1988. Inventive Pay-off from R&D: Organization Designs for Maximizing Efficient Research Performance, *Sociology*, 22(3), 171–193.

xxi   Mintzberg, H. and Quinn, B. 1996. *Strategy Process*, Prentice-Hall: Englewood Cliffs.

CHAPTER EIGHT

IN-PROCESS DESIGN CONTROLS: FLEXIBLE DISCIPLINE FOR COST-EFFECTIVE INNOVATION

Overview

This chapter profiles processes dealing with controls over the design of customer offerings during development operations. Process is a more dynamic and flexible form of control than inviolate standardized procedures for rigidly controlling behaviors. In-process Design Controls (IDC) refashions rigid mechanistic procedures into flexible and adaptive processes. "In-process" connotes dynamism in the mode of control so that stakeholders may adapt to emergent technical and market opportunities during their development journey. Process guides but does not dictate development activities. This flexibility enables cross-functional teams greater latitude in executing project plans to the extent they take partial ownership of adaptations of process guidelines and responsibility for outcomes. IDC enables development teams to exercise human judgment in executing projects instead of following standard procedures lockstep as so often occurs in mechanistic bureaucracies requiring rigid conformance with stage-gate procedures.

8.1. The Need for In-process Design Controls (IDC)

Flexible guidance is needed for cross-functional, product development team members because much of their work falls outside of the rules and hierarchy of their home departments. Integrating heterogeneous perspectives usually results in higher rates of invention. Disciplined control over the product development process increases the probability that ideas will be commercialized as products. Process provides a more flexible and enabling alternative to the rigid procedures typical of mechanistic procedures.[i] So long as process guides rather than mandates, product development teams may use them to retain focus, reuse knowledge, and track progress toward targets exercising their collective wisdom.[ii]

IDC enables cross-functional teams to be given greater latitude for executing project plans to the extent they take partial ownership of the process and responsibility for outcomes. When cross-functional teams are involved in both the improvement and maintenance of product development processes, IDC becomes a hybrid kind of control that is partially self-imposed. IDC enables enterprises to handle novel as well as routine products.

Process is a dynamic and flexible generation of practices that evolved from the rigid rules and procedures characteristic of mechanistic bureaucracies and sequential workflows. IDCs include methods for assessing markets, benchmarking, identifying customer needs, translating requirements into product specifications, such as Quality Function Deployment (QFD) and reviewing product designs. Process mapping is often used to eliminate unnecessary hand-offs and activities that do not add value. Updated processes are embodied in product development manuals as templates for team activities. Their intent is to foster repeatability, consistent with ISO 9000 procedures. However, the work or development varies by project, so human judgment is required.

Formal procedures are embedded in the operations of mechanistic bureaucracies. However, for dynamic, complex work, the rule often does not fit. Therefore, process mapping arose as a method for evaluating how work was actually done vs.

> A method of proven effectiveness is for cross-functional teams to collaborate in mapping the processes they plan to collectively use

how it should be done. Such mapping provides a grey area in which cross-functional teams can exercise some degree of judgment.

Although processes are common in goods industries, they are also increasingly deployed in services industries. For example, Morgan Stanley has a book of detailed maps of procedures as well as processes for executing financial transactions. But processes in services may also be helpful in managing tacit as well as explicit knowledge embedded in financial numbers. Many observers of services have found formal processes lacking, despite documented benefits from their deployment.[iii] However, some note the need for flexibility in the rules of the development process.[iv] A synthesis of these viewpoints might be that, on average, greater controls are needed, but they should be deployed more as dynamic processes than as rigid rules.

8.1.1. *Mechanistic vs. organic design system controls*

The default mode of control in mechanistic bureaucracies is standard procedures. The purpose is to ensure that critical operations deemed necessary for realizing the product can be readily monitored to minimize variability. Traditionally these checks are rationally based on a logical sequence of stages like a relay race where one function performs an action and hands the baton to the next specialist and so on down the value chain. Stage-gate systems are often used to enforce compliant behaviors at various points along the product development value chain. Lock step observance of standard procedures may be the most appropriate mode of control so long as strategic objectives are relatively stable.[v]

In environments characterized by dynamic and complex changes, greater latitude in human judgment needs to be allowed in development decision-making. Complex dynamic tasks provides the rationale for the deployment of organic organization practices so teams may make appropriate adaptations to process guidelines. However, people on a journey to develop radically new product seldom voluntarily try to map their route in advance. Leading creative people in new development journeys is difficult because often the team seeks unrestricted travel in directions of their own choosing with little regard for bureaucratic procedures. Some managers capitulate to the mantra of "hire smart people and get out of the way".

In many organic organizations, "ad hoc" development occurs in a *laissez-faire* environment. Often the norm is "just get it done however you can". The relaxation of bureaucratic procedures, however, does not mean that controls are absent in organic organizations. Rather controls are based on peer exchanges and often reinforced by professional knowledge bases and norms.

The downside to the organic approach to development is that sometimes the viable concepts are slow to crystalize and frequently impractical. The generation of ideas may be profuse, but the yield of actionable ones that may be commercialized relatively few. The dynamic pursuit of strategic performance objectives by diverse stakeholders in organic settings can easily descend into chaos without a process providing a conceptual map guiding activities. People in organic organizations with open communications may input an overwhelming amount of information from external as well as internal sources and swamp capabilities unless structured processes are used for systematically integrating knowledge.

8.1.2. *IDC as an enabler for ESI: The axis of the composite model*

To avoid stifling creativity by bureaucratic rigidly, process was devised as soft form of control for guiding the exercise of human judgment. IDC is a flexible means of guidance enabling cross-functional teams to

> Bureaucratic procedures preclude human judgment. Processes should guide rather than coerce decisions

adapt activities to cope with unanticipated obstacles or seize emergent opportunities instead of having to march in lock-step formation down a serial path. However, the discipline that process provides needs to be in the form of flexible guidance instead of rigid, inviolate procedures so that human judgment can be exercised creatively within pre-agreed boundaries.

IDC falls in between the two extremes of mechanistic and organic practices by providing guidance that is disciplined, yet flexible for helping cross-functional teams use methods of proven effectiveness for transforming ideas into outputs. Although every journey is unique and uncertain, process codifies knowledge from prior travelers facilitating discoveries and the commercialization of ideas. Reuse of process knowledge as well as prior know-how helps creative people focus on what really needs to be discovered without unnecessary reinventions. The adaptability of IDC is important for innovation because new opportunities as well as unforeseen obstacles typically emerge during the execution of product development projects.

Creative individuals often bridle at the notion of any kind of constraint. Ironically, however, the flexible discipline of process measured as IDC is actually positively associated with innovation in both the goods and services data. The axis of the composite model is a synergistic bond between the organic organization of human creativity to cross-fertilize ideas with the discipline of mechanistic bureaucracies exercised in softer forms. The innovation paradox is that the flexible constraint of process has a moderating effect on the cross-fertilization of ideas. The axis of the composite model is synergistic benefit from the combination of creative human judgment and dynamic process.

Synergy between IDC and ESI occurs in both the goods and services data. IDC and ESI have significant correlations with performance. But their combinatory impact on performance is greater than the sum of their separate effects in both datasets. Synergy between IDC and ESI is schematically illustrated in Figure 8.1 for six stages of a development sequence and documented for both studies in prior publications.[vi]

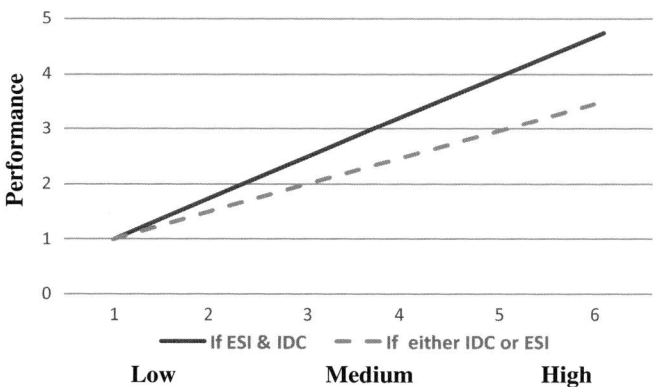

Figure 8.1.   Illustration of Synergies between ESI and IDC

Synergies between ESI and IDC explain why some enterprises are able to outperform others by achieving both kinds of generic competitive advantage simultaneously, efficiency in time and cost as well as innovation. Synergy is possible so long as the organization is purposively structured

> The axis of the composite model is synergy between the organized creativity of people and processes which guide but do not dictate human judgment

and process provides flexible guidance instead of rigid "procedure", which underscores the value of IDC.

8.2. IDC in Operation

A principal value of IDC is focusing development on adding value to customer offerings. Processes include methods for identifying customer needs, translating requirements into product specifications, and reviewing product designs. Processes also help guide team behaviors. Processes for managing development projects include charters, model plans, stage-gates with exit and entry criteria, and product reviews for helping teams stay on track. One way of keeping focus and reducing waste is the reuse of knowledge, such as prior standards and product performance specifications needed for market competitiveness.

An essential feature of IDC is continual improvement. Process mapping is often used to eliminate unnecessary hand-offs and activities that do not add value. Updated processes are embodied in product development manuals as templates for team activities. Their intent is to foster repeatability. Measures used for scoring IDC practices are shown in Table 8.1 for goods and services.

The IDC practices used in the goods data focus on the integration of socio-technical behaviors such as the combination of documentation and standards with collaborative reviews by employees. The focus of the practices was on the use of design standards, documentations and design reviews in which downstream functions like manufacturing participated. In the services data, processes were more inclusively measured and included a greater emphasis on project management methods including the identification of customer needs using QFD, goal setting criteria, and continuous process improvement.

Table 8.1.   In-process Design Controls

Goods:

- Use of design documentation.
- Increased use of design standards.
- Increased use of product design reviews in the last 5 years.
- Level of manufacturing participation in design reviews in eight stages of product development process.

Services:

- Benchmarking best-in-class companies.
- Using structured processes for identifying customer needs and translating into requirements (e.g., QFD).
- Setting performance criteria for projects.
- Setting standards for the performance of products.
- Institutionalizing systematic reviews for development projects.
- Mapping/blueprinting processes to reduce non-value added activities.
- Measuring conformance with processes.
- Improving documentation of processes.
- Institutionalizing continuous improvement processes.

These measures of process have significantly positive correlations with time compression and cost reduction in goods (0.45) and services (0.52).

8.2.1. *IDC in goods industries*

Measures of IDC are strongly correlated with performance in both the goods and services datasets. Cases studies, however, have revealed many issues in the deployment of process in goods industries. In most instances, product development systems are either ignored or gamed to some extent. In a few instances, compliance with process is to the letter which often means that development teams executed activities to check procedural boxes some of which did not add any value for which customers were willing to pay.

One of the reasons for lack of use is that the systems are often complex and very difficult to use. The criteria for exit and entry into stage-gates can be daunting and

> Rigid deployment of stage-gate procedures may hamper performance, especially innovation

extraordinarily time consuming. Some complain that compliance with the process is more difficult work than developing the product itself. The basic problem is that many managers demand conformance with rigid procedures masqueraded as flexible "processes".

The logic of creating a concept and realizing it as a product is actually rather basic. One of the best practices used by leading companies is to devise a model plan template that can be customized as needed for developing a specific product.

Model Process Templates at Stanley
A simple process template at Stanley helped people understand that strategy formulation was a reiterative process that needed collaborative engagement up-front. Stanley's process template helped development teams look strategically before they leapt. Because their people used a basic process that they were trained to understand, teams developed products with significant strategic advantages. Their rate of success in launching new offerings far outpaced their competitors.

8.2.2. *IDC in services*

Much of the literature on NSD has focused on process. The formalization of stage-gates occurred first in goods industries, but rapidly spread to services. Most research shows benefits from processes. However, a downside is that some companies in goods as well as services regard stage-gates as the essential feature of their product development system and neglect other factors such as the organization of people organized in cross-functional teams who accept collaborative responsibility for achieving strategic goals. A one-track focus on control as the essential component of development systems misses the synergistic opportunities of the composite model whereby processes have interactions with the organization of people (ESI) and tools (CIT) for achieving innovation as well as cost savings.

A primary conclusion to be drawn from studies of new services is the importance of the quality of development process.[vii] However, process excellence requires experienced people, functional co-ordination, adequate resources, and top management support. A lack of expertise in the skills and processes required to undertake NSD restricts firms' ability to exploit the opportunities open to them.[viii] Several researchers have noted the need for flexibility in the rules for development processes.[ix] A synthesis of these viewpoints might be that, on average, greater controls are needed, but they should be deployed more as dynamic processes than as rigid rules.

The "structuring of activities" by formalization, standardization, and hierarchy has been replaced in many corporations by processes that are more flexible and enabling because team members may more easily change product development plans in response to emergent contingencies. Such flexible forms of guidance are needed for cross-functional product development team members because much of their work falls outside of the rules and hierarchy of their home departments. Disciplined control over the product development process increases the probability that ideas will be commercialized as products.

To implement a strategy of rapid product introduction, it helps to have mature, repeatable processes that are continually improved such as the one that evolved at Chase retail banking. Many service enterprises devised model templates for managing product development projects, such as stage-gates with entry and exit criteria. These new processes usually resulted in greater reliability consistent with research showing that financial service firms adopting defined stage-gates for product development have better track records.[x] The value of mature, repeatable processes that are continually improved may be illustrated by events at Merrill Lynch.

Processes at Merrill Lynch

A vice president was made responsible for creating and maintaining a global product development process. Initiatives included devising product development templates made available on their intranet. The templates included business case analyses and stage-gates with recommended entry and exit criteria. A cross-functional committee was formed to review new product development proposals for process conformance at two stages, the early idea stage and the pre-launch stage. Although businesses were not required to submit their new product ideas for review, records were kept that compared those that did with those that did not. Analysis of the records provided evidence to document the benefit of conformance with the review process. Innovations using the process were over 5 times as likely to succeed. The intranet and the flexible software templates enabled product reviews to be conducted using common global processes.

Having processes in place is not the same as using them effectively. In Financial Services Company, XO, manuals for product development were developed to standardize processes and provide guidelines including stage-gates. One reason was because initiatives in cross-functional teaming without processes had resulted in some degree of chaos and uneven outcomes. However, the teams resisted using the new processes. The struggle to get teams to actually use process manuals continues today. This case illustrates the need of coupling process improvements with changes in organization, and vice versa, to achieve synergy.

8.3. Process as a Strategic Approach

Process, as opposed to rigid procedures, is conducive for innovation. Service enterprises with a strategy of developing radical new products are likely to deploy IDC (0.56).

> Strategic planning is essential and in dynamic environments a continuous process

The more enterprises deploy IDC, the more likely they are to develop innovative offerings (0.45), a relationship which is even stronger in synergistic combination with early simultaneous influence.

Enterprises forming a dedicated group for new service development (NSD) were more likely to deploy IDC (0.33) and pursue a strategy of radical innovation (0.35) and as well as making major modifications to existing offerings (0.56). The advantages of process for increment innovation are quite strong for enterprises innovating by making major modifications to existing offerings. A rapid, reiterative approach to differentiation provides an alternative path to innovation that may complement targeting radically new developments. Enterprises in the service sample adopting a major modification approach were successful in part because they executed rapid development cycles akin to the approach of plan, do, check, and act (0.67). The tortoise beat the hare so to speak by persistently making major modifications to existing offerings instead of trying to make big jumps. Enterprises adopting a strategy of making major modifications to existing offerings are also more likely to deploy IDC (0.55). Moreover, IDC has significant interaction effects with both differentiation and delivery performance under the contingency of a strategy of making major modifications.[xi]

A strategy of targeting radically new offerings, while associated with IDC (0.54), has no interaction effects with it. One reason may be that existing processes may be helpful guides, but need to be overridden by human judgment. For achieving radically new innovation, it is the deployment of ESI, OTS, and other organization practices that enables diverse functions to collaborate for developing radical innovations.

8.4. Processes Instead of Procedures for Realizing Objectives

Large corporations achieve strategic goals far beyond the capabilities of isolated individuals by dividing labor and structuring activities into narrowly defined bits controlled by prescribed procedures. Such procedures provide a means for achieving strategic objectives so long as the work is standard, repeatable, and can be reduced in complexity by breaking tasks down into simpler acts. To the extent work is standardized, mechanistic bureaucracies are appropriate for efficient operations. However, such narrowly defined roles preclude opportunities for most employees to engage in thinking about how their actions contribute to the strategic objectives of the enterprise.

As a new and more dynamic economy has emerged in recent decades, strategy formulated by top executives in corner offices is insufficient for guiding decisions of employees in development operations. As products and services have become much more complex and dynamic, strategy becomes the responsibility of a large proportion of stakeholders, especially in product development. In such environments, stakeholders engaged in development need to exercise judgment in formulating strategic ends and aligning them with means.

A principal reason many enterprises in dynamic markets do not realize strategic objectives is because their employees are hamstrung by rigid procedures, many of which do not add value for which customers are willing to pay. As a result, as many as 90 percent of enterprises fail to achieve their strategic objectives in major ways according to some estimates.[xii] Yet many executives resist converting to more organic modes of management as the environmental context of their enterprise changes. They typically gloss over prior shortfalls in strategic achievement last year rather than engage in postmortem examinations that might lead to transformation of their development system. As a result, they fail to deploy process as flexible guide for product development execution and cling to the routine of mechanistic bureaucracy.

The need for transforming rigid bureaucratic procedures into enabling processes is critical for realizing enterprise strategies in dynamic markets. To compete in environmental conditions characterized by Moore's Law (twice the performance at half the cost in half the time), complex knowledge must be rapidly exploited for innovations in product and process. To compete in complex, dynamic markets, cross-functional teams need to be engaged in shaping the strategic ends toward which their work is directed. Process plays a critical role in helping teams achieve strategic objectives by focusing creative ideas on targets and proven means of achieving them. Flexible but disciplined processes fostering reuse of best-known methods for product development and careful assessment of risks helps teams achieve strategic aims. The combinatory benefits of IDC and cross-functional teaming are best realized by appropriate alignment between objectives and means for achieving them.

Alignment between ends and means sounds simple, but is actually difficult to do. As suggested in Figure 8.2, enterprise strategy may be easily known by employees and stockholders in most enterprises. However, many employees pay scant attention to strategy because they are bogged down in checking boxes to indicate compliance with bureaucratic procedures. Many employees in development projects either blindly follow procedures to the letter or execute development projects using whatever means seem to work. Conforming employees try to achieve the ends targeted by the enterprise using acceptable procedures. However, others

Figure 8.2.   Adaptations of Ends and Means

simply abandon strategic intent as well as game procedures so that their conformity is a sham.[xiii]

Retreaters: Seldom are employees in product development engaged in strategy formulation. Often they are overwhelmed by complex rules that smother any creative ideas they might consider initiating pertinent to strategy. One adaption is to retreat by going through the motions of conformance with procedures for product development specified by others supposed directed toward ends they do not know or care about. Some retire on the job by doing enough to keep from being fired, but have neither their heart nor mind in their work. Theirs is not to reason why, but just to do or die. When employees give up on helping further enterprise strategy because they are lost in the forest of a myriad of rigid rules, unnecessary costs are expended and innovative opportunities missed.

Ritualists: Many employees enact their bureaucratically prescribed roles to the letter of specified procedures. They are ritualists who conform to all the required rules and procedures without assessing the extent to which strategic goals are being served. The result is that many

> Employees in mechanistic bureaucracies avoid punishment if they do as they are told, but the employer loses the benefit of their minds

development operations are successful, but the product subsequently dies because of a lack of innovative adaptions to dynamic and complex market demands. Ritualistic behavior is most common in mechanistic bureaucracies, but also occurs in politically biased enterprises where a dominant leader or coalition determines policy with little or no input from others.

Improvers: Many employees are committed to the strategic goals of their enterprise. However, they improvize if they are burdened by bureaucratic rules and procedures that get in the way of efficient execution of their strategically focused work. Successful development staff in many companies keep double books of their processes, one for managerial review and one for themselves. For example, middle managers at a world-renowned aerospace facility stop their day jobs 2–4 weeks ahead of a procedural audit to achieve high marks. Then they quickly revert back to the way they do their work effectively. Needless to say, this is a wasteful burden. Managers are often willing to turn a blind eye to procedures so long as their subordinates just get the job done right. But if improvised methods go wrong and expose the enterprise to risk, innovators get the blame. Such a lack of collaboration between management and development teams mean that procedures do not become converted to dynamic processes. Lessons learned in actual execution are not incorporated into continuous improvement because nobody wants to reveal how the tasks were actually accomplished if they worked around standard procedures. Innovations simplifying and improving processes remain under the table.

Aligners: On the upside, many employees are committed to the strategic goals of their enterprise and contribute to continually improving the means used for achieving them. This alignment is the essence of the concurrent execution of strategy and potentially very synergistic.

> Concurrent development systems engage their employees in understanding and helping formulate strategy at least at the operating level

The advantage of IDC is that empowered team members are enabled to adapt the means of developing customer offerings in ways that optimize the strategic creation of value. Processes that do not add value for which customers are willing to pay are wasteful and simplified or eliminated. The axis of the composite model is synergy between strategically focused cross-functional development teams responsible for the processes they use and their continual improvement. The axis of the composite model is alignment between the organizations of people and the processes they continually improve to achieve strategic aims.

8.5. Conclusions

For many practitioners in development operations, stage-gate procedures for governing the behaviors of various functions is the dominate feature of the system. Stage-gates and rigid procedures are beneficial for performance if customer offerings are relatively standardized and differentiated on the basis of cost. However, rigidly prescribed role behaviors may be deleterious in enterprises competing in dynamic, complex environments. To the extent enterprises are affected by contingencies requiring innovation and the exploitation of complex knowledge, greater flexibility is required for exploiting human capital. Therefore, process is an enabler of human judgment and not a substitute for it to the extent that enterprises target a strategy of innovation that requires the development of new features. Some employees become so frustrated with the strategy of their enterprise as well as the means of achieving it that they rebel. Their options are to try to transform their enterprise from within or join another one which might be one they establish on their own.

Notes

[i] Adler, P. S. and Borys, B. 1996. Two Types of Bureaucracy: Enabling and Coercive, *Administrative Science Quarterly*, 41(1), 61–89.

[ii] Garvin, D. A. 1993. Building a Learning Organization, *Harvard Business Review*, 71(4), 78–91; Graessel, R. and Zeidler, P. 1993. Using Quality Function Deployment to Improve Customer Service, *Quality Progress*, (Nov), 59–63; Melan, E. H. 1985. Process Management in Service and Administrative Operations, *Quality Progress*, 18(6), 52–59.

[iii] de Brentani, U. 1993. The New Product Process in Financial Services: Strategy for Success, *International Journal of Bank Marketing*, 11(3), 15–22.

[iv] Edvardsson, B., Haglund, L. and Mattsson, J. 1995. Analysis, Planning, Improvisation and Control in the Development of New Services, *International Journal of Service Industry Management*, 65(2), 24–35.

[v] Cooper, R. G. and Edgett, S. 1999. *Service Product Development*, Perseus: Cambridge.

[vi] Hull, F. 2004. Innovation Strategy and the Impact of a Composite Model of Service Product Development on Performance, *Journal of Service Research*, 7(4), 167–181; Hull, F. M., Collins, P. D., and Liker, J. K. 1996. Composite Forms of Organization as a Strategy for Concurrent Engineering Effectiveness, *IEEE Transactions on Engineering Management*, 43(2), 133–142.

[vii] Cooper, R. G., Easingwood, C. J., Edgett, S., Kleinschmidt, E. J. and Storey, C. 1994. What Distinguishes the Top Performing New Products in Financial Services, *Journal of Product Innovation Management*, 11(4), 281–299; de Brentani, U. 1991. Success Factors in Developing New Business Services, *European Journal of Marketing*, 25(2), 33–59.

[viii] Kelly, D. T. and Storey, C. 2000. New Service Development: Initiation Strategies, *International Journal of Service Industry Management*, 11(1), 45–62.

[ix]   Edvardsson *et al.* 1995. *Op. cit.*

[x]   Cooper *et al.* 1994. *Op. cit*; Cooper and Edgett. 1999. *Op. cit.*

[xi]   Hull, F. 2004. Innovation Strategy and the Impact of a Composite Model of Service Product Development on Performance, *Journal of Service Research*, 7(4), 167–181; Clark, K. B. and S. C. Wheelwright. 1993. *Managing New Product and Process Development: Text and Cases*, Free Press: New York.

[xii]   Mintzberg, H. and Quinn, B. 1996. *Strategy Process*, Prentice-Hall: Englewood Cliffs.

[xiii]   Merton, R. K. 1968. *Social Theory and Social Structure*, Free Press: New York.

CHAPTER NINE

COMPUTER INFORMATION
TECHNOLOGIES

Overview

Practices exploiting Computer Information Technology (CIT) provide a means of accomplishing tasks that would otherwise be more difficult, if not impossible. The effects of CIT on performance are synergistic as well as direct. Electronic modes of communication help team members from diverse functions and locations exchange information. Processes may be electronically distributed and continually updated. However, CIT is a double-edged sword in that it can augment either mechanistic and/or organic forms of enterprise design. The key for harnessing the value of CIT for realizing a composite system lies in melding socio-technical factors in development operations.

9.1. The Use of Tools and Technologies

Tools and technologies are necessary but insufficient drivers of successful development of customer offerings. Computer Information Technology (CIT) helps create value by transforming inputs into outputs whether physical objects, data, or people are involved.[i] The growth in the capability of tools and technologies for transformation of inputs into outputs as well as for aiding decisions has been exponential. Despite remarkable capabilities, CIT *per se* offers relatively little competitive advantage because technologies have grown widely available at cheap prices that they offer relatively little differentiation. Competitive advantage from CIT comes from wisdom in using capabilities as enablers instead of drivers in the development of new customer offerings. The synergistic effects of CIT are more important in many ways for product development performance as an enabler of dynamic processes and electronic communications among cross-functional team members.

Successful developers need to fully exploit the capabilities of computer-based tools to be more analytical and to embody knowledge in professional standards, technical procedures, hardware, software, and communication formats. Tools and technologies for product development have undergone revolutionary changes. Computer automated design (CAD) makes visualization of Solid models of physical products possible so that a great variety of design alternatives may be explored in early stages at relatively low cost. Programmable automation has transformed manufacturing in goods industries from rigid, hard automation to flexible, dynamic controls.[ii] The emergence of soft, programmable automation makes the realization of socio-technical synergies more feasible between functions that work with intangible ideas, such as product designers, and physical objects, such as manufacturers, e.g., CAD/CAM systems.

Computer technologies are increasing deployed in designing physical objects, data, and people, including intangible dimensions of human thought as well as overt behaviors. People may be treated by surgical robots, learn online, tracked by electronic monitors, etc. Services enterprises have been greater consumers of computer tools than goods industries. Many kinds of service involve a physical aspect where transformation of things is part and parcel of the service offering. Tools supporting design and delivery are helpful in service sectors with physical infrastructures such as aircraft interiors and medical surgery suites.

Service developers not only design things, but also programmes for the transformation of data which is even more amenable to automation than physical goods. Even though the applicability of computer tools to the intangible aspects of people is difficult, human thought structures and behaviors are increasingly being modeled for the design of service offerings. Decision support systems not only aid engineers in goods industries, but also service development staff using tools for discounted cash flow analyses, algorithms for predicting purchasing decisions, etc. Fuzzy logic and other nascent software capabilities lead several researchers to envision even greater use of simulation modeling in future service designs.[iii]

Delivery processes are particularly important for many kinds of services especially those in which the exchange is tantamount to the product itself. Yet computer tools are increasingly replacing human interfaces for service delivery, such as internet banking, program trades, airline self-check-in, software applications, etc. Econometric models can analyze data to predict customer behaviors and map optimal delivery processes.

9.2. Mechanistic vs. Organic Dimensions of CIT

A principal issue in the deployment of CIT is that of two cultures which socio-technical theories attempted to bridge.[iv] To some extent, these competing perspective play out in the distinction between goods, which are often more technical, and services, which may be more humanistic, especially to the extent interpersonal relationships are entailed in delivery. Contrasts between goods and services often parallel the divide between the two cultures. But as noted in the typology in the opening chapter, a techno-mindset has applicability across both sectors. Similarly, some goods companies are socio-centric in focusing on customer experiences and supporting services. New business models have the opportunity not only of including developers of goods and services in the same group at the outset of the value creation cycle, but also of integrating people and tools in the development process.

Prior to the advent of programmable automation, most tools and technologies were congruent with the mechanistic type, such as assembly-lines where hard automation dictated behaviors. However, the recent emergence of soft, programmable automation has revolutionized transformational technologies. Today, mental as well as physical value creation activities may be managed by computer programs serving as mechanistic substitutes for bureaucratic controls. Tools and technologies may be mechanistic determinants of behaviors not only in manufacturing, but also in many service operations. For example, product life cycle management (PLM) systems may be used to program the activities of development teams in goods and services. PLM systems are often deployed in mechanistic systems in ways that preclude human judgment because exit from one gate to permit entry to another is controlled by automated check lists.

By contrast, systems PLM in organic organizations may enable teams to make more complex, creative decisions. People in organic organizations may use computer tools as aids for innovation by exploring creative options virtually as well as in actuality, e.g., visualization of prototypes, simulations, animated service models, etc. The wealth of information available via information management sources enables creative people to evaluate a plethora of design options. If organic teams lack strategic structure, however, individualistic exploitation of tools and technologies may be focused on niches applications that hamper systemic compatibility in developing common architectural standards.

In composite systems, computer tools are used for optimizing the creation of value throughout the cycle from concept to consumption. Visualization and simulation software is used to create and evaluate orthogonally different designs as a set of alternatives. Downstream functions, such as manufacturing and service, participate in virtual modeling. For example, product designers can create virtual prototypes and simulate how maintenance staff can best service equipment. Service developers can analyze customer behaviors and try to empathetically identify features to better fulfill their needs and deliver value more effectively. Designers operating in a composite system seek to use CIT for enabling human creativity and guiding activities so that customer offerings optimize the mix of innovation and cost-effectiveness.

A barrier to the deployment of CIT in composite systems in both sectors is that Information Technology (IT) function is poorly integrated with the social groups responsible for developing customer offerings. Often the dominant coalition in large-scale enterprises is rooted in either the technical IT camp or a socio-centric camp integrating diverse functional stake-

> Although IT departments in some enterprises are initiators of product development, in others they are estranged from the functions they nominally serve, which hampers the use of enabling tools in development operations

holders. The socio-centric camp may include technical professionals, but their techno perspective is mediated by the collective nature of the team

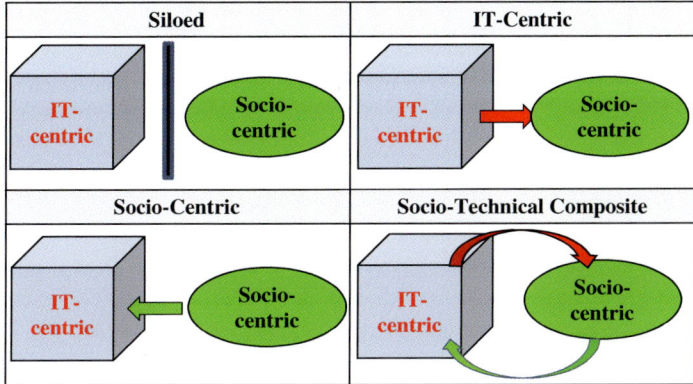

Figure 9.1.   Typology of Socio-Technical Relationships

responsibility for developing customer offerings. In goods, a product development group integrates diverse stakeholders. In services, NSD groups are cross-functional stakeholders whose objectives typically transcend functional boundaries between IT and other departments. Four alternative interrelationships are illustrated in Figure 9.1.

9.2.1. *Silo-centric development systems*

In functionally segregated development systems, the IT department as well as others are often segregated. Integration of NSD with the IT function was the exception rather than the rule in most of our case studies. Typically, the service development function did not involve the IT function early on. One result was friction between product development and the IT function analogous to that between design and manufacturing engineers in goods industries. In most other cases, each development project went separately to the centralized IT department for the resources to introduce their new offering, which resulted in conflicting priorities and political squabbles. Competition for IT resources sometimes led to Balkanized solutions. In others, the economies of scale that could be potentially realized by exploiting common CIT capabilities was lost such as was the case at a company we will call Amalgamated Financial Trust (AFT).

AFT
In Bank AFT, the centralized IT function was underutilized with many divisions purchasing the same programs it had available. Considerable duplication of effort occurred and rework was often necessary because of incompatible systems. With a 100 million-dollar carrot of new, integrated services, the centralized IT function tried to woo the bank's businesses back into its fold. But each business persisted with their homegrown systems that they knew and controlled directly. Technical support for product development and delivery remained fragmented and lacking system-wide alignment. Dozens of its strategic business units found ways around the centralized IT function by building specific applications to support the development and delivery of their own offerings.

In silo development systems, relationships across departmental boundaries may be intermittent and determined by upper managers using command and control across different hierarchical lines of authority. A case at what we will call STAD Bank illustrates this uncoordinated scenario.

Technocratic Push at STAD Bank
The management at an international bank decided to develop a bevy of new products. The president appointed some people from finance and econometricians to generate new offerings. These technocrats worked largely solo with little contact with other employee or customers. Of the six launches, two were scrapped because the IT department could not support them cost-effectively, two were subsequently declared illegal, and two offered customers so little in differentiated value that sales were minimal. The financial engineering of the offerings may have been well conceived, but the lack of cross-functional integration and customer input doomed the bank's initial effort to innovate. They fired the people tasked with new service development (NSD) and conservatively stuck to their traditional customer offerings.

9.2.2. *IT-centric development systems*

A techno-centric approach to development is common in goods industries, but also occurs in services as well. Recently PLM systems have been deployed not only in the development of goods, but also services. The risk is that PLM systems may be mechanistically deployed so as to inhibit creative decision-making by

> PLM may serve either as an enabler of creative product development and/or as a tool for enforcing assembly-line rigidity

organic teams and transform processes into electronically enforced procedures. In some goods industries, CIT can be used as a control mechanism that often stifles creativity. For example, AMATA, one of the largest producers of electronic equipment in the world, purchased smaller competitor that was taking market share partly because they have systematically deployed the composite model. Subsequently the larger corporation imposed rigid controls on its acquisition with the result that organic exploitation of it locally grown CIT capabilities was replaced by mechanistic controls.

PLM System Control at AMATA

A global manufacturer of electronic equipment imposed a computer automated version of stage-gates to electronically police compliance with exit and entry criteria by subordinate locations. The imposition of the new PLM system radically changed development team meetings at one of the acquired sites. Previously the team openly discussed design issues and options among themselves. Now their attention is focused on a screen controlled by directors from a HQ location. Discussion now focuses on understanding the content displayed on the screen and ticking boxes to indicate compliance with externally determined criteria. The acquired site is struggling to retain the capability of its locally adapted CIT systems for supporting organic practices.

In principal, CIT in goods industries can help design better services. For example, warranty repair information at vehicle manufacturers such as Ford is regularly fed back to designers to preclude future defects. The opportunity for using CIT to better integrate the design of goods and services may be enhanced by PLM systems. However, a socio-technical approach where people exchange information face-to-face as well as electronically seems more likely to optimize the benefits of CIT. Much information about service involves tacit knowledge that is difficult to program. A case study of RADS Corporation suggests that interpersonal as well as computer automated information exchange is needed for integrating the design of goods and services. In this case, a technocratic perspective dominated a development process that failed to adequately incorporate the social side of services in up-front development decisions.

PLM System Control at RADS

A large aerospace development group of over a 100 people has only a single person representing the service function. The service department is segregated in a different division of the corporation and exerts relatively little input to early engineering design decisions despite the fact that the bulk of company profit is derived from after-sale support. Lack of strategic alignment among functional groups results in product designs being thrown over walls with little reciprocal interactions. Consequences include high manufactured costs and low profit margins from post-sale services relative to competitors. To improve, the corporation is deploying a PLM system attempting to capture downstream data for inclusion in engineering design decisions. But the data only indirectly deals with the soft dimensions of customer experience, which are intangible and virtually impossible to capture adequately in a computerized control system. An engineering mindset by the dominant coalition makes customer empathy difficult to achieve. RADS seems kind of stuck in an engineering mindset despite growing concern that its competitive rivals make relatively more from services than they do.

9.2.3. *Socio-centric development systems*

IT is regarded as an afterthought in many socio-centric development systems. This often leads to lack of socio-technical collaboration which suboptimize the development and delivery of customer offerings. At DTD Bank, various groups were responsible for developing customer offerings, but they did not routinely engage the IT function in up-front decision-making.

Information Technology Disintegration at DTD Bank

A director of product development was appointed to integrate the activities of a NSD group and coordinate its requests for IT resources. However, the IT function resisted complying with the priorities and schedule of the new product development group, which resulted in missed market opportunities. One reason was because the decision process was so serial that the IT group received a work request only after the development group had made its final decisions. To change this, the development group tried to engage IT early in their decision processes and encouraged them to write prototype programs prior to release of final specifications. Before this change could be implemented, however, line managers from IT and other specialist departments rebelled at the notion of a central product development group and had it disbanded. All responsibilities for new product development reverted back to functional departments.

(Continued)

(Continued)

Yet the need remained to achieve a more integrated product development process. Therefore, a higher level position was created at the VP rank to oversee product development. Although this position lacked command over the resources allocated to the various businesses, some of the computer-aided processes for product development were created and used more effectively than in the past.

9.2.4. *Composite development systems*

Seldom in our case studies did development groups closely coordinated activities with the IT function. Exemplars include American Express and Chase retail banking which routinely included representatives from IT on development teams. Several companies introduced increasingly sophisticated software to provide a common tool for product data management and communications among cross-functional team members, including IT. Moreover, they experimented with rapid prototyping to develop design rules for developing products that could be more quickly ramped-up to volume delivery schedules.

The successful application of computer tools to product development decision-making is illustrated by the evolution of collaboration between development groups and the IT function at Morgan Stanley.

Socio-Technical Integration at Morgan Stanley

Many lines of business constituted separate development groups at Morgan Stanley. Because they competed with one another for essential IT resources, conflict was endemic. To resolve tensions and optimize resource utilization, all NSD groups began participating in weekly user group meeting with the directors of the IT department. Members of the user group collaboratively prioritized the utilization of IT resources. Each group understood the capabilities of the IT function as well as the needs of others seeking vital IT services. This social solution however lacked its technical complement. Development groups perpetually experienced difficulty in predicting whether products would make money as past practice was to give customers pretty much what they wanted. To have a more systematic basis for prioritizing projects than so-called horse trading, the businesses collaborated in developing a modeling program for simulating profit and loss over the life cycle of use on their intranet. This common tool aiding NSD decisions was adopted and utilized by all the development groups which enhanced their capabilities for making early decisions affecting the priority of development. Socio-technical integration was high because the user group augmented its collaborative prioritization of projects using a sophisticated simulation tool to which all parties subscribed.

The need to co-develop goods with services is illustrated by the first generation of ATMs widely used in US banking. This early project not just increased their awareness of product development practices in goods companies, but underscored the interconnectivity between goods and services.

9.3. Prior Research on CIT in Innovation

Research has posited that high levels of knowledge dispersion can increase the effectiveness and efficiency of decision-making and implementation, and impact innovation performance.[v] As dispersion levels increase, a project team's shared mental models become unified, cross-functional understanding and co-operation is enhanced, resulting in timely, cost-effective decisions that improve the short-term financial performance of development activities.

CIT enables people to share information in multiple forms, for example, messages, structured data, diagrams, text-based documents, models, and image data, files and documents. Communication systems comprise dynamic components such as expert and decision-support systems, groupware, intranets, and document management systems.[vi] Such systems aid coordination and collaboration helping organizations increase the productivity of their knowledge-intensive processes. A wide variety of people may view similar content. The extent to which they also exchange ideas stimulates innovative solutions to service problems and opportunities.

Communication systems can act as both asynchronous and synchronous forms of communication. Computer mediated communication can play an important role in facilitating personal communication via mechanisms such as electronic bulletin boards and chat rooms.[vii] These facilitate contact between the person seeking knowledge and those who may have access to the knowledge and can accelerate and broaden the knowledge sharing that happens through socialization. Most communication systems (e.g., intranets) have memory and search functions allowing the retention and retrieval of information. Such communication is important as it can stop service development teams wasting resources on finding solutions to problems that may have already been solved by other groups or projects teams.[viii] This memory function can be especially valuable in the medium to long term because knowledge from one innovation project can be of use years later in another project.[ix]

While knowledge is recognizably created, codified, and transferred during a NPD project, researchers have observed that the experience and know-how that task group members acquire during the life cycle of one particular project can also be transferred in subsequent projects and programs.[x] Effective recording, storing, and reviewing of information from market research and product testing studies are related to new product success.[xi] Such knowledge management activities enable potential problems with the product to be spotted earlier and corrected prior to launch.

9.4. CIT and Project Management

Project management tools are helpful not only for development teams, but also for managing a wide variety of organizational activities, such as an event, relocation, etc. Since all activities compete for resources enterprises need to appraise and prioritize its projects. Consequently a discipline of project portfolio management has evolved. Historically, however, service firms have not treated project portfolio management as an important process and there is little consistency in approach even within firms. Research shows that a wide range of tools are employed to manage project portfolios (see Figure 9.2).[xii]

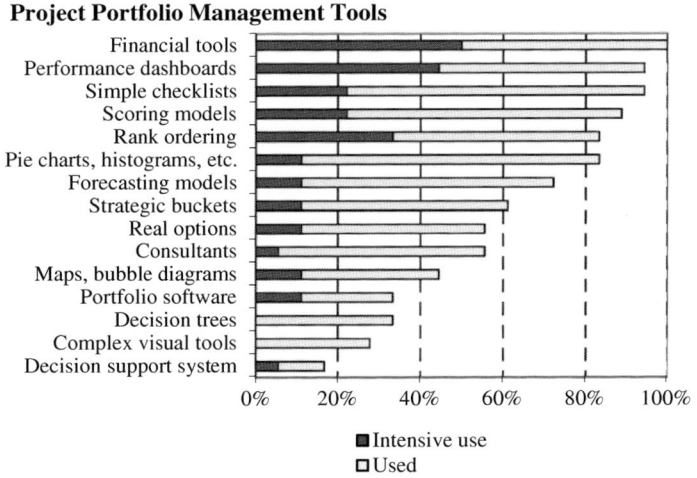

Figure 9.2.   The Usage of Project Portfolio Management Tools
Source: Storey and Harborne, 2012, p. 107.

This research shows that the least intensively used tools were the more complex systems-based tools such as decision support systems; decision trees; portfolio management software and real options. The most used management tools were standard financial calculations e.g., NPV, IRR, ROI. Next were simple checklists; performance dashboards; rank ordering; basic visual tools e.g., histograms, pie charts; and scoring models. Furthermore, the simple tools were employed as both decision-making and discussion tools, while the more complex tools were used purely for discussion.

There is considerable cynicism about the usefulness of complex software systems. A manager from a major firm commented that "*senior management believe that software can solve all management problems if the right system is purchased*",[xiii] a sentiment echoed by other interviewees in large firms. However, the more complex tools took time, training, and perseverance to be adopted throughout firms. The research found integration issues resulting from immature business processes, general perceptions of over-complication, and senior divisional manager resistance. In addition, firms felt that they have been through a cycle of introducing tools before, only for them to be withdrawn and another approach taken. This has been described elsewhere as the "sheep dip" approach — in one year the "sheep dip" is total quality management (TQM), the next year it is balanced scorecard, and the following year it is portfolio management.

9.5. CIT in Goods and Services

The capabilities of tools and technologies are combinations of hardware and software. Computer applications are versatile and range from electronic data manipulation and exchange to computer management of physical transformation. The CIT practices used in the good data focus on data exchange and computer capabilities for integrating upstream design with downstream and manufacturing.

In the services data, measures of CIT practice were expanded and include an additional focus on information capabilities for project management as shown in Table 9.1.

Practices are significantly correlated with performance, measured as time compression and cost reduction (0.40). These practices are significantly correlated not only with time and cost performance (0.36), but also innovation measured as new and upgraded features (0.28).

Table 9.1.   Computer Information Technology

Goods:

- Increased use of electronic databases
- Increased use of Computer Automated Design (CAD)
- Increased use of Computer Automated Manufacturing (CAM)
- Increased Coupling of CAD/CAM
- Automaticity of manufacturing capability, i.e., extent of computer controls
- Increased use of electronic databases

Services:

- Company internal communications via e-mail or other computer networks
- Distributed databases online to multiple functions
- Common software for project management
- Common software for process mapping
- Management Information Systems/Expert Systems
- Updating existing IT systems
- Building online databases with lessons learned and best practice templates
- Linking electronically with customers, e.g., EDI, computer networks, etc.
- Linking electronically (EDI) with externals, e.g., suppliers, partners, etc.

9.6. CIT as Enablers of Early Simultaneous Influence (ESI) and In-process Design Controls (IDC) in Composite Systems

Cross-functional organization is enabled by electronic communications. Especially in large corporations, the capability of diverse functions to communicate asynchronously up-front and throughout the value realization stream is a valuable capability. The discipline of flexible process is enabled by computer-based information systems that permit plans to be rapidly adapted and shared globally.

ESI is enhanced by CIT which provides asynchronous communications and speedy access to vast treasure troves of information. CIT is especially important for integration by helping people from diverse functions collaborate with one another. The confluence of computer information tools with interpersonal teaming is illustrated by collaborative design capabilities at the European Space Agency facility in the Netherlands. Creative designs are collaboratively architected and evaluated by cross-functional teams on their own computer terminals with line-of-sight to a commonly visible screen. CIT can act as both asynchronous and synchronous forms of communication. Technologies support communications throughout the organization regardless of time or location, and the continual improvement of development processes. It is suggested that a lack of appropriate CIT tools is a reason why financial organizations have not been more successful at innovating,[xiv] and it has been found that IT choices directly affect both the speed of the NSD process and the general effectiveness of the firm's innovation activities.[xv]

The rise in computing power coupled with highly capable software applications supports both the discipline of mechanistic practices along with the creativity of organic ones. For example, CIT enables processes to be more flexible and adaptive, which softens mechanistic constraints. CIT enables team members to communicate information with one another asynchronously as well as simultaneously, which provides mechanistic discipline to the organization via commonly shared knowledge. Software for handling imprecise information with fuzzy logic makes socio-technical explicit integration in new service development more feasible.

IDC is greatly facilitated by CIT because control of development can be transformed from inviolate procedures to flexible processes because electronic modification is relatively quick and easy. CIT enables processes for product development to be communicated as living documents that can be updated and changed much more easily than hard copies. Stage-gate product development systems are routinely online as well as access to a host of decision support systems enabling developers to augment human judgment by reusing knowledge from those with past experience. Knowledge management systems are available in various forms, such as in internal as well as external Wiki formats for best known methods.

9.6.1. *Socio-technical issues in composite development*

Tension between social and technical approaches to development is common. Groupthink in marketing groups can lead to faulty development decisions. An engineering-centric perspective may occur in services as well as goods when offerings are designed by technocrats with little up-front input by customers at the concept stage. Technocratic solutions to service development may neglect the intangible dimensions of customer experience. The saga of developing new credit card offerings provides an illustrative case of the difficulties in balancing socio-technical perspectives at American Express, a global leader in best practices for service development. Technology-based models that do not correspond very well with the way people in real-world settings actually make decisions may be risky. This case

> Socio-technical integration enables humans to exploit the enabling capabilities of tools and technologies while a tech push approach dampens creative options

provides a cautionary note on over-reliance on technocratic solutions that may obfuscate empathy with customers.

CIT Problems at American Express

A major financial corporation embraced the concept of cross-functional teaming and established a diverse group of key stakeholders in the up-front development of a new diversified offering. Protracted discussions took place week after week partly because development processes were unused even though most team members had been trained to do so. As time stretched out, team members accepted a technocratic approach for assessing the marketability of various offerings. They paid participants to play a kind of computer game to gather data on *voice of the customer*. Game participants gave many of the variegated offerings staggeringly high ratings. A computer automated scoring system weighted potentially marketable options. A launch was rolled based on features receiving top ratings. But the new offering was an abysmal failure resulting in millions of dollars in losses. The reason was that social factors were neglected because the computer simulation game failed to capture intangible factors affecting how customers actually make choices in real-life experience. *Design for experience* was not used to empathize with people in real world settings. One reason they jumped at a technocratic solution is because their extensive cross-functional team meetings were observed as wandering rather aimlessly for months because of the lack of disciplined processes. Subsequently they adopted IDC and ultimately resurrected their initial failure by a developing a complex set of targeted offerings catering to specific market segments. The successful launch occurred after they integrated the troika of practices in the composite model in development operations: ESI, IDC, and CIT.

9.6.2. *Contingency factors affecting CIT*

Tools and technologies entail more than just physical equipment and software. CIT entails a wide array of capabilities that are potentially more beneficial if adapted to fit with the needs development groups have in designing new offerings. The challenge is particularly great in services where offerings are often based on tacit rather than explicit, codified knowledge. CIT capabilities are needed for exploiting game theories and fuzzy logic as well as automated transformations. Technologies may be codified in various forms of knowledge which vary in their mode of management. Some types of knowledge are regulated by professional standards that are determined and maintained by organizations of peers. Such professional knowledge is often highly codified and explicit, which lends itself to computer archives and file transfers. Other kinds of professional knowledge may involve considerable proportions of tacit knowledge that is somewhat idiosyncratic so is less amenable to codification. Often tacit knowledge is needed when people are the object of transformation. Tools ranging from physical devices for transformation to algorithms and simulation model are needed to help exploit embedded technological knowledge.

9.7. Conclusions

Socio-technical integration is more likely to create innovative business solutions than either a technocratic or a social-centric approach. Tacit knowledge and the idiosyncrasies of human behavior provide a greater challenge in many ways than designing new kinds of physical objects. A socio-technical approach to development is likely to optimize outcomes in the development of goods and/or services. The resolution of socio-technical tensions provides synergies which proffers the composite model with its capabilities for developing innovative offerings cost-effectively. To the extent CIT is used to enable processes to be dynamic and adaptive, the cost advantages associated with mechanistic forms of system design may be realized. To the extent CIT supports organic communications among cross-functional team members and enhances rather than constrains their creativity, innovative customer offerings are likely to be developed. The cardinal rule is that tools and technologies are enablers, not drivers of successful development systems.

Notes

[i]   Collins, P., Hage, J., and Hull, F. 1988. Technical Systems: A Framework for Analysis, Research, in *Sociology of Organizations*, Bacharach, S. and DiTomaso, N. (Eds.), JAI Press: Greenwich, Vol. 6, pp. 81–100.

ii   Collins, P. and Hull, F. 1986. Technology and Span of Control, *Journal of Management Studies*, 23(2), 143–164; Hull, F. and Collins P. 1987. High Tech Batch Production Systems: Woodward's Missing Type, *Academy of Management Journal*, 30(4), 786–797.

iii   Edvarsson, B. and Olsson, J. 1996. Key Concepts in New Service Development, *Service Industries Journal*, 16, 140–164.

iv   Snow, C. P. 1959. *The Two Cultures*, Cambridge University Press: London. Trist, E. L. and Bamford, K. W. 1951. Technological Content of the Work System Defences of a Work Group in Relation to the Social Structure and of Coal-Getting, *Human Relations*, 4, 3–38.

v   Moorman, C. and Miner, S. A. 1997. The Impact of Organisational Memory on New Product Performance and Creativity, *Journal of Marketing Research*, 34, 91–106.

vi   Wijnhoven, F. 1999. Development Scenarios for Organizational Memory Information Systems, *Journal of Management Information Systems*, 121–146.

vii   Alavi, M. and Leidner, D. E. 2001. Review: Knowledge Management and Knowledge Management Systems: Conceptual Foundations and Research Issues, *MIS Quarterly*, 25(1), 107–136.

viii Ramesh, B. and Tiwana, A. 1999. Supporting Collaborative Process Knowledge Management in New Product Development Teams, *Decision Support Systems*, 27(1/2), 213–236.

ix   Garud, R. and Praveen R. N. 1994. Transformative Capacity: Continual Structuring by Intertemporal Technology Transfer, *Strategic Management Journal*, 15(5), 365–385.

x   Meyers, P. W. and Wilemon, D. 1989. Learning in New Product Development Teams, *Journal of Product Innovation Management*, (6), 79–88.

xi   Lynn, G. S., Skov, R. B. and Abel, K. D. 1999. Practices that Support Team Learning and Their Impact on Speed to Market and New Product Success, *Journal of Product Innovation Management*, 16(5), 439–454.

xii   Storey, C. and Harborne, P. 2012. Project Portfolio Management: Prioritising Resources for Change, *International Journal of Entrepreneurship and Innovation Management*, 16(1/2), 98–113.

xiii Storey and Harborne. 2012. *Op. cit.*

xiv   Vermeulen, P. and Dankbaar, B. 2002. The Organisation of Product Innovation in the Financial Sector, *Service Industries Journal*, 22(3), 77–99.

xv   Froehle, C. M., Roth, A. V., Chase, R. B. and Voss, C. A. 2000. Antecedents of New Service Development Effectiveness: An Exploratory Examination of Strategic Operations Choices, *Journal of Service Research*, 3(3), 3–17.

SECTION D

CONFIGURING INVESTMENT IN HUMAN CAPITAL TO OPTIMIZE VALUE

CHAPTER TEN

PATTERNS OF SIMULTANEOUS INFLUENCE AND THE CONTINGENCY OF RADICALNESS

Overview

A strategy of developing radical offerings is often a vital method for gaining competitive advantage. Innovation, however, is demanding of human capital. Fortunately, the services data provides a rich opportunity for exploring how influence by 10 functions affects innovative performance at three phases of the development cycle. The goal of this chapter is to provide guidance for deploying total simultaneous influence to optimize innovative development throughout the life cycle, from concepts to post-launch augmentation. Early Simultaneous Influence has positive impacts on performance at the concept phase that is even stronger under the contingency of radicalness in both the service and goods datasets. However, only in the services data does influence by some functions have a positive association with performance at the post-launch phase. The intangibility of some services provides opportunities for augmenting offerings in innovative ways. Therefore, performance is measured not only for differentiating features, but also delivery. Profiles of the role 10 functions play in developing and delivering service offerings note the extent to which each is affected by the contingency of radicalness. As detailed below the engagement by some functions enhances performance even more so under the condition of radicalness, and affects delivery as well as differentiation performance.

10.1. Investing in Human Capital for Radical Innovation

A rapidly growing number of service enterprises are attempting to differentiate themselves from competition by offering new features. Although Moore's law was formulated for the semiconductor industry, the demand for new features has rapidly affected the service sector. One reason is because computer information technology is increasingly pervasive. In an earlier era, many service enterprises relied upon traditional offerings. Today many are attempting to rapidly innovate. A growing number are consolidating responsibility for NSD into a cross-functional group, a practice common in goods industries. However, the development of new offerings remains Balkanized in the majority of service enterprises where one functional department or another takes the lead in development within the confines of a mechanistic hierarchy.

Managers tend to closely oversee expenditures. The issue with regard to innovation, however, is that most of the opportunities to innovate occur at the front-end where only a relatively small percentage of funds are expended. As the development cycle progresses, much more money is spent. Under-managing the front-end and over-managing the back-end of the development cycle is common. However, human capital is needed throughout the development cycle, especially at the front-end. The more complex the development, the greater the need for human capital of all kinds. Novelty is a driver of complexity and the need for human capital. In goods companies manufacturing small batches or service companies varying their offering based on interpersonal delivery, the need for the management of human capital is relatively high for achieving success.[i]

Total simultaneous influence is an expansive concept integrating activities from the seeding of concepts to post-launch augments. The wellspring of innovation is the creative input of diverse people from heterogeneous functions. The cross-fertilization of ideas is optimized by multifunctional engagement. Early simultaneous influence at the concept phase is critical for innovation as a wider array of options are available at the outset of the development cycle. However, many functions are required

> Skimping on human capital at the concept phase limits innovative thinking about new ways of creating value

to realize a product concept in actual practice and especially in services where delivery processes are an important dimension of value added. Cross-functional collaboration in value development stretches from concept to customer delivery and requires continual feedback among functions.

To optimize return on investment, multiple functions not only need to be engaged, they must also actively cross-fertilize their ideas. To achieve innovation in a high-performance system, the key is to build collaboration so that:

> *People from different functions accept personal*
> *responsibility for project development outcome*
> *regardless of their individual job role.*

Getting cross-functional teams to take collective responsibility for project outcomes seems simple, but it is extremely difficult to achieve. Mechanistic bureaucracies rely on a serial approach where each individual enacts their role serially and separately. Structuring horizontal exchanges requires proactively building cross-functional collaboration. Collaborative responsibility is best achieved by building organic bonds up-front among people responsible for designing, building, and servicing customer offerings. Extensive cross-functional collaboration in creating and developing offerings is very strongly associated with innovative offerings that are also cost-effective because stakeholders from all points in the value stream are engaged throughout the cycle.

A lack of understanding of the value innovation brings to competitive advantage over the life cycle of customer offerings is a barrier to the adoption of concurrent methods of development. Most managers view up-front expenditures for engagement by downstream functions as unnecessarily wasteful rather than a proactive investment. The retention of a serial, non-concurrent approach to development is illustrated by the rarity of adoption of Toyota methods of product development that rely on early simultaneous influence. Many industrial firms have emulated their manufacturing practices, but relatively few realize that much of the same kind of thinking may be applied upstream to the development process.[ii] However, a few enterprises have engaged multiple functions up-front to consider multiple kinds of alternatives at the concept phase using methods such as set-base design to compare orthogonally different options.[iii] Open consideration of alternative design options at the front-end enables implementation of a 3P, a Toyota approach to design whereby all stakeholders throughout the value stream are engaged throughout the cycle. The advantages of Toyota development methods, such as 3P, are derived from a socio-technical approach. People and technologies are so closely interwoven that tactile and non-verbal experiences among stakeholders intimately bonds them together. Genie Industries is one of the most successful exemplars of 3P methods.

3P Methods at Genie Industries

Genie has an area on its shop floor that is walled off during phases of new product development. Everyone from the most creative designers to the operational employees who will build and service the product are collaboratively engaged from the outset and throughout the process. All functions collaborate in reiteratively designing a customer offering first in paper/cardboard, then wood, and finally metal. The plasticity of paper and to a lesser extent wood (or 3D printer models), enables creative ideas to be prototyped at low cost and risk. The product is not only innovative, but also low cost because expensive back-end quality and service issues have been addressed up-front. The final prototype works the first time and could actually be put to use by customers.

The generation and use of tacit information in socio-technical development is quite applicable to the design of services. Many services involve physical aspects and even if not, various design and delivery scenarios may be developed by a team of multifunctional collaborators. The generic principle behind concurrency and methods such as 3P is a reiterative approach to multiple design options by a wide variety of stakeholder functions who take responsivity for the customer offering during its whole life cycle from creation to after sale service.

10.2. Barriers to Collaborative Development

A common barrier to holistic development of customer offerings in goods and services is mechanistic bureaucracy. It is the default form of organization for any large-scale enterprise and places employees in a hierarchical structure with defined role expectations. What is startling is how easily delimited roles provide a bureaucratic *gestalt* for contextualizing work so that employees fail to realize opportunities for cost-effective innovation. The limitations the bureaucratic mindset places on human creativity have been not only documented in scores of studies, but also demonstrated repeatedly in experiential simulations. As noted below, people easily define their role in ways that limit collaboration and creativity occurs in simulated scenarios.

Simulating Development Operations

In DevSim, an experiential simulation of development and delivery operations in a hypothetical corporate enterprise, participants are assigned to perform roles commonly found in large organizations of all kinds, e.g., CEO, CFO, marketing, quality control, finance, sales, delivery, supplier, customer service, etc. Each participant is provided with a description of the role they are asked to enact. However, the initial operational structure typifies mechanistic bureaucracies with hierarchical, serial communication patterns. The customer offering is producible, but there are opportunities for improving its design and delivery that are missed because of a lack of collaboration. In over 40 simulations, participants from major corporations attempted to conscientiously execute their prescribed roles. However, in every instance, a high percentage of deliveries to customers were often late or defective. As performance suffered, each incumbent typically attempted to execute their role ever more efficiently. Some sweated profusely, occasionally cursed, dashed between offices to speed things up, and occasionally cried. Only after a breakout workshop, did participants realize that focusing on executing their delimited roles often hampered the overall effectiveness of the enterprise as a system. For example, a participant enacting the role of CFO strictly enforced rules relating to due diligence in expenditures by denying funds requested for innovation since it was outside the authorized budget. The result of micro-managing and strict role enactment caused delays throughout operations and prevented innovative developments. A key insight noted by a senior VP of a major bank was, "How amazing! We imposed the prison on ourselves and this isn't even a real company". Participants during the breakouts were empowered to share their frustrations with one another and make improvements in the operating system. They collocated functions as needed, streamlined processes, and held more cross-functional team meetings. As they began to transform the simulated enterprise from a mechanistic bureaucracy to a concurrent operation, the key lesson learned by all was that collaboration among participants in all roles was necessary for innovatively optimizing performance. Customer satisfaction rose sharply and the time taken to develop an innovative offering dropped precipitously.

The simulation demonstrates that hiring functional specialists is a necessary but insufficient driver of performance. To gain innovative benefit from input by heterogeneous specialists, collaborative engagement is necessary which requires people to transcend the boundaries of their roles. Motivating people to take on responsibilities for project outcomes as well as their own job is difficult even in a simulation and even more so in a real world corporation.

Cost controls are a huge barrier for innovation following the great recession beginning in late 2007. Managers have become more reluctant to invest up-front to develop innovative offerings. By focusing on operational cost-cutting they have often precluded opportunities of developing innovative features for which customers are willing to pay more. They failed to realize

> Cutting costs often means shedding employees, but opportunities for organic growth depend upon investment in diverse forms of human capital up-front where returns on investment are the least certain

that concurrent engagement by multiple stakeholders in development and delivery throughout the value stream leads not only to top-line profits, but also bottom-line savings. Stakeholders in manufacturing and service delivery help get the design of new offerings right the first time and reduce costs over the life cycle. But if short-term cost reduction thinking prevails, managers are unlikely to allow downstream functions to participate up-front to develop innovative offerings cost-effectively. Cutting waste from the bottom line may occur at the expense of evaluating creative options upfront, which may also be money savers. The danger of a narrow focus on reducing operating costs while failing to invest in the future is illustrated by the case of 3M.[iv]

Cost-effective Innovation at 3M

3M has long prided itself on its "vitality index", the percentage of sales from new products introduced during the past 2 years. However, during a period where lean Six-sigma methods of design were rigidly deployed, the rate of new product introductions dropped precipitously to less than a quarter of the norm. Lean Six-sigma methods may be useful, however, so long as the total value equation is simultaneously examined: top line profits from new features as well as bottom line savings from waste. After a change in top management, 3M renewed its up-front investment in innovation, but realized even higher profit margins because they married the creativity of early cross-functional teaming with relatively more flexible deployment of processes for saving money thereby achieving socio-technical integration.

A recent upsurge in cost cutting has relied on Six-sigma quality methods and "Lean Principles" to cut costs. Lean practices deployed in production operations are being retooled for application to product development where they only partially apply because of the intangibility of creative ideas. However, the notion of eliminating waste, such as in unnecessary processes, is quite consistent with concurrency so long as Lean is deployed flexibly rather than as a rigid mandate as illustrated in the 3M case.[v]

10.3. Patterns of Total Simultaneous Influence

A high percentage of costs and innovative opportunities occur at the front-end of the development cycle. Therefore, it is advantageous for enterprises to engage diverse functions representing multiple points

> Many methods of cost-cutting may suboptimize the performance of the system as a whole

along the value stream at the front-end of the development cycle. Whether the function is engaged or unengaged is measured at three phases: concept, pre-launch and post-launch. The number of functions engaged at a phase indicates the degree of heterogeneity at a given phase of development. As shown in Figure 10.1, the average number of functions engaged in NSD declines over the three phases of the development cycle.

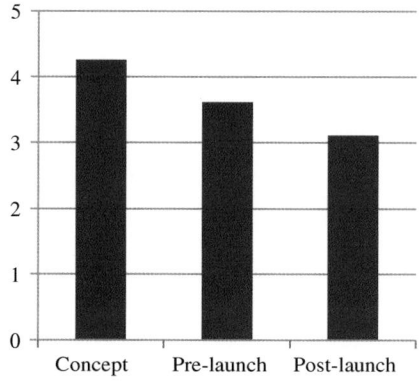

Figure 10.1. Average Number of Functions Engaged at Each Phase

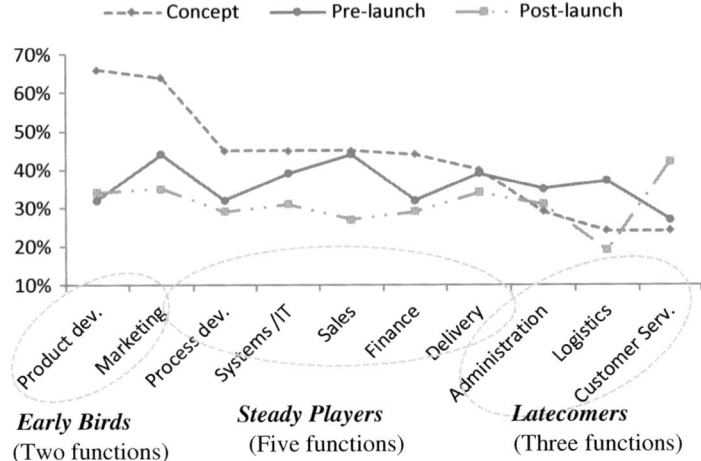

Figure 10.2.   Percentage of the Time Each of 10 Functions are Engaged by Phase

The percentage of time each of the 10 functions is engaged at the three phases is shown in Figure 10.2. The order in the figure is based on the percentage of representation at the up-front concept phase. At the concept phase, the most frequent function participating in development decisions is product development (66 percent) while the least is customer service (24 percent).

Two functions stand out as "early birds", product development and marketing. The product development function had the highest frequency of engagement at the concept phase. Five functions have a middling level of early engagement (ranging from 40 to 45 percent). These functions (process development, systems/IT, sales, finance, and delivery) are labeled "steady players" because their level of engagement is a kind of plateau and is relatively constant throughout the development cycle, never falling below about 30 percent.

Three functions are labeled "latecomers" because their engagement at the concept phase is below 30 percent, but rises subsequently. These functions include administration, logistics, and customer service. Customer service is most frequently engaged post-launch.

Grouping the 10 functions into the categories of early birds, steady players, and latecomers makes discerning patterns easier as shown in

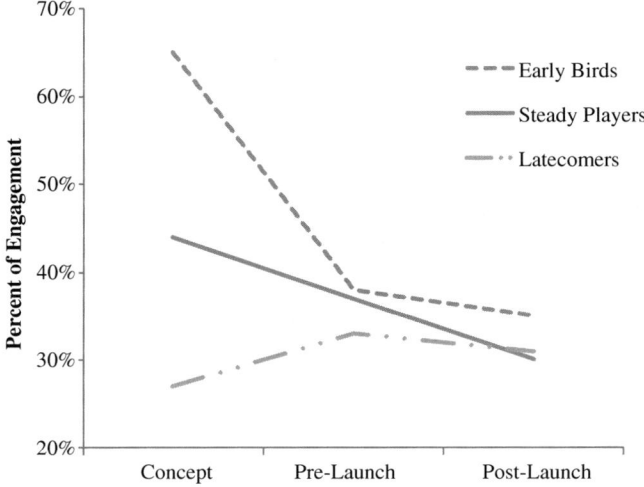

Figure 10.3.   Engagement by Early Birds, Steady Players, and Latecomers at Each Phase

Figure 10.3. The pattern for early birds is a lazy L. The pattern for steady players is a gently sloping decline. The pattern for latecomers rises for the pre-and post-launch phases.

Early bird functions are more often involved in decisions than any other functions at the Concept Phase — over 60 percent of the cases. However, involvement by early birds declines sharply at the Pre-launch Phase.

Steady player functions exhibit a roughly homogeneous pattern of involvement. Each is involved in product development decisions at least 40 percent or more of the cases at the Concept Phase. Each declines to approximately 35 percent or less at Post-launch Phase, a slight decline. Among steady players, the systems/IT, and sales functions are slightly above the average for the group.

Latecomer functions are more involved subsequent to the Concept Phase. Latecomers exhibit a slightly inverted V-pattern. Involvement peaks at the middle phase just prior to release of the product for sale. Among latecomers, customer service has a level of influence that is higher than that of others in the group.

10.4. Simultaneous Influence and Performance

ESI was measured earlier as engagement at the concept phase of four key functions: marketing, process development, finance, and customer service. As shown in Figure 10.4, high performing service enterprises were more likely to be engaged in NSD at the concept phase of the development cycle. However, the average level of engagement by all 10 functions is associated with high performance at the concept phase although the contrast is not as strong as for the four key functions.

To configure a winsome development team, which of the 10 functions offer the greatest benefit? One way to decide is to compare your enterprise with the average deployment in human capital in the service database. However, emulating the average may offer little or no competitive advantage. So what functions do high performers engage more often than others?

Measures of innovation performance in the services dataset capture two dimensions of performance (see Chapter Five, Table 5.3): (A) Differentiation — measured as time, cost, quality, and novelty; (B) Delivery — measured as time, cost, and quality. Overall innovation performance combines the two dimensions. Because the nature of value added differs to some extent for the differentiation of offerings pre- and post-launch, the impact of simultaneous influence by diverse functions is

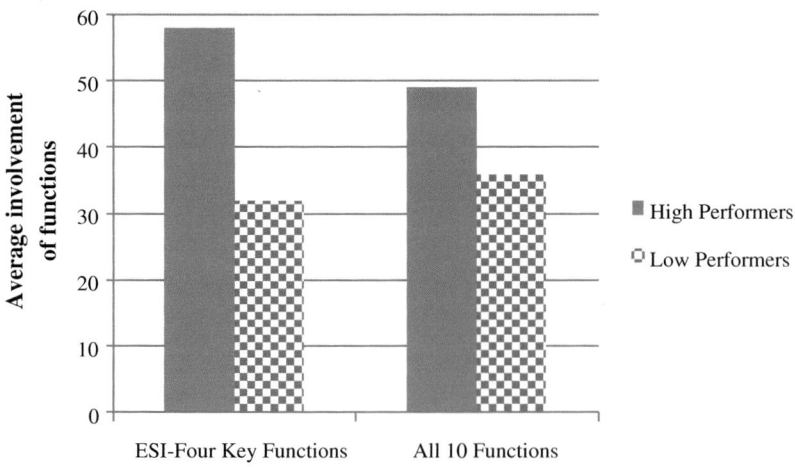

Figure 10.4.   ESI at the Development Concept Phase: High vs. Low Performers

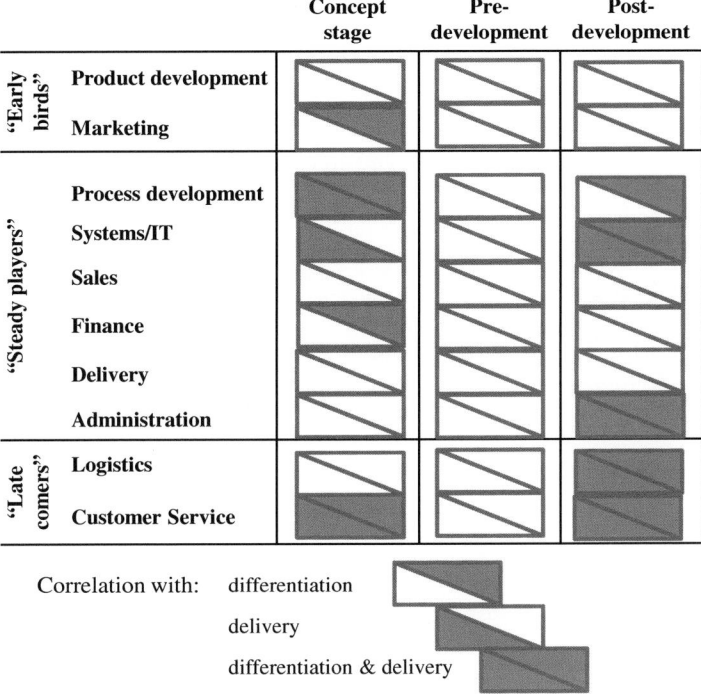

Figure 10.5.   Significant Correlations of Function with Performance

analyzed separately for each of the two performance components, differentiation, and delivery. The importance of delivery in services was emphasized by the positive effect of engagement by some functions post-launch had on performance in contrast to goods, where products may require physical reworking.

Correlations for engagement for each of the 10 functions with differentiation and/or delivery are summarized in Figure 10.5. If a function has a significant correlation with both differentiation and delivery performance, the whole square is blackened. If significant correlation is only with differentiation performance, a diagonal wedge points to the left. If significant correlation is only with delivery performance, a diagonal wedge points to the right.

Fifteen significant correlations were observed, seven at the concept phase, none at pre-launch, and eight at post-launch. Seven of the

10 functions had a significant correlation with performance. Some were relatively more important for differentiation, others for delivery. One option is to think about functional engagement by phase in your enterprise and assess whether any benefit might accrue from more heterogeneous input in instances where correlations are statistically significant.

10.5. Radical Strategy and Investment in Human Capital

This chapter builds on a contingency theory of strategy and system design. This theory suggests that the more dynamic and technologically complex markets become, the more likely large-scale corporations are to shift their product development system toward the organic rather than the mechanistic end of a continuum of design in order to innovate.[vi] Virtually every aspect of life is accelerating at a faster pace. This speeding up of change has challenged service firms to adapt quickly to new developments in their environment, such as deregulation, globalization, new technologies, mergers, and other factors driving hyper-competition.[vii] Therefore, some service enterprises have adopted a deliberate strategy of developing highly radical service offerings.

Service enterprises pursuing a strategy of radicalness are likely to need greater input of human capital as prior knowledge is inadequate. Developing novel service products requires the creation of new knowledge and/or the reworking of prior know-how to achieve a differentiated customer offering. Therefore, the benefits from investment in human capital are greater to the extent enterprises target a strategy of developing radical products. Enterprises with relatively high levels of commitment to such a strategy should have relatively greater levels of investment in human capital than otherwise. As shown in Figure 10.6, comparisons show that enterprises targeting a strategy of radicalness invest more in diversified human capital for all three groupings of functions.

The need for collaborative integration along the development cycle is likely to be higher when customer offerings entail complex unknowns and risks. Cross-fertilization of ideas by diverse functions is a proven way not only for stimulating ideas, but also for precluding downstream risks. Cross-functional collaboration is the tap root of innovation and requires

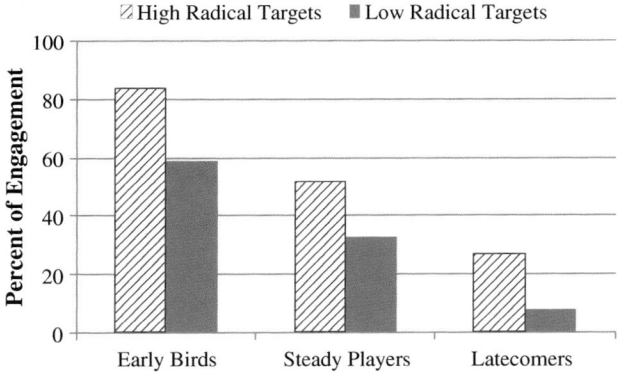

Figure 10.6.   Degree of Collaborative Engagement by Radical Strategy

engagement by all hands along the value stream. The development of new customer offerings is arguably the most complex business activity in large-scale enterprises because of the number of functions involved and the impact of their influence throughout the value development stream.

10.5.1. *Radicalness as moderator of human capital pay-off*

As shown above, enterprises with the strategic intent of innovation engage more functions on average than those without this target. But do enterprises deploying more human capital actually achieve higher levels of performance?

Results of moderated regression analysis show that enterprises achieving high differentiation performance deploy more overall simultaneous influence than others for every grouping at all three phases with the single exception of *latecomers* at the front-end as shown in Figure 10.7 where statistically significant interaction effects are designated by a darkened circle. Delivery performance is omitted because the only interaction effect is for Steady Players at the pre-launch phase. With this single exception, the benefit of simultaneous influence for differentiation performance under the contingency of radicalness holds for all three groups at all three phases.

The impact of simultaneous influence by early birds at the concept and post-launch phases is significantly stronger under the contingency of

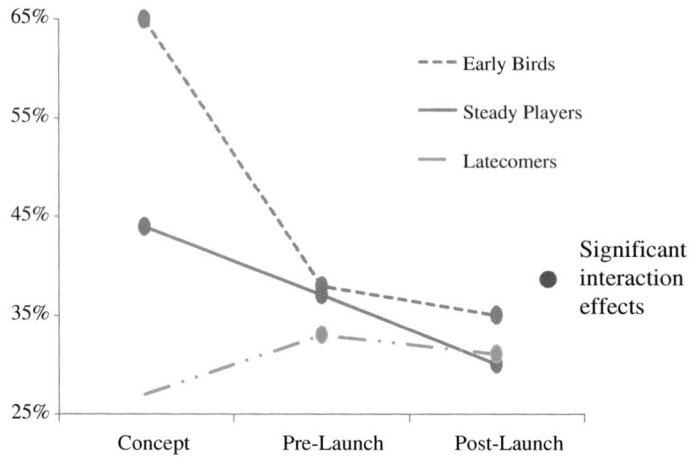

Figure 10.7. Impact of Simultaneous Influence on Differentiation Performance Moderated by Radicalness

radicalness. The inference is that engagement by early birds is not only beneficial at the front-end, but also post-launch if the development entails novel offerings.

Steady players have a stronger association with differentiation performance at all three phases: concept, pre-launch, and post-launch. This result suggests benefit from increased levels of engagement throughout the development cycle for this group of functions.

Latecomers have a stronger association with performance at the pre-launch and post-launch phases. This result suggests benefits from earlier engagement of latecomer functions to the extent enterprises pursue radicalness.

Engagement by some functions is synergistically beneficial for performance to the extent the enterprise pursues a strategy targeting radical innovation. In the next sections, 25 instances are reported in which participation by a given function has a synergistic impact on performance under the contingency of a strategy of radical development. If engagement by a given function boosts performance, the moderated interaction effects add strength to the argument for investment in its deployment for building capabilities for developing radically new offerings.

10.5.2. *Impact on differentiation performance*

The results of moderated regression for each of the 10 functions in combination with a strategy of radicalness show 18 significant interactions, all but one of which is positive. The percentage increase in multiple R square is shown graphically for significant effects for the 10 functions. All of the 10 functions have a significant interaction effect with differentiation performance at one or more of the three phases.

Concept phase (Figure 10.8a): The interaction effect is strong for marketing, e.g., 10 percent additional variance explained in differentiation performance, and moderate for IT systems. By contrast, the interaction for the delivery function is negative despite its strong positive interaction at the pre-launch phase. A possible explanation is that the delivery function in many enterprises is a relatively routine activity so that early engagement may provide limited value to design decisions.

Pre-launch phase (Figure 10.8b): Nine of 10 functions have significant interaction effects with the sole exception of product development. This pattern of results argues strongly for greater simultaneous influence prior to launch.

Post-launch phase (Figure 10.8c): Six functions have significant interaction effects with differentiation performance: product development, marketing, process development, administration, and customer service.

10.5.3. *Impact on delivery performance*

Radicalness also has moderating effects on delivery performance. However, they are fewer in number, 7 vs. 18. The seven interaction effects are all positive except one as shown in Figure 10.9. As is the case for differentiation performance, most are at the pre-launch phase.

Concept phase (Figure 10.9a): Product development has a significant interaction at the concept phase. By contrast, the delivery function has a slight negative interaction. As noted for differentiation performance above, and also for types of knowledge in the next chapter, early engagement is generally a good practice, but the delivery function seems to be exceptional in these data in this regard.

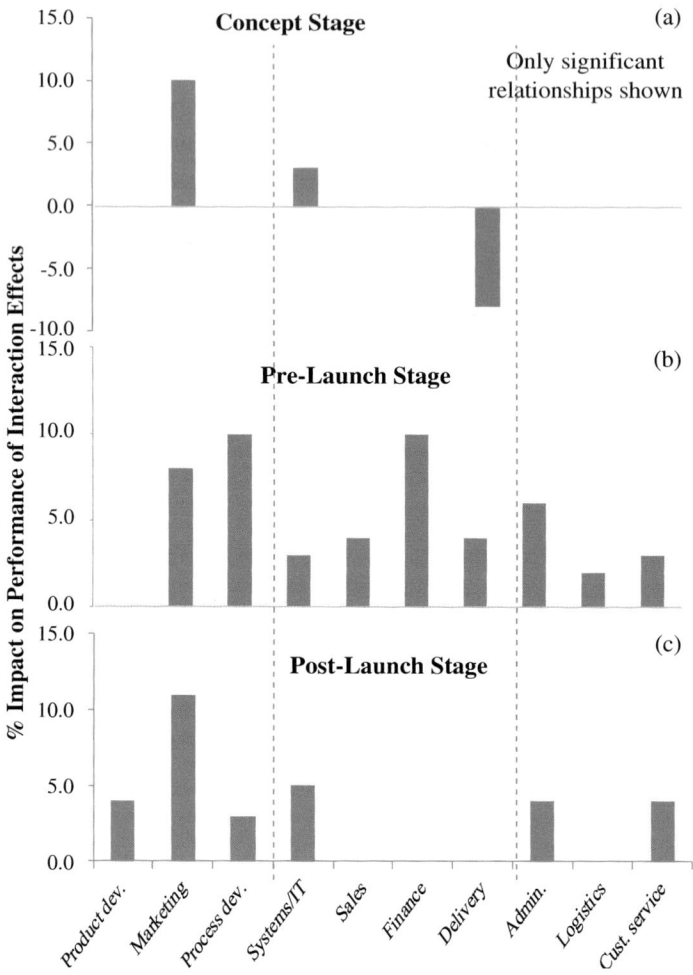

Figure 10.8. Interaction of Functions with Radical Strategy at Different Stages (Differentiation Performance)

Pre-launch phase (Figure 10.9b): Four interactions are significant: product development, marketing, sales, and finance. Extra engagement by the two early birds is consistent with the reverse side of the coin for ESI and suggest advantages from downstream engagement. The engagement of the finance and sales function pre-launch is probably beneficial for assessing cost benefits of new offerings prior to post-launch risks.

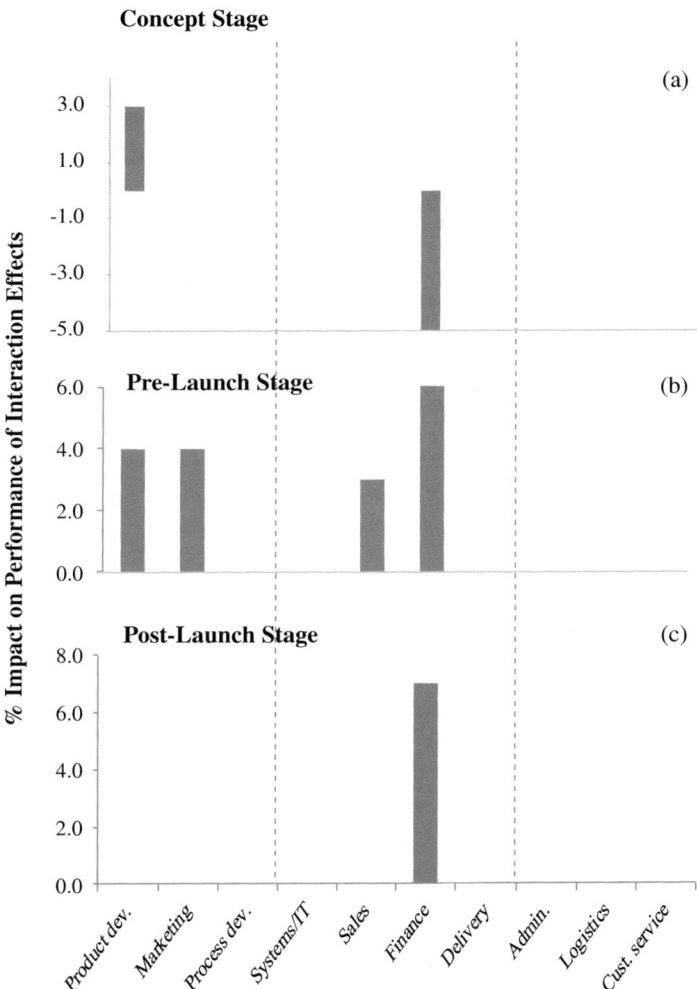

Figure 10.9. Interaction of Functions with Radical Strategy at Different Stages (Delivery Performance)

Post-launch phase (*Figure 10.9c*): The finance function has the only significant interaction, but it is rather strong. The need for post-launch evaluation of new launches is probably beneficial especially to the extent feedback may help modify subsequent offerings.

10.6. Conclusions

The input of human capital from diverse functions is the driver of developmental performance in services as well as goods. The hallmark of organic practices is cross-functional integration. Such integration is critical at the outset. But collaboration needs to occur throughout the development cycle which in services may entail augmented offerings post-launch.

The results of analysis support the thesis that the organic organization of cross-functional collaboration is a strong predictor of performance. All 10 functions had at least one or more significant relationships with either differentiation and/or delivery performance at one or more of three phases of the development cycle. These results are potentially useful for guiding managers in configuring innovative development teams in services.

Notes

[i]   Collins, P. and Hull, F. 1986. Technology and Span of Control, *Journal of Management Studies*, 23(2), 143–164; Hull, F. and Collins, P. 1987. High Tech Batch Production Systems: Woodward's Missing Type, *Academy of Management Journal*, 30(4), 786–797; Woodward, J. 1981. *Industrial Organization: Theory and Practice*, Oxford University Press: Oxford.

[ii]   Morgan, J. and Liker, J. 2006. *The Toyota Product Development System: Integrating People, Process, and Technology*, Productivity Press: New York; Womack, J. P., Jones, Daniel T., and Roos, D. 2007. *The Machine that Changed the World*, Simon and Schuster: New York.

[iii]   Sobek, D. K., Ward, A. C. and Liker, J. K. 1999. Toyota's Principles of Set-Based Concurrent Engineering, *Sloan Management Review*, Winter, (40), 2.

[iv]   Hindo, B. 2007. At 3M, A Struggle between Efficiency and Creativity, *Bloomberg*, June 10.

[v]   Byrne, A. 2012. *The Lean Turnaround*, McGraw-Hill: New York.

[vi]   Burns, T. and Stalker, G. M. 1961. *The Management of Innovation*, London: Tavistock; Lawrence, J. and Lorsch, P. R. 1967. *Organization and Environment*, Harvard University Press: Cambridge.

[vii]   D'Aveni, R. A. 1994. *Hypercompetition*, Free Press: New York.

CHAPTER ELEVEN

KNOWLEDGE STRATEGY AS A CONTINGENCY AFFECTING NSD BEST PRACTICES

Overview

Knowledge is increasingly evolving as a key factor differentiating customer offerings. How knowledge is exploited in developing and delivering service offerings provides the basis for competitive differentiation. Ultimately the provider gains and retains customers by offering services with greater value than competitive alternatives. Differences for which customers are willing to pay are ultimately backed-up by some type of knowledge capability affecting the experience of customers. However, the value proposition of service offerings varies widely. One type of customer offering is valued because of explicit knowledge that is embedded externally in codified forms. An alternative type deals with tacit knowledge which is often internal to the personal skills and capabilities of people developing and delivering services. The extent to which the troika of practices in the composite model are contingent upon the type of knowledge for which customers are willing to pay is explored. Computer Information Technology (CIT) practices are postulated as best suited for exploiting explicit, codified knowledge. Conversely, human capital associated with Organic Team Structure (OTS) is presumed to be relatively more effective for offering customers value from tacit knowledge.

11.1. Heterogeneity in Services

Variety in service offerings makes generalizations difficult because not all services are the same. The service sector is quite heterogeneous. Enterprises vary considerably in terms of the nature of the service act and on the degree of interaction between the service organization and the customers. However, to date there has been little attempt to investigate differences in development approaches among types of services.[i] Yet leading researchers argue that differences among services warrant further research.[ii]

Because the diversity of service offerings is poorly understood, it has proved difficult to identify general principles for managing operations and marketing practices across different service firms.[iii] One solution is the application of contingency theory. Contingency theories test how variation in system capabilities differentiates performance outcomes depending on situational factors. For example, it has been found that a more cross-functional approach to product development is needed under conditions of uncertainty.[iv] This contingency approach closes a gap in the product development literature that has been characterized as the failure of a "one size fits all approach to innovation".[v]

Lack of understanding of contingency factors may be a reason why recent research on service innovation competence yielded inconclusive findings regarding the importance of particular development factors and their relationship with NSD performance.[vi] Goldstein *et al.*[vii] postulate that a major deficiency in the NSD literature is a lack of research linking business strategy and service development. Strategy has been found to be an important moderator of the link between marketing capabilities and performance.[viii] It has been suggested that classifications of the strategy deployed and the nature of the service rendered could help provide operationally useful rules for new service design.[ix] This approach builds on strategic choice theory that envisions a deliberate role for managers in making decisions with critical impacts on performance.[x]

11.2. Value Creation Strategy Based on Knowledge

The strategy for a service firm accounts for not only its mission and long-term objectives, but also how it delivers value to its customers in comparison to other firms in the marketplace.[xi] Generic strategies have been identified that transcend traditional industry classifications[xii] and may prove a fruitful way of dealing with the diversity in services. However, there is little guidance on optimal dimensions for measuring strategy. It is argued that services theory needs to take a knowledge management perspective as knowledge is considered the most important resource that a firm can control.[xiii] Knowledge competencies are the main determinants of superior performance as they are rare, valuable, and difficult to imitate leading to a sustained competitive advantage.[xiv] It is a firm's knowledge competencies that provide value to its customers. Therefore, this chapter explores how two types of knowledge resources enable firms to offer varied kinds of service offerings and strategically differentiate themselves from competitors.

> Value is ultimately based on knowledge whether imbedded in physical objects, data, or tacitly emergent from inter-personal exchanges

11.2.1. *Tacit idiographic knowledge*

A strategy based on the sharing of tacit knowledge relies principally upon personalization through direct person-to-person contacts. Many services require an interaction between the service provider and the customer, and in some circumstances interaction amongst customers as well. Sometimes the service product is essentially its delivery process. This is especially true when the customer is the direct recipient of the service, often undergoing transformation during the transaction, e.g., education, psychiatry, hairdressing. One of the difficulties of competing on tacit knowledge is that quality is reliant on human idiosyncrasies. Quality is more uncertain and often cannot be objectively judged. Therefore, the risk to the customer is higher and features such as service guarantees become critical in providing value to customers.[xv]

Tacit knowledge is more effectively employed when services need to be adapted to unique customer needs, for example, to solve unique problems of customers when no standard solutions are available.[xvi] For services that involve judgmental decisions by the service provider the main factors behind new service success is the quality of the service experience and the expertise of front-line staff.[xvii] Customers and staff come together in a socialization process where tacit knowledge is combined in new and different ways to create shared meanings.[xviii] This mixing of tacit knowledge often includes subtle qualities like trust that are hard to measure. An advantage of competing on tacit knowledge is that it is harder to copy by competition because of "sticky information", i.e., information that is costly to acquire, transfer, and use in a new location.[xix] Organizations competing on the basis of tacit knowledge are able to win in the marketplace by service offerings providing knowledge-based solutions tailored to the needs of diverse customers.

11.2.2. *Explicit nomothetic knowledge*

This strategy entails making tacit knowledge more "explicit" via codification. Firm's adopting an explicit knowledge strategy translates information into externalized forms that can be used readily by others. It is a "people-to-docs" approach where knowledge is codified and stored in databases. This is suitable for a production or standardization approach where "economies of reuse" occur so that knowledge is not created unnecessarily. This is more than simply storing knowledge in databases, documents, and the like. It is embodiment of tacit knowledge into processes, routines, and procedures.[xx] Organizations that have high levels of explicit knowledge create value by codifying and building this knowledge into technical and service systems that are often automated. Professional service firms have been found to employ an explicit knowledge strategy where knowledge is pigeon-holed into applications in conformance with pre-defined operating procedures, e.g., accountancy standards, medical care, legal precedents, etc.[xxi] Similarly some advertising firms use internet software to standardize webpage production for customers.[xxii]

Many firms competing on explicit knowledge are key players in the information economy. Often firms will directly sell their knowledge base, e.g., information and research services. Firms may also embody their knowledge in hardware and software. For example, IT services typically include buying a mix of product and service activities. It has long been recognized that IT/IS can give service firms a competitive advantage by lowering costs and/or enhancing differentiation.[xxiii] Knowledge capabilities embedded in both hardware and software is also required to deliver a seamless communication experience via multiple customer "touch-points". Similarly self-service technologies are being introduced by service firms to add value via enhanced customer service, enabling direct transactions, and/or customer self-learning.[xxiv] Codification enables the standardization of service design and delivery. It makes growth simpler, reduces costs, and makes quality management easier. Service firms competing with a codification strategy are able to win in the marketplace because of superior capability for delivering knowledge-based solutions in a relatively standardized, easy to consume format.

Knowledge strategy may offer service firms a positional advantage having a direct impact on the service concept and value proposition offered to customers. It is argued that different service concepts require different approaches to their design and management.[xxv] Therefore, how effective new service development (NSD) practices are contingent on the firm's knowledge strategy is explored. However, tacit knowledge is difficult to measure objectively because of its myriad manifestations although it is somewhat more easily done for explicit knowledge. One solution is to examine the elements of the service offering that provide competitive advantages.[xxvi]

11.3. Knowledge and Human Engagement

Considerable research has been conducted on the ratio of personal vs. impersonal input required for optimizing system performance. Pioneering research by Woodward[xxvii] showed that industrial organizations making bespoke or customized batches required relatively high levels of managerial intensity to be successful. If knowledge from one operation to the next is not reused, a codified knowledge base is lacking for repeated applications. Managerial decisions are constantly required for dealing with idiosyncratic situations and input from the people doing the work is necessary. Batch producers that skimped on human capital were low performers because they "undermanaged". They failed to appreciate that tacit knowledge is complex and intensively personal. By contrast, if knowledge can be codified for reuse in massive operations that can be routinized, relatively less human capital is needed. Low performers in mass production operations wastefully "over managed" because they failed to transform tacit knowledge to codified forms of knowledge providing explicit guides for repeated actions.[xxviii]

Utilizing tacit knowledge in services is typically demanding of human resources because the knowledge base and/or the point of application involve unknowns and uncertainties. Judgment and/or interpersonal skills are needed for applying non-codified knowledge lacking in idiosyncratic situations. The ad hoc application of tacit knowledge means that planning is difficult. Scripting and pre-set processes are likely to have imprecise applications. Ironically, planning is often needed when the offering involves multiple options that may or not be required depending upon the course of the application. The general pattern is that the more contingent the offering is on tacit knowledge, the greater is the need for multifunctional engagement. Exploiting explicit knowledge typically involves codifying knowledge so that services may be rendered with greater standardization. In some cases human interfaces are relatively impersonal and scripted. In other cases they are computer automated. The general pattern is that the more the offering exploits explicit knowledge, the less the need for multifunctional engagement and managerial oversight.

To the extent the same principles apply to services as well as goods, the level of human capital deployed should be contingent upon the type of knowledge technology. The notion of a uniform span of managerial control or standard allocation of human resource is a relatively common practice, even by renowned corporations such as DuPont. Relative to uniform standard, high performers over-staff if the operation utilizes tacit knowledge, but under manage if explicit knowledge is exploited.

11.4. Knowledge Strategy Dimensions and Operationalization

Many ways of classifying knowledge are complex and difficult to operationalize. This research explores a relatively simple approach focusing on what types of service provided the basis of value for customer purchases. The question was worded as: "To what extent do the following add value to your service products for which customers are willing to pay?" The list of categories of value was very generic (see Table 11.1). However, analysis

Table 11.1.   Explicit vs. Tacit Knowledge Value: Exploratory Indicators

Explicit knowledge value:

• Professional knowledge
• Knowledge bases, e.g., research
• Hardware
• Software
• Communications

Tacit knowledge value:

• Personal service
• Convenience
• Guarantees
• Transactional changes

The items in the factor for explicit knowledge were fairly inter-correlated (alpha = 0.79). The items for tacit knowledge were more weakly correlated (alpha = 0.66). Two kinds of value added grouped in a miscellaneous factor: leisure and transportation.

showed that they could be readily grouped into two factors which were captioned "Explicit Knowledge" and "Tacit Knowledge".

Despite the generality of the categories of value, the two factor groupings, each has correlations with profiles of service enterprises that are surprisingly consistent with the notion of value added by explicit vs. tacit knowledge.

One factor dealt relatively more with explicit, nomothetic knowledge, such as professional codification, research-based information, know-how embedded in hardware, software programs, and communications associated with electronic transmission capabilities.

One may speculate that the other factor was associated with a personalization strategy in service offerings. Personal service obviously is likely to include tacit dimensions. The value customers place on convenience varies by person. Guarantees usually involve some degree of trust that is emotive as few customers read legal documents, such as car rental agreements in their entirety. Transactional changes may entail negotiations with varying degrees of impersonal interchange and emotional involvement.

Although these exploratory indicators of tacit explicit vs. tacit knowledge strategies need considerable improvement in future research, the extent to which the indicators available in this research analysis differentiate the two types is appreciable. Although these two knowledge strategies are slightly correlated ($r = 0.27$), the structure and practices of enterprises exploiting these types of knowledge vary considerably despite the fact that customer offerings often involve some mixture of both.

Enterprises pursuing tacit vs. explicit knowledge strategies display a collage of contrasts. A thematic difference is the relative reliance upon people vs. technology. To achieve differentiation based on tacit knowledge, enterprises need to organize and manage a relatively complex configuration of human resources. By contrast, enterprises adding value based on explicit knowledge use relatively more impersonal means in developing and delivering services as shown in Table 11.2.

Table 11.2.   Tacit vs. Explicit Strategy Practices

Practices	Tacit knowledge strategy enterprises	Explicit knowledge strategy enterprises
Performance outcomes	Delivery	None significant
Multifunctional engagement functions engaged	Marketing; Process development; IT systems; Sales; Finance; Administration; Logistics; Customer service	Marketing; IT systems
NSD decision-making Stakeholders responsibility Locus of decision-making	Cross-functional team Decentralized SBU units	Executive Director Central HQ staff
Business Critical Functions Key tasks required to retain customers	Customer Service; Information Technology; Logistics; Finance; Marketing; Sales	Product Development; Information Technology
Customer linkages Mode of exchange Delivery support	Personal Service in person or by telephone	Electronic networks Electronic communications
Improvement initiatives Methods	Business Process Reengineering; ISO conformance with processes	Total Quality Management
Key functions responsible	Customer service; Administration; Logistics	None specified

Performance Outcomes: The only significant correlation between type of knowledge utilized and performance is tacit knowledge with service delivery ($r = 0.31$). This association is consistent with the notion that tacit knowledge often entails interpersonal exchanges that are associated with delivery. One reason explicit knowledge may lack a significant association with performance is that CIT are far more standardized than tacit knowledge utilized by many service firms to differentiate themselves from competition. This association is consistent with the notion that services valued by customer because of tacit knowledge are likely to entail idiographic applications of know-how in delivery processes. Sometimes the essential value of the offering is closely intertwined with its delivery. Although some service delivery is impersonal, others may involve interpersonal exchanges some of which may be recurring. By contrast, technical capabilities are generally more easily reverse engineered than competitive advantages based on organization and management practices which are trickier to emulate.

Multifunctional engagement: The contrast between personal vs. impersonal modes of adding value is underscored by comparing how the two categories of enterprise differ in their engagement of 10 functions. Eight of 10 functions are engaged in enterprises using tacit knowledge vs. two for those exploiting explicit knowledge.

> Developing customer offerings exploiting tacit knowledge is demanding of diverse forms of human capital

Both engage marketing, which is business essential, and IT Systems. But enterprises exploiting explicit knowledge engage almost all of the other functions.

Decision-making: Enterprises reliant on explicit knowledge are less likely to have a functional department responsible for NSD. Instead headquarters relies upon functions in departments reporting directly to them, such as marketing and IT systems. Tacit knowledge enterprises decentralize NSD to cross-functional teams which are often collocated and rewarded as a group. By contrast, the development of customer offerings based on explicit knowledge is more likely to be directed by staff centralized at headquarters.

Business critical functions: Enterprises utilizing explicit knowledge are especially reliant upon the customer service function and logistics even though IT systems are also important. Dealing with idiosyncratic situations is associated with the engagement of analytic functions such as marketing and finance. The sales function is also important because of personal relationships between provider and customers are often involved. By contrast, enterprises exploiting explicit knowledge are most reliant upon IT systems directed by a centralized product development function.

Customer linkages: Relationships with customers help explain the differential importance of functions in the two types. For enterprises reliant upon tacit knowledge, much of the relationship is handled face-to-face or by telephone. One may infer that this type often entails ongoing transactions that are relatively more amenable to augmentation after sale than technical kinds of value added. They are less likely to "reach their customers via electronic networks" and unlikely to operate internationally. By contrast, enterprises reliant upon explicit knowledge develop electronic networks and depend relatively more on electronic communications, e.g., "Use electronic means of communication to support the delivery of the service product to customers".

Competitive challenges for each type of knowledge strategy differ. Tacit knowledge is relatively more reliant on relationships with customers. Dealing with idiosyncratic customer differences is very demanding of customer support and requires administrative oversight because of a myriad of exceptional circumstances. To reduce variation in customer exchanges, enterprises exploiting tacit knowledge try to devise standards for service delivery, including logistical support. From a knowledge management perspective, the struggle is to transform idiosyncratic, tactic knowledge into standardized, codified knowledge to realize economies of scale and ensure reliable service. Interestingly, enterprises exploiting explicit knowledge did not cite any specific function responsible for improving their competitiveness. One reason is that quality is often built into the electronic networks of information and communications systems upon which they rely for delivering the bulk of their services.

Improvement Initiatives: As the pace of change has accelerated in the service sector, many enterprises have deployed initiatives to improve performance. In services utilizing tacit knowledge, process is often particularly critical, and especially so if interpersonal relationship are entailed in the delivery of augmented offerings. Methods of improvement include conformance with ISO standards and business process reengineering. Key functions responsible for such process improvements include customer service, administration, and logistics.

Enterprises pursuing a strategy of explicit knowledge are more likely to adopt Total Quality Management (TQM) methods. This approach often includes techniques for statistical quality control which is frequently used by financial service organizations to monitor transactions and reduce risk.

The contrast between the two types is consistent with the presumption that the deployment of human capital is contingent upon the knowledge technology involved. These differences add validity to the type of knowledge strategy as they are consistent with the notion of how each approach drives the service offering.

11.5. Knowledge Strategy and the Composite Model

The contrasting structure and practices of the two types of knowledge exploitation has implications for the human capital component of the composite model. OTS is demanding of human capital because people are pulled out of defined functional roles are working as collocated team members rewarded for their project instead of departmental contributions. Deploying a strategy utilizing tacit knowledge requires diverse specialists to handle varied value creation opportunities with a heterogeneous customer base. Early simultaneous influence is helpful for developing services based on tacit knowledge entails idiosyncratic transactions requiring customer contact not only before sale, but also after the initial transactions. By contrast, transactions for enterprises exploiting explicit knowledge are more likely to be codified and processed electronically.

Strategic context presumably has associations with the deployment of practices in the composite model. The significant correlations in Table 11.3 show that enterprises exploiting tacit knowledge are more likely to deploy all elements of the composite model, and especially OTS. The association between a tacit knowledge strategy and OTS is plausible because collaboration among people from diverse functions is required for developing customer offerings. OTS facilitates the exploitation of human judgment which is often required for applying idiographic knowledge. Similarly services based on tacit knowledge require relatively

Table 11.3.   Correlations of Knowledge Type with Composite Model Practices

Organic organization	Tacit knowledge strategy	Explicit knowledge strategy
OTS		
Cross-functional Teaming	0.32	—
Collocation	0.39	—
Group rewards	0.28	—
Composite Model		
ESI	0.36	—
IDC	0.27	—
CIT	0.21	0.30

more up-front planning and involvement to counter the problems of reliability and control. Hence In-process Design Controls (IDC) is associated with tacit knowledge.

By contrast, the only significant correlation between strategy and practice for enterprises exploiting explicit knowledge is with CIT. This association is consistent with the notion that explicit knowledge can be codified and embedded in software, firmware, and physical accoutrements for delivering services. Enterprises exploiting a strategy based on explicit knowledge often rely upon impersonal electronics. These differences are consistent with the deep-rooted distinction between nomothetic and idiographic forms of knowledge.

The need for various kinds of human capital varies depending upon the knowledge strategy of the enterprise. Engaging functions to exploit a tacit knowledge strategy may require expensive investments in human capital. OTS provides a framework for cross-functional integration along the value development stream. But how much of which kinds of human capital are needed for exploiting a tacit knowledge strategy? The greater the pursuit of a strategy exploiting tacit knowledge, the greater the need for human capital is likely to be. Conversely, the more enterprises target a strategy exploiting explicit knowledge, the less the need for human capital is likely to be.

A tacit knowledge strategy is likely to have a somewhat distinctive profile in terms of the kinds of human capital deployed. Enterprises pursuing a tacit knowledge strategy have positive correlations with the index measuring ESI (marketing, process development, finance, and customer service) at the concept phase ($r = 0.36$) and with an index of *late simultaneous influence* (Marketing, Process development, Systems support/IT, Administration, Logistics, and Customer service) at the post-launch phase ($r = 0.24$).

Functions deployed by enterprises with a tacit knowledge strategy focus on post-launch and up-front engagement presumably to ensure delivery processes work. Process developers and customer service functions are correlated with a tacit knowledge strategy at the concept and post-launch phases. This is consistent with the notion that tacit knowledge entails interpersonal exchanges that may benefit from up-front analysis of guiding processes and early input from people dealing directly with customers after launch as well as administrative oversight. Enterprises pursuing a tacit knowledge strategy are more likely to have marketing engaged at the concept phase and sales pre-launch.

Enterprises exploiting explicit knowledge are likely to display a different profile than those with a tacit strategy. Theoretically, investment in multifunctional engagement is more necessary to the extent knowledge utilized is explicit. To the extent computer tools and technologies replace some kinds of skills; the need for human capital should be lower on average although some functions may be more necessary. Explicit knowledge has a modest negative correlation with the average level of deployment of all 10 functions ($r = 0.22$). The only specific function having a significantly negative correlation with explicit knowledge is marketing at the pre-launch phase ($r = -0.23$). One may speculate that customer offerings programmed by it required less marketing input.

11.6. Effects of Knowledge on Innovation Performance

According to contingency theory, the design of development systems should be a means congruent with strategic objectives. High performing

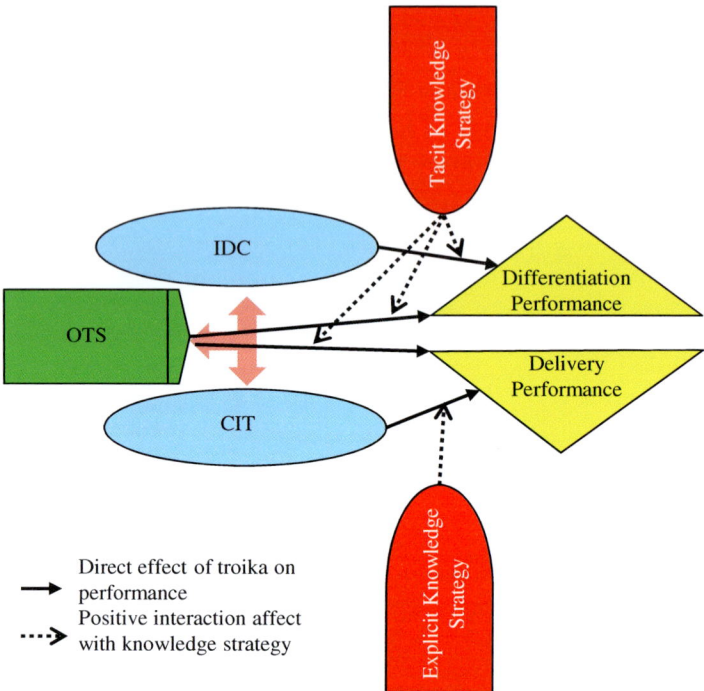

Figure 11.1.   Impact of Composite Model on Performance Moderated by Knowledge Strategy

systems should deploy elements of the composite model most appropriate for effectively exploiting the type of knowledge adding value for which customers are willing to pay. Therefore, the associations between development system and performance outcomes are tested for the moderating effects of knowledge type. In moderated regression analyses, each element of the troika has an impact on performance that is moderated by the contingency of knowledge strategy as shown in Figure 11.1.

11.6.1 *OTS*

The contingency of tacit knowledge strategy moderates the impact of human capital on both differentiation and delivery performance. This result is consistent with the presumption that people are vital repositories of tacit knowledge because of difficulties in codifying applications in idio-syncratic situations. Presumably the value of tacit knowledge is heavily reliant upon its personal delivery to customers. This hypothetical interaction effect may be summarized as follows:

> *The more tacit the knowledge adding value strategy, the greater the impact of human capital (OTS) on differentiation performance.*

The primary factor in the development of successful new services is the creation of an innovative environment where ideas and open communication are encouraged by supportive management.[xxix] OTS empowers people from diverse functions with responsibility for executing specific service development projects. It is characterized by open communication which helps cross-fertilize ideas and stimulates creative solutions to complex problems. Research in the service sector stresses the importance of involving and empowering front-line staff throughout the development process.[xxx] This allows constructive ideas to improve not only the service, but also the processes of developing and delivering them. Cross-fertilization of ideas among diverse functions is especially at the outset of the development process where the opportunity for innovation is the greatest.[xxxi] Cross-functional communication also builds commitment for the project and reduces the amount of risk and uncertainty surrounding it.[xxxii]

If the firm's strategy is based on exploiting tacit knowledge, the impact of organic practices on performance is presumed to be relatively greater. The services offered are relatively more interpersonal, idiosyncratic, and are amenable to augmentation during delivery. Downstream functions such as operations staff and customer service need to be involved early in the development process for the effective implementation and delivery of new services. Team based practices are more necessary to the extent the service product entails human factors and opportunities to spontaneously react to emergent situations transcending the capabilities of programmed actions. Also cross-functional teamwork is needed when dealing with subtle and imprecise information. For example, it has been found that established interrelationships are needed for sharing knowledge during service development and that this increased in importance when tacit knowledge was high.[xxxiii] Following this line of reasoning one may speculate that the benefit of an OTS is relatively greater for service firms employing a personalization strategy.

11.6.2. *CIT*

The contingency of an explicit knowledge strategy moderates the impact of tools and technologies, but only on delivery performance. This result is consistent with the presumption that nomothetic knowledge can be codified for transmission. Presumably the content delivered is heavily reliant upon the analyses and transformations of codified information. This interaction effect may be summarized as follows:

The more explicit the knowledge adding value strategy, the greater the impact of tools /technologies (CIT) on performance.

CIT has been found to directly affect both the speed of the NSD process and the general effectiveness of the firm's innovation activities. [xxiv] CIT enables NSD plans to be dynamic and continually updated throughout the development process.[xxxv] The effective recording, storing, and reviewing of information generated during development has been shown to have a positive relationship with further new product successes.[xxxvi] In addition, service developers are able to be more analytical in their decision-making by using computer-based simulations, e.g., econometric modeling, discounted cash flow analyses, etc.[xxxvii] CIT is also embedded in the delivery of new service offerings either in the form of hardware e.g., ATMs, or software, e.g., risk analyses for life insurance.

11.6.3. *IDC*

The contingency of a tacit knowledge strategy moderates the impact of process on differentiation performance. The competitive advantages of deploying process to help standardize services helps achieve economies of scale and abets reliability. IDC provides flexible discipline for managing idiosyncratic service situations where options need to be evaluated and narrowed. Hypothetically, tacit knowledge may more readily be rendered into processes than tacit knowledge.

The more tacit the knowledge adding value strategy, the greater the impact of processes (IDC) on performance.

Services based on tacit knowledge require relatively more up-front planning and involvement to counter the problems of reliability and control. Paradoxically, the more uncertainty associated with the new service under development, the more a disciplined, but flexible process is needed to help reduce risk. NSD processes need to be dynamic and flexible because rigid rules and procedures can stifle creativity.[xxxviii] Conversely, as explicit knowledge is easier to plan and program into computer-based systems,[xxxix] formal processes may add relatively less value during development. Therefore, higher levels of IDC are hypothesized as relatively more important for new services based on a personalization strategy than a codification strategy.

11.7. Knowledge Contingencies in the Deployment of Human Capital

How much of which kinds of human capital are needed for exploiting a tacit knowledge strategy? The greater the pursuit of a strategy exploiting tacit knowledge, the greater the need for human capital is likely to be. Conversely, the more enterprises target a strategy exploiting explicit knowledge, the less the need for human capital is likely to be. Explicit knowledge strategies affect the need for human capital, often by automating some tasks while creating others. But which functions are made redundant by an explicit knowledge strategy and which are more needed? Moreover, at which phases of the development stream are functional role more or less necessary?

The average influence of all 10 functions is largely uncorrelated with performance. However, type of knowledge has several contingent relationships moderating the effect of functional engagement by one or more of the 10 functions on either differentiation and/or delivery performance.

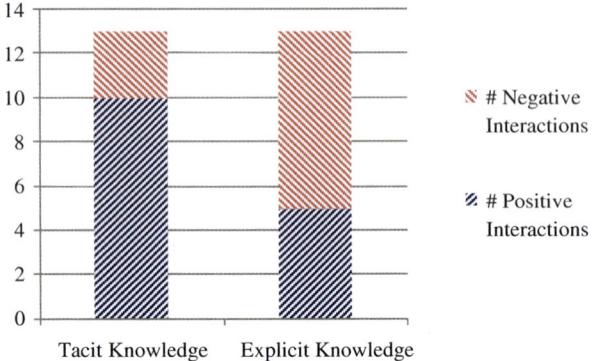

Figure 11.2. Number of Statistically Significant Interactions between Functional Engagement and Innovation Performance

Tacit knowledge has 13 significant interaction effects, 10 of which are positive. Explicit knowledge also has 13 significant interactions effects, but eight are negative. This contrast is summarized in Figure 11.2 and is consistent with the presumption that explicit knowledge is relatively demanding of human capital while tacit knowledge reduces the need for some kinds of functions but not others.

11.7.1. *Effects on differentiation performance*

For each of the three phases, interaction effects are compared for tacit vs. explicit knowledge for differentiation performance. The results are shown in Figure 11.3.

(A) Concept phase

As shown in Figure 11.3a at the concept phase, three functions have significant interaction effects with *tacit knowledge,* two positive and one negative. The effects for the product development function and IT systems are positive. To exploit tacit knowledge, greater effort in conceptualizing the offering is likely to be needed up-front to design value which may involve idiosyncratic applications. The positive interaction of IT systems may be due to efforts in transforming tacit knowledge into explicit knowledge. Many kinds of information technologies are deployed

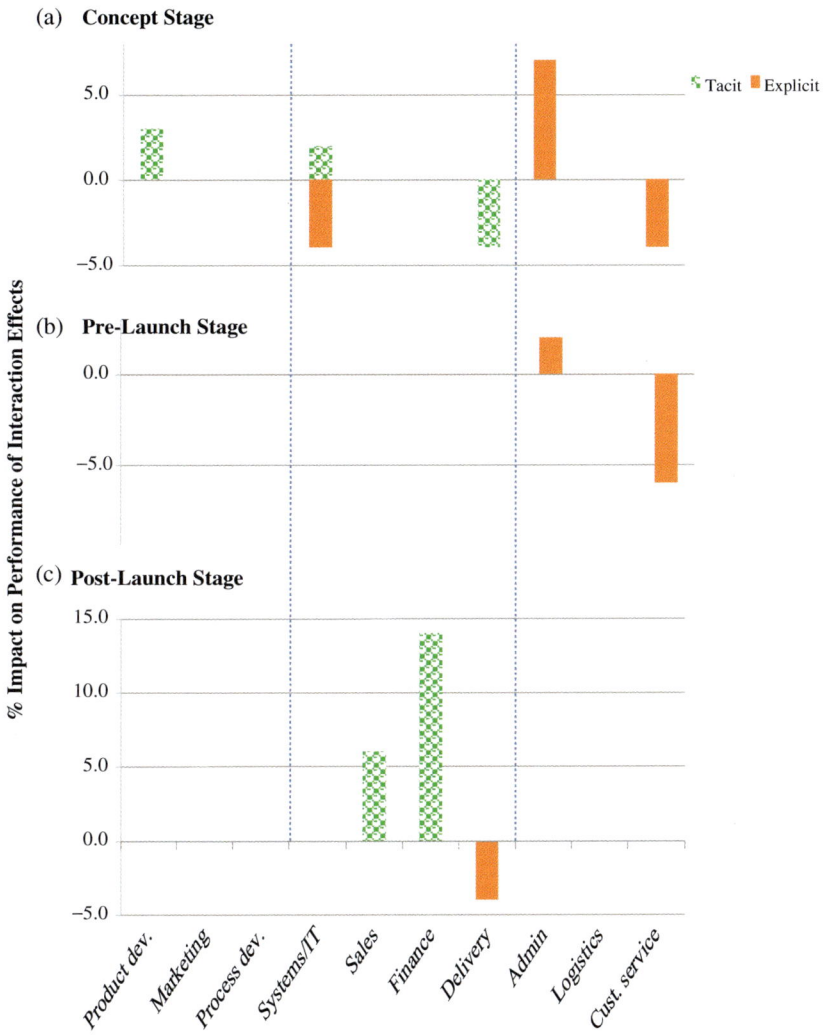

Figure 11.3. Effect of Knowledge Strategy on Differentiation Performance

in increasingly sophisticated ways to codify qualitative knowledge. The delivery function has a modest negative interaction. To the extent their function is routine, early engagement may be less valuable for designing offerings at the concept phase.

For *explicit knowledge*, three functions have significant interaction effects contingent on explicit knowledge, one positive and two negatives.

The positive interaction effect for administration is sizable. One explanation is that as knowledge gets codified as explicit, the ratio of administrators to human employees increases, a so-called "robot effect".[xxxix] Automation substitutes for the actions of direct workers, yet the outputs need managerial coordination. The interaction effect for customer service is appreciably negative, which is consistent with the notion that computer tools and technologies reduce the need for personal contact by service support personnel because a higher proportion of value is added electronically. Surprisingly, the other negative interaction effect is for IT systems. On the one hand, one might presume that the more explicit the knowledge exploited, the greater the need for IT staff. On the other hand, the involvement of IT/systems may drive efficiency considerations that limit differentiation performance. Also overstaffing may occur if a level of maturity is reached in codification without subsequent reduction in personnel as their marginal utility declines.

(B) Pre-launch

Only two interactions are significant for functional engagement at the pre-launch phase with *explicit* knowledge as shown in Figure 11.3b. These two interactions reprise the pattern consistent with the robot effect, positive for administration and negative for customer services noted above at the concept phase.

(C) Post-launch

As shown in Figure 11.3c, two functions have significant interaction effects at the post-launch phase with *tacit* knowledge, both positive. The sales and especially the finance function have fairly strong, positive interactions which may be related to the need to preclude post-launch risks with the idiosyncratic nature of offerings exploiting tacit knowledge. Also creating value from tacit knowledge requires negotiations between sales and finance functions to ensure offerings provide favorable returns. One small negative effect is for the delivery function if knowledge is *explicit*. This is consistent with the notion of the robot effect. One possibility is that people engaged in the delivery function may be redundant to the extent computer automated mechanisms are the means of transfer to customers.

11.7.2. *Effects on delivery performance*

For each of the three phases, interaction effects are compared for tacit vs. explicit knowledge with delivery performance. More interaction effects are observed for delivery than differentiation performance as shown in Figure 11.4.

(*A*) *Concept phase*

Four interaction effects are significant if knowledge is *tacit*, three positives and one negative as shown in Figure 11.4a. The interaction effects are positive for process development, logistics, and customer service. All three of these functions seem to have an obvious link with interchanges between provider and customer. Augmentation during service delivery is not an added extra but often an integral part of the total offering entailing tacit knowledge. Unlike tangible products, where the physical product can be sold without any elements of augmentation, the service product cannot exist without service augmentation, in one form or another. This is because the service is not created until the customer interacts with the service organization, its systems, and/or staff. Processes, logistics, and customer service are all elements that help create this augmentation at the point of delivery.

Surprisingly the delivery function has a modest negative interaction if knowledge is tacit. To the extent the delivery function normally performs relatively routine operations, the idiosyncrasies associated with providing tacit knowledge to customers may be experienced as an extra burden which they are unprepared to take on. For example, delivery staff may view innovation in dealing with customer idiosyncrasies as increasing their workload and resist augmentation activities which might be better performed by those provided with training in interpersonal skills.

Three interaction effects with delivery performance are significant if knowledge is *explicit*. The strong positive interaction with administration

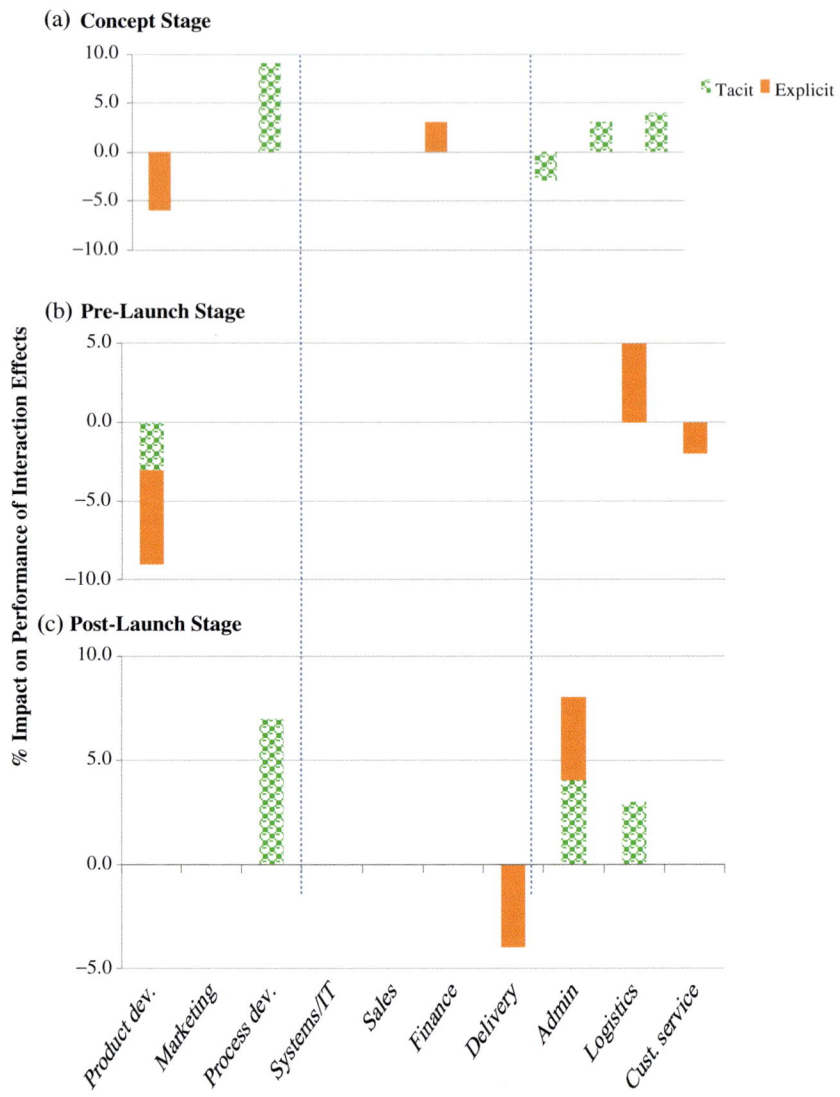

Figure 11.4. Effect of Knowledge Strategy on Delivery Performance

and negative with customer service is consistent with the notion of the robot effect. The negative interaction with IT systems seems surprising. But this was also observed for delivery performance and the reasons may be similar.

(B) Pre-launch phase

As shown in Figure 11.5b, the negative with customer service is consistent with the notion of the robot effect which was also observed at the concept phase for delivery and both the concept and pre-launch phases for differentiation. Somewhat puzzling are the negative interaction effects for product development with delivery performance with both tacit and explicit knowledge. One possibility is that engagement by product development function pre-launch may be later than optimal as one might think their input could be relatively more valuable at the concept phase consistent with the notion of ESI.

The logistic function has a positive effect. Logistics can be a highly technical discipline extending computer automated applications to networks and managing distribution in ways consistent with the delivery of explicit knowledge.

(C) Post-launch

Five positive interactions are observed for delivery performance with *tacit* knowledge: process development, sales, finance, administration, and logistics. All of these seem easy to link with the tasks of augmented service offerings. Although no interaction effect was observed for customer service, their level of engagement is high on average and also significantly correlated with delivery performance.

The only negative interaction effect is for delivery if knowledge is *explicit*. Perhaps this function is somewhat redundant to the extent deliveries become computer automated.

These interaction effects present a fairly compelling argument for the extra deployment and training of personnel in functions for augmenting services if tacit knowledge affects the value of the delivered offering.

11.8. Augmented Offerings: Explicit and/or Tacit Knowledge

Delivery of services offers many opportunities for admixtures of explicit and tacit knowledge. For example, students in a classroom may passively take notes and have little or no interpersonal interaction with the instructor.

On the other hand, some students may ask questions in class, visit the instructor during office hours, and establish some degree of interpersonal relationship. Without coming to class and taking notes, the student is less likely to engage the instructor in exchanges which include tacit as well as explicit knowledge. Of course some subjects such as physics may deal with more explicit knowledge than say psychology. But even in the instance of physics, when instructors provide personal experiences relating to their experiments or ask probing questions to help students grasp factual information, tacit knowledge is involved.

Opportunities for differentiating service offerings is trending toward greater exploitation of tacit knowledge for enhancing customer experiences. The value of customer offerings seems likely to be

> Personal skills for empathetically dealing with people is key for exploiting many kinds of tacit knowledge

increasingly driven by tacit relative to explicit knowledge. Because experience is an emergent property arising from interactions between provider and customer, the importance of delivery performance relative to the differentiation of features also seems likely to rise in importance. Service design is a rapidly growing field of study and application that focuses particularly on service delivery and the quality of the augmented offering. Some dimensions of the augmented offering may be standardized, others may be highly idiosyncratic.

The human chemistry between provider and customer is often an extraordinarily important source of competitive advantage. Customer experiences in the airline industry provide insightful examples. One of the best known success stories in aviation is Southwest Airlines. While operations are lean and efficient, flight attendants are permitted to improvise and joke even during the safety demonstration. Although Southwest record of on-time arrivals is not at the top, customer satisfaction remains extraordinarily high because the carrier caters to their concerns even at the opportunity cost of letting passengers check bags for no charge. The ambiance on their flights is humane and personable.

A case study of an airline merger highlights the vital role human chemistry plays in competitive advantage. One author repeatedly traveled between two cities with a choice between two non-stop options. Carrier A was one of the top five in size in the US aviation industry and offered frequent flights. Carrier B had fewer flights and less commodious planes. However, the author as well as a great many other fellow passengers preferred to fly on the smaller carrier. Subsequently the larger carrier purchased the smaller one.

Delivery Experiences at Northwest Airlines

Although flight attendants in the merged airline served passengers wearing identical uniforms, some seemed to be so much more pleasant than others. Based on their conversations and behaviors, the author began to play a guessing game as to the provenience of the flight attendants based on their non-verbal behaviors and conversations with passengers. The author correctly guessed the attendant's employer prior to the merger in 21 of 23 instances.

The two exceptions were instructive. One flight attendant has just started within the week and had little opportunity to become jaded by the culture of the acquiring carrier. The other attendant had such an angelic personality that the observer found it hard to imagine how bad any situation would have to be before her service behavior would turn sour. One of the most telling confirmations were statements made by pilots. For example, several said that when flight attendants came into the cockpit to offer snacks or to chat, we knew they were from the acquired carrier. These friendly behaviors never happened before the acquisition. Another indicator was complaints by flight attendants from the acquired carrier who resented being "written up" by their new mangers for sitting on the arm of a seat to chat with passengers. Two even complained about being written up for "thank you" to those who were putting trash in the bag as they passed through the aisle toward the end of the flight.

The case illustrates how interpersonal interactions affect customer experiences. Often a high percentage of the experience is non-verbal. The flight attendants from the acquired company read the faces and gestures of passengers. The reflections in the social mirror were almost always mutually pleasing. The delivery of passengers from point x to point y was the same after the acquisition. But but the positive emotions and pleasing ambiance experienced by the author deteriorated within a year after the acquisition..

11.9. Conclusions

The pattern of positive and negative interaction effects based on the type of knowledge reveal a complex pattern that is mostly explicable. The most important finding is that five functions in addition to customer service need to be relatively more engaged to enhance delivery performance under the contingency that a tacit knowledge strategy is pursued.

The importance of administration under the contingency of explicit knowledge for explicit knowledge is consistent with well-established findings that the span of control widens with the deployment of automation, the so-called robot effect. Often the codification of knowledge into explicit forms reduces the need for interpersonal interactions from customer service.

At the post-launch phase, finance and sales functions seem to be of particular importance under the contingency of tacit knowledge. Perhaps their involvement is particularly important because cost benefits are difficult to assess. Augmented offerings have emergent properties that can only be best evaluated during delivery experiences.

Despites the tangled web of positive and negative interactions based on type of knowledge, the upshot is that optimal configuration of investment in human capital for performance needs to take knowledge contingencies into account. As many services are becoming more personalized, the role of key functions for service providers is increasingly important for augmenting customer offerings.

Notes

[i]   Johne, A. and Storey, C. 1998. New Service Development: A Review of the Literature and Annotated Bibliography, *European Journal of Marketing*, 32(3/4), 184–251.

[ii]   Lovelock, C. and Gummesson, E. 2004. Whither Services Marketing? In Search of a New Paradigm and Fresh Perspectives, *Journal of Service Research*, 7(1), 20–41.

[iii]   Chase, R. B. and Apte, U. M. 2007. A History of Research in Service Operations: What's the Big Idea? *Journal of Operations Management*, 25, 375–386.

[iv]   Olson, E. M., Walker, O. C., and Ruekert, R. W. 1995. Organizing for Effective New Product Development: The Moderating Role of Product Innovativeness, *Journal of Marketing*, 59(January), 48–62.

[v]   Barczak, G., Griffin, A., and Kahn, K. B. 2009. Trends and Drivers of Success in NPD Practices: Results of the 2003 PDMA Best Practices Study, *Journal of Product Innovation Management*, 26(1), 3–23.

vi Menor, L. J. and Roth, A. V. 2007. New Service Development Competence in Retail Banking, *Journal of Operations Management*, 25, 825–846.

vii Goldstein, S. M., Johnston, R., Duffy, J., and Rao, J. 2002. The Service Concept: The Missing Link in Service Design Research? *Journal of Operations Management* 20(2), 121–134.

viii Olson, E. M., Slater, S. F., and Hult, G. T. M. 2005. The Performance Implications of Fit Among Business Strategy, Marketing Organization Structure, and Strategic Behavior, *Journal of Marketing*, 69(3), 49–65.

ix Chase and Apte, 2007. *Op. cit.*

x Child, J. 1997. Strategic Choice in the Analysis of Action, structure, Organizations and Environment, *Organization Studies*, 18(1), 43–76.

xi Goldstein *et al.*, 2002. *Op. cit.*

xii Zahra, S. A. and Pearce II, J. A. 1990. Research Evidence on the Miles–Snow Typology, *Journal of Management*, 16(4), 751.

xiii Roth, A. V. and Menor, L. J. 2003. Insights into Service Operations Management: A Research Agenda, *Production & Operations Management*, 12(2), 145–164.

xiv Barney, J. 1991. Firm Resources and Sustained Competitive Advantage, *Journal of Management*, 17(1), 99–121; Grant, R. M. 1996. Toward a Knowledge-Based Theory of the Firm, *Strategic Management Journal*, 17(Winter Special), 109–122.

xv Lidén, S. and Sandén, B. 2004. "The Role of Service Guarantees in Service Development", *Service Industries Journal*, 24(4), 1–20.

xvi Salmi, P., Torkkeli, M., Ojanen, V. and Hilmola, O-P. 2007. "New product creation process of KIBS firms: A case study", Paper presented at Tekes Seminar on Innovation in Services: Challenges and Opportunities for Economies, Industries and Firms, 27–28 April, Haas School of Business, Berkeley.

xvii Storey, C. and Easingwood, C. 1998. The Augmented Service Offering: A Conceptualisation and Study of its Impact on New Service Success, *Journal of Product Innovation Management*, 15(4), 335–351.

xviii Nonaka, I. 1994. A Dynamic Theory of Organisational Knowledge Creation, *Organization Science*, 5(1), 14–37.

xix Von Hippel, E. 1994. Sticky Information and the Locus of Problem Solving: Implications for Innovation, *Management Science*, 40(4), 429–440.

xx Grant. 1996. *Op. cit.*

xxi Mintzberg, H. and Quinn, B. 1996. *Strategy Process*, Prentice-Hall: Englewood Cliffs.

xxii Salmi *et al.* 2007. *Op. cit.*

xxiii   Bharadwaj, S. G., Varadarajan, P. R., and Fahy, J. 1993. Sustainable Competitive Advantage in Service Industries: A Conceptual Model and Research Propositions, *Journal of Marketing*, 57(4), 83–99.

xxiv   Bitner, M. J., Ostrom, A. L., and Meuter, M. L. 2002. Implementing Successful Self-Service Technologies, *Academy of Management Executive*, 16(4), 96–108.

xxv   Roth and Menor. (2003). *Op. cit.*

xxvi   Roth and Menor. 2003. *Op. cit*; Storey and Easingwood. 1998. *Op. cit.*

xxvii   Woodward, J. 1965. *Industrial Organization: Theory and Practice*, Oxford University Press: London.

xxviii   Hull, F. and Collins, P. 1987. High Tech Batch Production Systems: Woodwards Missing Type, *Academy of Management Journal*, 30(4), 786–797.

xxix   de Brentani, U. 1993. The New Product Process in Financial Services: Strategy for Success, *International Journal of Bank Marketing*, 11(3), 15–22.

xxx   Storey and Easingwood. 1998. *Op cit.*

xxxi   Goffin, K. 1988. Evaluating Customer Support During New Product Development An Exploratory Study, *Journal of Product Innovation Management*, 15(1), 42–57; Hull, F. M. 2003. Simultaneous Involvement in Service Product Development: A Strategic Contingency Approach, *International Journal of Innovation Management*, 7(3), 1–32.

xxxii   Lievens, A., de Ruyter, K., and Lemmink, J. 1999. Learning During New Banking Service Development: A Communication Network Approach to Marketing Departments, *Journal of Service Research*, 2(2), 145–64.

xxxiii   Hansen, M. T., Mors, M. L., and Løvås, B. 2005. Knowledge Sharing in Organizations: Multiple Networks, Multiple Phases, *Academy of Management Journal*, 48(5), 776–793.

xxxiv   Froehle, C. M., Roth, A. V., Chase, R. B., and Voss, C. A. 2000. Antecedents of New Service Development Effectiveness: An Exploratory Examination of Strategic Operations Choices, *Journal of Service Research*, 3(3), 3–17.

xxxv   Sethi, R., Smith, D. C., and Park, C. W. 2001. Cross-Functional Product Development Teams, Creativity, and the Innovativeness of New Consumer Products, *Journal of Marketing Research*, 38(1), 73–85.

xxxvi   Lynn, G. S., Skov, R. B., and Abel, K. D. 1999. Practices that Support Team Learning and Their Impact on Speed to Market and New Product Success, *Journal of Product Innovation Management*, 16(5), 439–454; Ramesh, B. and Tiwana, A. 1999. Supporting Collaborative Process Knowledge Management in New Product Development Teams, *Decision Support Systems*, 27(1/2), 213–236.

xxxvi Edvarsson, B. and Olsson, J. 1996. Key Concepts in New Service Development, *Service Industries Journal*, 16,140–164.

xxxvii Cooper, R. G. 2008. The Stage-Gate Idea-to-Launch Process-Update, What's New, and Nexgen systems, *Journal of Product Innovation Management*, 25(3), 213–232; Olson, Walker and Ruekert. 1995. *Op. cit.*

xxxviii Salmi *et al.* 2007. *Op. cit.*

xxxix Hull, F. 1977. *Task Uniformity, Technology and Organization Structure*, Dissertation, Columbia University.

CHAPTER TWELVE

ORCHESTRATING COLLABORATIVE INFLUENCE

Overview

Investment in human capital is critical for enterprises in general and many services in particular. Because investing in the diverse functions to develop a new service may be expensive, enterprises often undermanage by skimping on human capital and/or failing to deploy functions appropriately for achieving their strategic objectives. Sometimes over managing occurs if functions are engaged when and where they do not add value. Therefore, results from four analyses are summarized to provide guidelines for orchestrating the configuration of human capital. The goal is to optimize investment in 10 kinds of functional expertise. First, which functions do high performers deploy more than low performers and at what phases? Second, which functions have relatively greater impact on performance for enterprises pursuing a strategy of developing radically new offerings? Third, which functions need to be more engaged to the extent enterprises exploit knowledge in their offerings? Fourth, which functions are relatively more important for developing competitive advantage in one or both by developing differentiating features or improving delivery processes? Finally, the role of each of the 10 functions in new service development (NSD) is profiled and contributions to performance detailed. A case example illustrates each role.

12.1. Configuring Human Capital

Creating value for customers, especially via new offerings, is very demanding of human capital. Executives need to orchestrate collaboration among a large number of diverse functional specialists. Executives need to manage development systems so that the cumulative value of the output offering exceeds the sum of the separate inputs by individual employees. To achieve high levels of value added, people from varied functions and different ranks need to take collective responsibility as a team for transforming inputs into outputs.

Given the expense of human capital, a tendency is to under-invest at the front-end where relatively little of the actual development is done. However, it is axiomatic that most costs are committed and opportunities for innovation arise during the defining and fleshing out the concept of the offering. Consequently, high performers tend to over-manage their front-end relative to low performers. To the extent high-performers optimize the design of their offering up-front, their downstream costs are lower. By contrast, low-performers tend to over-manage the back-end of their development cycle because they focus on managing money rather than opportunities.

> Up-front investment in human capital differentiates high from low performers

The guidelines for investing in human capital highlighted in this chapter suggest that the need for diverse collaboration is greater on average to the extent enterprise strategy targets radically new development. Moreover, exploiting tacit knowledge is often demanding of interpersonal deployment of human capital, especially post-launch where customer offerings may be augmented during delivery. Exploiting explicit knowledge reduces the need for some functions because computer automated transformations and deliveries supplant the need for some kinds of personnel. But the administrative requirements for managing operations in explicit knowledge development remain high despite reduction in some kinds of work because the need for coordination remains high.

A framework for systematizing the complexity faced by executives in managing NSD may be illustrated using an orchestral metaphor. Each player performing a functional role in an ensemble may uniquely contribute to the performance as a whole. But it is their collaboration with players of instruments with other capabilities that creates the composite sound intended by the composer. Although the composition is consumed when played by the ensemble, some set pieces are explicitly codified in repertory for reuse. Other compositions may be jazzy improvizations stimulated by ad hoc audience interactions sparking tacit emotions which result in performances impossible to closely replicate.

To orchestrate NSD (New Service Development), a first requirement is familiarity with 10 instrumental roles and their contribution across three phases of performance. Second, how groups of function collaborate to optimize differentiation and delivery performance within each phase needs to be considered.

1. Role volume depends on the phase of the composition being performed, some are pianissimo, others forte. Some roles need to be played more forcefully up-front than subsequently, and vice versa, depending on the phase.
2. Compositions vary in terms of radicalness. Some are newly created. Others modify existing compositions in interpretative ways, making them practically new. Novelty of composition and performance also affects the volume of players enacting their roles. For example, some new compositions may need more improvization after initial concerts because of the experimental nature of the creation and/or interactions with audiences.
3. Extant compositions vary according to the subtlety and structure in ways which are loosely analogous to contrast between the exploitation of explicit vs. tacit knowledge.

   - Most compositions are either faithful renditions of earlier works or minor modifications of them. Structured compositions like military marches, national anthems, traditional dance music often emphasize rhythmic brass sounds syncopated by serial percussion. Volume is likely to be delimited for many players in this type of composition.
   - Nuanced compositions may be played in a variety of ways to elicit subtle emotions. They are relatively more likely to deploy woodwinds and stringed instruments than brass and percussion. Each player in the ensemble needs to modulate their volume to optimize the effect of the composition as a whole.

4. Orchestral music may continue to be delivered impersonally or personally after a formal concert. Post-concert and informal delivery methods

vary in ways that are also somewhat analogous to the contrast between explicit and tacit knowledge.

- Historically some compositions were automated for impersonal delivery via orchestrion.[a] More commonly today they are captured in a variety of digital recordings for discretionary listening by customers.
- Compositions may be more personally modified in delivery, such as improvizations, adaptions during encores, follow-on jam sessions, and musical events engaging audiences as participants.

Musical offerings, somewhat like services, may be divided into two major segments. In applying the orchestral metaphor to service offerings, the initial focus is on differentiation prior to concert performance. This includes new work, adaptive features, or quality precision to make the offering distinctive. Innovation may occur pre-launch and/or in delivery.

For managing development projects, the orchestration function needs to be performed not by a single conductor, but a core team or lead players. For example, at The Stanley Works, all development teams were required to have four functions take responsibility for the entire development cycle: development engineering, marketing, manufacturing, and purchasing. Although the optimal composition of core teams vary by industry, their deployment is a proven predictor of success. However, core teams need to be relatively small and compact, ideally 4–6 people. Those engaged with the project may go to any core team member and get most if not all of the answers to their questions. As illustrated in Figure 12.1, core team members are responsible for networking with others whose knowledge is vital for the success of the project.

Ensuring that the right players of each instrument are in the right positions is essential for the quality of the composition as a whole.[i] Members of core teams not only need to take responsibility for the project, but also distribute ownership to others who need to be accountable, consulted, and informed. Each core team member needs to ensure that stakeholders peripheral to the core team are appropriately engaged especially as

---

[a] Orchestrion refers to machine that plays music and is designed to sound like an orchestra or band.

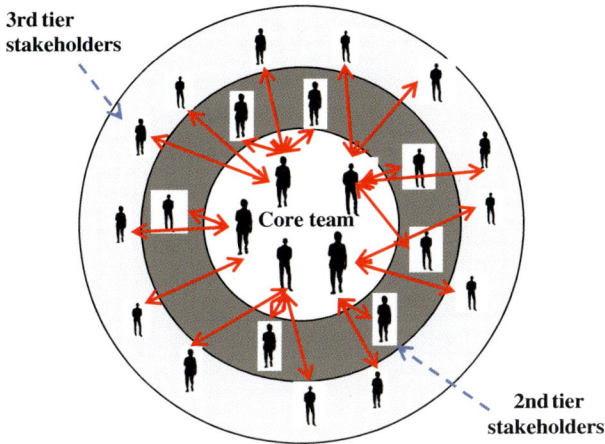

Figure 12.1. Core Team with Responsibilities for 2nd and 3rd Tier of Stakeholders

the need for contributions by specialized functions varies in time and quantify over the development cycle.

A wide variety of stakeholder mapping methods are available. All stakeholder maps are more effective if used as a method for visual management. All stakeholders need to understand the work breakdown structure over the course of the development cycle interdependencies to ensure appropriate levels of collaborative exchange.[ii]

12.2. Configuring Human Capital for Differentiation Performance

Service enterprises compete by providing services that differentiate their offerings from those of others. Differentiating features include time to market, lower cost, higher quality, and innovative features. This section suggests ways of configuring cross-functional teams for developing offerings with competitive advantages. Because many NSD projects are intensive of human capital, ensuring appropriate engagement by heterogeneous functions is a success factor. Enterprises scoring relatively high in differentiation performance generally deploy more of 10 kinds of functional expertise at one or more phases. The need for greater heterogeneity in NSD may be estimated by aggregating the positive contributions to variance explained in differentiation performance from three separate analyses:

1. **Correlation**: strength of association with performance (square of the coefficient = % variance explained).
2. **Radical innovation multiplier**: percentage of additional variance in differentiation performance explained when a function is engaged in enterprises targeting radically new innovative development.
3. **Tacit knowledge multiplier**: Percentage of additional variance in differentiation performance explained when a function is engaged in enterprises exploiting tacit knowledge.

Figure 12.2 aggregates the variance each of these three explains in differentiation performance. These results are merely suggestive because the bars shown simply sum up each effect separately instead of integrating the results from a single multivariate equation.[b] The advantage of this segregated display is that readers may select the functions they wish to consider deploying as enterprises vary in their pursuit of a radical strategy and/or the exploitation of tacit knowledge.

Correlation: Some enterprises achieve higher differentiation performance because they engage function at phases where others do not. Examples include marketing, process development, administration, and customer service at the concept phase as shown in the blue striped bar in Figure 12.2. Engagement by each of these functions at the concepts phase predicts approximately 10 percent of the variance in differentiation performance. Enterprises failing to engage such functions up-front might have a rethink.

No correlations were statistically significant at the pre-launch phase. However, five significant correlations are shown as explaining variance in differentiation performance at the post-launch phase: Process development, information technology (IT) systems, administration, logistics, and customer service.

---

[b]Adding variance explained by the correlation with the innovation and tacit knowledge multipliers provides an estimate of benefits from deploying specific functions. Because radical innovation and tacit knowledge are uncorrelated, the sum is an approximation of the maximal benefit from deployment of a given function.

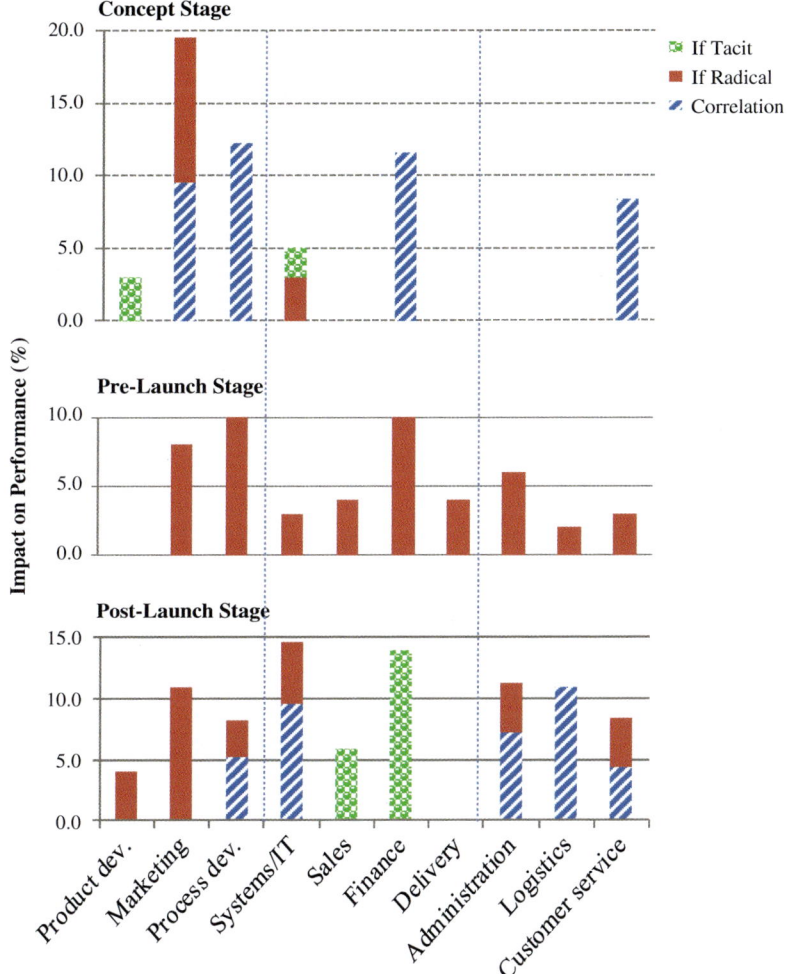

Figure 12.2.   Percent Variance Explained in Differentiation by Phase

Radical innovation multiplier: If enterprises pursued a strategy of developing radically new offerings, all 10 functions had at least one interaction effect explaining significant amounts of additional variance in differentiation performance at one or more of the three phases. A single exception is a negative interaction for the delivery function at the concept phase. By contrast, engagement of the delivery function at the pre-launch phase has a positive interaction. This result is consistent with the organic thesis that heterogeneity is a key driver of innovation.

At the concept phase, enterprises with engagement by marketing and IT systems were more likely to achieve high differentiation performance. This result provides support for the ESI hypothesis especially because these functions are not only critical for NSD, but also because they are the most likely departments to launch new offerings largely on their own initiative.

At the pre-launch phase, 9 of the 10 functions have significant interaction effects with differentiation performance if developments were radically new. This result is also supportive of the ESI hypothesis even though engagement occurs after conceptualization.

> Pursuit of a strategy of radical innovation is more likely to succeed if many diverse functions are engaged prior to launch

Engagement by all steady players and latecomers has advantages for delivery performance if the enterprise strategy involves radical offerings.

At the post-launch phase, engagements by product development, marketing, process development, and systems IT have positive benefits. This is consistent with the flip-side of the coin of the ESI hypothesis. Upstream functions need to take responsibility for the downstream consequences of their decisions and be engaged with post-launch outcomes. All stakeholders along the value stream need to take collaborative responsibility from concept to the final phases of development.

Tacit knowledge multiplier: If enterprises pursue a strategy of exploiting tacit knowledge, additional human capital may be needed because of the idiosyncratic nature of value added. At the concept phase, engagement by product development and IT systems have positive interaction effects impacting differentiation performance if the design involves tacit knowledge. However, early engagement of the delivery function has a negative interaction effect.

No significant interactions were observed at the pre-launch phase. However, at the post-launch phase, sales and finance have fairly strong interaction effects. As discussed below, one reason for the need for engagement by sales and finance may be to assess the cost-benefit of offerings involving tacit knowledge which are idiosyncratic and therefore difficult to calculate *a priori*.

Exploiting explicit knowledge reduces the need for some kinds of functional involvement. But the interaction effects for engagement by the administrative function at the concept and pre-launch phases are significantly positive for differentiation performance. This result is consistent with the so called "robot effect" whereby tools and technologies reduce some human capital needs at the doers level, but increase demands for executive coordination.

12.3. Configuring Human Capital for Delivery Performance

Service enterprises also compete by providing superior delivery. Valued characteristics of delivery performance include time, cost, and higher quality. This section suggests ways executives might consider configuring cross-functional team to achieve advantages based on service delivery relative to competitors. Figure 12.3 aggregates the variance three factors explain in delivery performance.

Correlation: Enterprises achieving higher delivery performance are more likely to engage two functions at the concept phase, process development and customer service. These functions appear to have a relatively plausible role in enhancing delivery performance. No-correlations were significant at the pre-launch phase, which is similar to the results for differentiation performance. Four functions are more likely to be deployed by enterprises strong in delivery performance: Systems IT, Administration, Logistics, and Customer Service. These functions may prove especially important for either ensuring delivery quality and/or augmenting customer offerings.

Radical innovation multiplier: The only positive interaction effect at the concept phase is for the product development function. At the pre-launch phase, product development has an interaction effect with delivery performance as does marketing, sales, and especially finance. Finance is the only function with a significant interaction effect on delivery performance post-launch. Opportunities for product development to collaborate with logistics and customer service at the up-front concept phase seem to have a plausible link with superior delivery performance.

Tacit knowledge multiplier: Enterprises pursuing a strategy of exploiting tacit knowledge achieve higher levels of delivery performance if functions

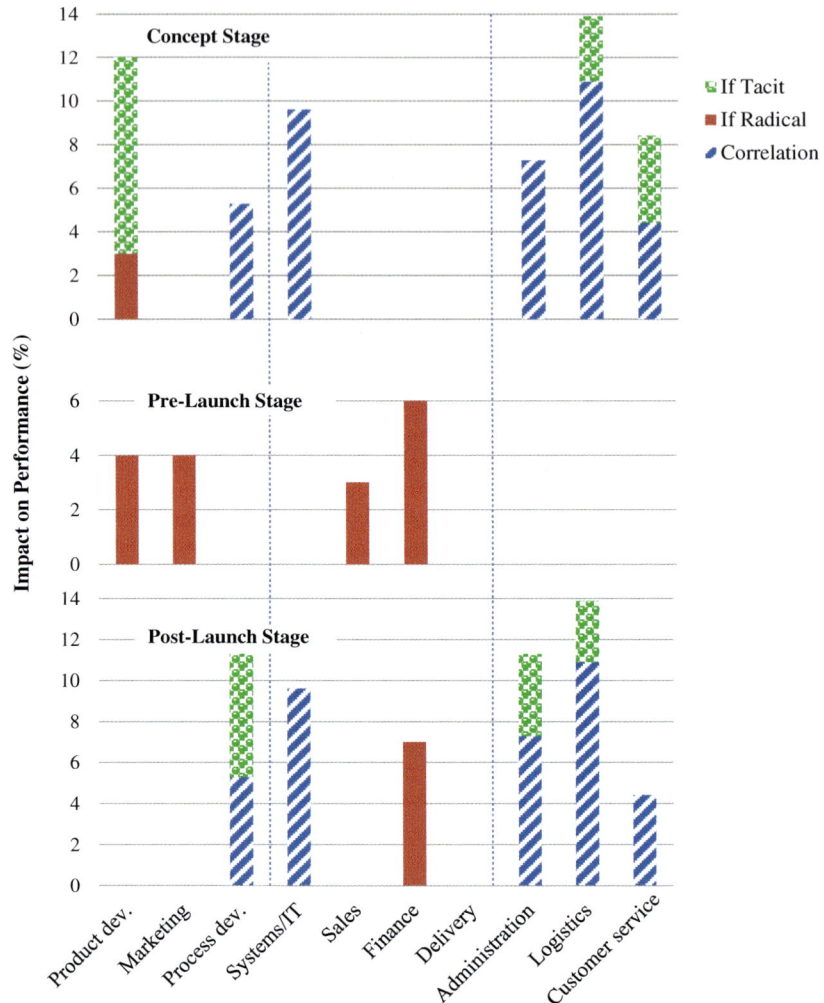

Figure 12.3.   Percent Variance Explained — in Delivery by Phase

connecting with customers are engaged, such as systems IT, logistics, and customer service (but not delivery). At the pre-launch phase, product development has a modest negative interaction effect. At the post-launch phase, three functions had positive interactions, process development, administration, and logistics. The interaction effect of process development is relatively strong and may be of particular importance for augmented customer offerings. Although no interaction effects were observed post-launch for customer service for tacit offerings, the presence of this vital function is relatively strong, correlated with delivery performance and has an interaction effect when engaged at the vital concept phase. High levels of investment in human capital are needed post-launch for achieving delivery performance especially if knowledge is tacit because of the idiosyncratic nature of augmented service offerings.

12.4. Configuring NSD Teams

This section integrates results from analyses of the three principal drivers of investment in 10 kinds of human capital. This overview provides context for a follow-on section where the contributions of each of 10 functions are detailed one by one. It's a snapshot of the forest, so to speak, before detailing each tree.

What are the patterns of relationships between human capital and performance that may help your enterprise enhance its competitive capability by deploying the right functions at the right time? Which functions are most likely to affect the kind of performance most likely to enhance your competitive advantage, differentiation, and/or delivery?

High performers are more likely to deploy 9 of 10 functions based on adding variance explained by correlations and multiplier effects for radical development and exploitation of tacit knowledge as shown in Figure 12.4. This summary effect holds for both differentiation and delivery, especially the former.

Marketing has the strongest summary effect on differentiation performance, nearly 40 percent. But it contributes only modestly to delivery process performance. If differentiation and delivery, performance are considered in tandem, process development and finance are the most predictive functions followed by systems IT, customer service, and administration.

Marketing and finance functions are correlated with differentiation performance only at the concept phase. Their importance early-on is consistent with the axiom that most opportunities and costs are determined at the up-front phases of the development cycle.

A bipolar pattern of correlations is observed over the development cycle. Several significant correlations occur between functional engagement

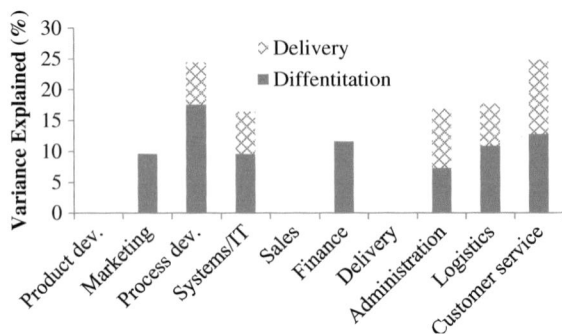

Figure 12.4.   Variance Explained in Performance by Function

and performance occurs at the concept and post-launch phases, but not at the middle, pre-launch phase. One reason may be that many service offerings are relatively minor improvements. High performers with a maintenance strategy of making minor improvements to existing offerings have relatively high levels of ESI at the concept phase, presumably to the exercise of due diligence, but then revert to low levels of engagement for the remainder of the cycle.[iii]

Investing in heterogeneous input of human capital at the pre-launch phase, however, is particularly important if pursuing a radical strategy. Nine of 10 functions have significant impacts on differentiation performance at the pre-launch phase under the contingency that the development is new. Interestingly, four relatively analytical functions have interaction effects with delivery performance for radicalness: product development marketing, sales, and finance. Making radical changes to offerings seems to require considerable due diligence prior to the launch of novel offerings. Thus, the pre-launch phase seems to be a particularly opportune juncture for investment in heterogeneous inputs of human capital to the extent enterprises pursue a strategy of radical innovation.

> Pre-launch scrutiny is especially beneficial for radically new offerings

Enterprises with extra investment in marketing at the concept and post-launch phases get payback in differentiation performance. The need for marketing engagement at the concept phase seems obvious. However, such up-front functions also need to be engaged post-launch when the results of new introductions are experienced by customers, and especially so if the service offering is being augmented. Other functions that are associated with post-launch benefits include finance and customer service, perhaps because the cost/benefits of customer experiences with new offerings needs to be optimized.

Offerings with tacit knowledge benefit form differentiation performance by engaging finance and sales functions post-launch. Presumably the cost/benefits of customer experiences, which are likely to be idiosyncratic, require extra evaluation and assessment activities. If the offering exploits tacit knowledge, engagement by process development at the concept and post-launch phases is beneficial for delivery performance. Sales and especially the finance function are highly beneficial for high delivery performance post-launch. Augmenting services though delivery processes post-launch is demanding of human capital not only for dealing with customers, but ensuring value is profitably added.

12.5. Profiles of Functional Roles in NSD

This section provides the reader with a profile of each of the 10 functions. The information is designed to help readers evaluate the value each may make to enterprise performance. The presumption is that each function plays a distinctive role in NSD. To capture distinctive dimensions, each is profiled as a solo instrument for adding value. The strength of each correlation with both differentiation and delivery performance is noted as well as contingency effects associated with radical innovation and type of knowledge. A case example illustrates the performance of each role in the context of enterprise operations.

12.5.1. *Product development*

In principal the product development function has formal responsibility for orchestrating the roles of the many players required to develop products using appropriate processes and enabling tools and technologies. Ideally the players in this function are so-called "T" people, who have not only in-depth subject matter expertise but are also able to be ambidextrous in engaging others from outside their domain in a common endeavor.

Chase Retail Bank

The appointment of a vice president for product development for retail banking at Chase was a key driver of their increased competitiveness. The new VP had a fairly wide breadth of experience and was able recruit representatives from other function to spent part or full-time in the NSD function she directed. The development of new customer offerings was aggressively pursued at a pace that surpassed rivals.

Several leading companies in the New York area appointed a VP for Product Development. Enterprises with a VP for product development generally deployed best practices for NSD. However, only about a third of the enterprises in the survey reported having someone responsible for new service development *per se*.[iv] Instead one or two departmental functions take the lead in developing new services without a formalized system for orchestrating cross-functional engagement.

- *Engagement Level and Correlations with Performance.* Product development has the highest volume of engagement of any of the 10 functions at the concept phase. Yet correlations with differentiation and delivery performance are insignificant. However, moderated regression analyses reveal that some contingencies affecting the relatively need for engagement.
- *Radicalness.* Engagement by the product development function is associated with higher levels of differentiation performance at the post-launch phase if enterprise strategy is focused on novelty. Interaction effects with radicalness occur for delivery performance at the concept and pre-launch phases.
- *Knowledge Type.* The level of engagement by the product development function has a positive interaction with differentiation performance at the concept phase if the knowledge is tacit. This suggests that somewhat higher levels of engagement may be appropriate up-front if the offering involves intangible idiosyncrasies. By contrast, engagement of the product development function at the pre-launch phase has negative interactions for both tacit and explicit knowledge. One possibility is that just before launch may be a bit late for anticipating and precluding delivery issues.

12.5.2. *Marketing*

Marketing is a key function which is vitally needed in any enterprise. Marketing has broad responsibilities for targeting appropriate customer segments offering profitable value. Marketing bears strategic responsibilities for ensuring due diligence from concept to delivery. In some enterprises, the marketing function is the department that acts almost solo in fulfilling the NSD role. The downside is that sometimes their dominance precludes appropriate engagement by others functions. On the other hand, many service enterprises suffer partly because new offerings are introduced by stakeholders from other departments without sufficient engagement of the marketing function.

Merrill Lynch

New kinds of product offerings originated from various departments and broker dealers. Most were not vetted beforehand by the marketing function. The decentralized nature of the business meant that originators of new ideas were not forced to submit to either a pre-launch marketing review or a development process review. A new program was development to provide voluntary advice on new product offerings. Employees with new ideas were encouraged to draft a business plan for review by a panel of experts. Within less than 2 years, the evidence was quite compelling that new offerings which were reviewed prior to launch made far more money than those which opted out and went to market on their own initiative.

- *Engagement Level and Correlations with Performance.* Almost two-thirds of service enterprises engage the marketing function at the concept phase. Such engagement is positively correlated with differentiation performance at the concept phase. This relationship is consistent with Axiom #1 which suggests that the key decisions need to be made up-front. Obviously marketing should have a lot of say in go/no go decisions.
- *Radicalness.* Greater engagement by marketing is strongly associated with higher levels of differentiation performance at all three phases if development strategy targets radicalness, e.g., an average of 10 percent added to variance explained. Marketing also has an interaction effect for delivery performance at the pre-launch phase if the offering entails

novelty. Why might this be? One possibility is that novel offerings may entail issues in delivery processes that are more expeditiously dealt with up-front. In sum, higher levels of marketing engagement have synergistic benefits for one or both kinds of performance at all three phases under the contingency of radical development.

- *Knowledge Type.* The level of engagement by marketing has no inter-action effects with the mode of knowledge exploited. This lack of contingency is somewhat surprising because one might suspect that the application of tacit knowledge entails many issues in market decisions.

12.5.3. *Process development*

One of the most important processes in large corporations deals with transforming concepts into customer offerings. This result is somewhat analogous to the vital role manufacturing engineering plays at the concep-tual level in goods industries. However, some service offerings are aug-mented post-launch while many sales of goods are delimited transactions. The delivery process can be tantamount to the product itself, which means that this function may play an outsize role post-launch. Process develop-ment is particularly important if interpersonal exchanges between the provider and customer are involved.

Citibank

Citibank's study of how people actually used ATMs lead to their optimizing design of electronic banking equipment and spaces. Student researchers drew socio-grams of behavioral patterns and conducted interviews to help engineers design better devices and architects to configure more user-friendly spaces. The results from mapping processes for optimizing customer experiences led to designs for automated banking facilities that were regarded by many as the gold standard in the industry.

- *Engagement Level and Correlations with Performance.* Less than half of service enterprises deploy a function with the explicit purpose of devising continually improved processes. This may be an important opportunity for improving competitiveness because engagement by process development is strongly correlated with differentiation at the concept phase and significantly so at the post-launch phase. Process is also correlated with delivery performance at the concept phase.

- *Radicalness.* If the enterprise is developing novel offerings, process is especially important for differentiation performance pre-launch, e.g., 10 percent additional variance explained. A lesser but significant interaction also occurs post launch. These contingency effects underscore the importance of process for adding value for many kinds of customer offerings.
- *Knowledge Type.* If value is added by tacit knowledge, engagement of the process function at the post-launch phase adds 7 percent more variance in delivery performance. Quite possibly process development collaborates with logistics and customer service which also have significant interactions at the up-front concept phase with delivery performance.

12.5.4. *IT systems*

IT has become an increasingly integral part of many services. Many customer offerings are designed with the aid of computer analyses. IT systems may provide not only the content of the customer offering, but also modes of delivery.

Market research suggested a great reluctance on the part of customers in considering the prospect of using ATMs. But once they became available, fears subsided rapidly and an increasing volume of financial transactions are handled through either automated tellers or internet transfers. Several new ventures have recently been launched that are based on new business models for electronic financial transactions.

- *Engagement Level and Correlations with Performance.* The level of IT engagement slopes downward over the development cycle. Yet IT engagement at the post-launch phase is correlated with both differentiation and delivery performances. This result is somewhat analogous to the role manufacturing engineering plays in goods industries where concepts must be designed in such a way that production problems are precluded. Greater engagement by IT systems has an even stronger effect on differentiation performance at the post-launch phase. Perhaps it is at this juncture that patches are developed to fix problems that were only apparent after initial customer use. IT often provides the dominant mode for delivering many services. This may be one reason high performers have more staff engaged in activities contributing to differentiation and delivery performance during the post-launch phase. These correlations suggest possible opportunities for greater IT involvement post launch.

- *Radicalness.* If the enterprise is developing new offerings, differentiation performance is higher at all three phases of the development cycle associated with engagement by IT systems. Many new products are built with IT systems, so some enterprises targeting a radical strategy are said to have higher performance associated with engagement of IT staff at the concept phase. Also customer support for ongoing technical transactions boosts the value of the service offering.

- *Knowledge Type.* High levels of engagement by IT systems at the concept phase are associated with a slight improvement in differentiation performance if the knowledge exploited is tacit. However, the association with delivery performance was relatively stronger. One reason may be that the idiosyncratic dimensions of tacit knowledge are far more difficult to programs than codified, explicit knowledge. One may speculate as to why IT is beneficial for development of offering with tacit knowledge. One possibility may be that IT is used to codify tacit, intangible knowledge. Perhaps writing programs incorporating fuzzy logic and other adaptations to deal with idiosyncrasies requires relatively more staff. Moreover, service design research is increasingly attempting to model human behaviors so that the deployment of IT systems for more effectively exploiting tacit knowledge may increase in the future.

12.5.5. *Sales*

People from the sales function are usually the tactical point of contact with customers in promoting the value proposition of the offering strategically formulated by marketing and/or other functions. They hone value propositions, typically generated by market research, into content for conveying competitive advantages to customers. To the extent they provide feedback to marketing and finance, their evaluation of the value of offerings is a dynamic process. If tacit knowledge of customer emotions are involved in augmented service offerings, the importance of sales input post-launch is especially critical. All too often sales personnel behave as order takers, but they may also act as forward observers of market intelligence as illustrated in the case studies summarized below.

Merit Investment Services

In several case studies of investment services, the financial advisor is also responsible for sales. Relationships develop between advisors and their clients what are based not only on explicit financial details, but also understanding of the dynamic life experiences of the investor. Needs of investors change over time, such as with age, family status, and economic employment. However, personalities also come into play as many financial decisions are made subjectively and may fail to optimize the use of codified knowledge in decision models.

- *Engagement Level and Correlations with Performance.* The level of engagement of sales by is lower than that of marketing at the concept phase, but identical at the pre-launch phase. However, engagement by the sales function has no significant correlations with performance. Perhaps service enterprises might benefit from exploring the ways the sales function may more proactively contribute to development decisions.
- *Radicalness.* Greater engagement by the sales function is associated with higher levels of differentiation and delivery performance at the pre-launch phases. Perhaps new product launches require extra preparation and training of sales forces. The sales function makes an important impact at the pre-launch phase to mitigate post-launch risk. If the offering is novel in either features or delivery, greater engagement by sales is associated with performance. The costs of a faulty launch may be exponential as suggested by Axiom #2.
- *Knowledge Type.* If value is added by tacit knowledge, the level of engagement of the sales function has a sizable interaction effect for differentiation and delivery performances at the post-launch phase. Perhaps the sales function is especially needed for following up on the extent to which customers understand and appreciate the value proposition entailed in offerings exploiting tacit knowledge. Moreover, the engagement of sales with customers may help in improving subsequent offerings involving tacit knowledge.

12.5.6. *Finance*

The finance function is important not just for actuarial tracking, but especially for making analytical projections over the life cycle in NSD decisions. Many new ideas may seem wonderful as concepts, but how they play out over a life cycle of development and delivery may be another story. Yet most of the activity of finance personnel is passive or reactive rather than proactive.

- *Engagement Level and Correlations with Performance.* The finance function is engaged at the concept phase in only 44 percent of the enterprises in the sample. Yet the only correlation of the finance function is for engagement at the concept phase with differentiation performance, which predicts almost 12 percent of the variance. This result is consistent with axioms #1 and #2 which suggest that the bulk of costs are committed up front. Up-front analyses by the finance function can save money over the life cycle. Constraints are best considered up front.[v] Prescient financial managers engaged at the outset represent an investment with measurable payback.
- *Radicalness.* Greater engagement by finance is strongly associated with higher levels of differentiation and delivery performance at the pre-launch phase if the enterprise pursues a novelty strategy. The introduction of novel features to offerings means that extra diligence may be needed prior to launch as costs and risks escalate exponentially afterwards. Extra effort in financial analyses pays-off at the pre-launch phase.
- *Knowledge Type.* A high level of engagement by finance has an extraordinarily strong effect (14 percent) on differentiation performance at the post-launch phase if the knowledge strategy is based on tacit knowledge. The effect is almost as strong for delivery performance. Teasing out cost/benefits of intangible value at the back end is often challenging if value is added by explicit knowledge. Staff costs for on-going customer interchanges can be quite expensive. Although tacit knowledge and radical strategies are uncorrelated with one another, both pose particular challenges for financial modeling because of unknowns and idiosyncrasies.

> **Morgan Stanley**
>
> As noted in the Morgan Stanley case, sales personnel often sold customize offerings to please customers without regard for life cycle costs. Pleasing the customer as rapidly as possible, however, was later found during a period of tight IT resources to suboptimize profits. Some of bespoke offerings lost money despite some innovations. To correct the problem, the finance function hired some programmers to develop algorithms for projecting life cycle costs. They developed an in-house financial modeling system to predict return on investment. A cross-functional team was formed to more rationally allocate resources relative to payback. The sales force was reined in and told that they had to price customized goodies to ensure a pre-set return on investment. As a result, fewer new offerings were sold, but rate of profitability rose sharply. The result from up-front calculations of cost/benefits was huge.

12.5.7. *Delivery*

Delivery is the activity of transferring offerings from provider to customer and is often a routine function. However, responsibility for delivery varies widely in services and is difficult to specify. In some instances, the deliverer of the services and the provider is one and the same, such as rendering personal offerings ranging from hairstyling to psychiatric counseling. In other instances the functions responsible for delivery are diffuse and difficult to identify, such as data services in which customers initiate automated transactions. Consequently, the role of the delivery function is highly ambiguous.

> **Federal Express**
>
> Federal Express invests considerable effort in scripting the behavior of their delivery personnel. People are training in minute detail on appropriate ways of greeting customers, gaining signatures, and even walking. For example, they are asked to walk deliberately and purposively, but never run or shuffle along slowly. Punctuality in delivery is reinforced by reliable interactions between the provider and customer.

- *Engagement Level and Correlations with Performance.* Engagement of those responsible for service delivery has a low flat pattern with a drop-off post-launch. From one perspective, this seems surprising because one might speculate that the level of engagement by delivery would be highest post-launch. This pattern may reflect the ambiguity in responsibility for delivery activities that may be handled by diverse functions in a myriad of ways from physical hand-offs to automated transfers. No significant correlations were observed. Because delivery activities do not seem to be as closely linked with a commonly understood functional role as others in the list of 10, interpretation of results is difficult. Therefore, attributions associated with this role are sketchy.

- *Radicalness.* If the offering is new, engagement by those delivering services is associated with differentiation performance especially at the pre-launch phase. Presumably those responsible for the delivery of novel features are able to perform better if engaged up-front prior to customer contact. However, engagement by the delivery functions at the concept phase has a negative interaction effect on differentiation performance if the offering involves novelty. The reasons for this negative interaction are unclear.

- *Knowledge Type.* Engagement of the delivery function has only negative interactions with performance and knowledge type. One modestly negative interaction is for engagement of the delivery function at the concept phase if the type of knowledge exploited is tacit. The reasons for this negative interaction are unclear as was also noted for radical offerings above. One possibility is that services with new features or tacit knowledge may require interpersonal skills for which occupants of this role are not trained, especially those involving interpersonal interactions post-launch. On other instances, negative interactions of the delivery function with differentiation and delivery performance at the post-launch phase seems plausible if one assumes that automated transfers reduce the need for personal.

12.5.8. *Administration*

Managerial oversight is exercised in many ways and typically includes interpersonal exchanges with diverse functions. The service administrative role is often executed in collaboration with others that are members of a managerial team in some instances. For example, service administration often involves the activities such functions as finance, IT systems, logistics, customer service, etc.

Quest Diagnostics
Quest is a medical diagnostics enterprise that has grown rapidly to dominate regional segments of the industry. Top management sought ways of improving and placed particular emphasis on quality management after setting some claims for faulty diagnostics and fraudulent billing. Teams of observers are sent to evaluate the quality and efficiency of operations, including customer intake facilities. Administrative functions are heavily engaged in evaluating options for improvement. The framework of Plan, Do, Check, and Act cycles of improvement is used. Customer intake operations have improved rapidly in terms of speed, quality of service, ambiance, and efficiency. One reason for the success of Quest is that they engage administrative executives in up-front planning and subsequently conduct assessments to check progress as a pattern of continuous improvement.

- *Engagement Level and Correlations with Performance.* The pattern for administrative engagement is a slightly inverted V-curve. Administrative engagement at the post-launch phase is significantly correlated with differentiation and delivery performance.
- *Radicalness.* If the offering is novel, administrative engagement has fairly strong effects on differentiation performance at the pre-launch and post-launch phases. Greater oversight and exercise of judgment in dealing with uncertainties and resolving unknowns seems an appropriate managerial function prior to delivery. Since the consequences of radical introductions are difficult to anticipate entirely, engagement to reassess the value of the offering pre- as well as post-launch seems necessary.
- *Knowledge Type.* If the knowledge is tacit, administrative engagement at the concept phase has significant benefit for differentiation performance. Administrative engagement has a modest impact at the post-launch phase on delivery performance. Curiously, administrative engagement at the concept phase has a slightly negative impact on delivery performance at the concept phase if knowledge is tacit. One possibility is that attempts to micro-manage the application of tacit knowledge prior to the information from idiosyncratic customer experiences is counterproductive. By contrast, if the knowledge exploited is explicit, administrative engagement has two positive interaction effects with differentiation performance at the concept and pre-launch phases. It also has a positive effect on delivery

performance post-launch. As discussed elsewhere, explicit knowledge may be codified and delivered electronically. While automation reduces the need for some kinds of personnel, administration is still needed of automated activities. A robot effect may occur whereby direct workers are less needed for providing services, but the deployment of tools and technologies may actually increase the need for administrators to coordinate and control inputs and outputs.

12.5.9. *Logistics*

The logistics functions deal with planning and assuring delivery of services to customers. Logistics is a subject matter of great diversity of applications. Although most commonly associated with physical objects, there are service applications as well. Often both are intertwined. The same principles for optimizing activities in time and space may be applied in a more abstract manner to intangible offerings.

There are innumerable examples of benefits from improved logistics. One of the most famous cases is that of Southwest Airlines which invented a new business model based largely on rapid turnaround times. Many manufacturers provide their customers with more rapid services by having components collaboratively assembled on site. The Bank of New York found ways of executing some kinds of federal transfers more rapidly and reliably than competitors. Urban Outfitters trains their staff to creatively rearrange their goods on offer so that customer can have continually refreshed displays. Improved logistics was also a key driver of the solution Citibank found in designing its automated banking facilities as noted above. However, some businesses rely upon logistics as a principal basis of competitive advantage.

Amazon
Amazon is well known as an online retailer. What is less appreciated is that they provide distribution services for many smaller companies who make deals directly with customers but rely upon warehousing and distribution by Amazon. An increasing number of these smaller businesses are also sharing the use of their web services. Logistical prowess provides Amazon with huge leverage in purchasing as well as the realization of economies of scale to offer the use of their infrastructure to smaller firms at a very competitive price.

- *Engagement Level and Correlations with Performance.* The pattern of engagement for the logistics function resembles an inverted V-curve. The bulk of logistics occurs at the pre-launch phase. However, the correlations for logistics engagement are significant with differentiation and delivery performance post launch. This suggests some potential benefit from higher levels of logistics engagement in designing as well as delivering services post-launch.
- *Radicalness.* Greater engagement by logistics is associated with higher levels of differentiation performance at the pre-launch phase if development involves novel features. Coupling with the strong positive correlation with logistics engagement at the post-launch phase with this interaction effect for radical offerings suggests a plateau pattern for post-concept development.
- *Knowledge Type.* If knowledge exploited is tacit, engagement by the logistics function has modest interaction effects with delivery performance at the concept and post-launch phases. Perhaps the difficulties configuring the transfer of intangible value requires extra human capital. Interestingly, if knowledge is explicit, logistics has a positive interaction effect with delivery performance at the pre-launch phase. Perhaps codified knowledge may be programmed for subsequent delivery by automated means at this phase.

12.5.10. *Customer service*

Customer service is usually considered only as a post-launch function. However, enterprises concerned with quality are likely to obtain input from this function in the NSD process to identify ways of improving customer satisfaction and identify latent needs. The Engagement of customer service from concept to delivery is essential for the notion of concurrency as involving life cycle engagement by key functions.

American Express

American Express is only one of many corporations that record interchanges between their service personnel with customers. However, their analysis of these data is often more sophisticated than most as many enterprises use recordings principally to police their own employees. AMEX uses recordings of inter changes

---

(Continued)

American Express (*Continued*)

with customers very proactively to help service personnel optimize their responses. Their call center personnel are typically domestically located and many have a relatively high esprit de corps. AMEX not only analyzes categories of customer complaints, but also attempts to classify the kinds of emotion associated with them. Many surveys have rated customer service by AMEX employees as tops in their industry.

- *Engagement Level and Correlations with Performance.* Engagement by customer service is lowest of the 10 functions at the concept phase, but ranks the highest post-launch at 42 percent of enterprises in the sample. However, high performers in both differentiation and delivery have relatively higher levels of engagement by customer service not only at the post-launch phase, but also at the up-front concept phase as well.
- *Radicalness.* If the enterprise strategy focused on novelty, engagement of customer service at the concept and post-launch phases has an even stronger impact on differentiation performance. Presumably customer service helps others responsible for development gain better understanding of experience in orders to make innovative improvements.
- *Knowledge Type.* If tacit knowledge is exploited, input by customer service at both the concept and post-launch phases has a positive impact on delivery performance. Customer service is presumably able to help improve the design of delivery. The importance of their role is likely enhanced to the extent the delivery of the offering involves idiosyncrasies of dealing with interpersonal transactions. Observations by customer service personnel may provide intelligence for follow-on NSD much like forward observers on battlefields relay current information.

Notes

[i]   Collins, J. C. 2001. *From Good to Great,* William Collins: US.

[ii]   Mitchell, R. K., Agle, B. R., and Wood, D. J. 1997. Toward a Theory of Stakeholder Identification and Salience: Defining the Principle of Who and What really Counts, *Academy of Management Review,* 22(4), 853–888; Turner, J. R., Kristoffer, V., *et al.* (Eds.) 2002. *The Project Manager as Change Agent,* McGraw-Hill Publishing Co.: London.

ⁱⁱⁱ Hull, F. 2003. Simultaneous Involvement in Service Product Development: A Strategic Contingency Approach, *International Journal of Innovation Management*, 7(3), 1–32, Figure 4.

ⁱᵛ The percentage of enterprises with an NSD function was negligible in a comparable London sample. See Tidd, J. and Hull, F. 2003. *Service Innovation: Organizational Responses to Technological Opportunities & Market Imperatives*, Imperial College Press: London.

ᵛ Goldratt, E. M. 1996. *Production: The TOC Way Work Book*, New Haven, Avraham Y. Goldratt Institute: CT.

SECTION E

CHAMPIONING TRANSFORMATION FOR TVD DESIGN CAPABILITIES

CHAPTER THIRTEEN

STRATEGIC DRIVERS OF CONCURRENT SYSTEM DESIGN

Overview

How does transformation take place from a mechanistic bureaucracy to a concurrent system of development for exploiting the capabilities of the composite model? Scenarios for transformation vary, but there are some events which are common to many journeys. Strategic responses to environmental dynamism drive a series of changes infusing horizontal integration into vertical hierarchies. A chart sketches a hypothetical path of events starting with environmental context and culminating with the emergence of the composite model of new service development (NSD). The competitive environment of services has become increasingly turbulent in recent years. Enterprises with superior capability for adapting to environmental changes are likely to enjoy competitive advantages because they more agilely adapt to changing threats and opportunities. The adoption of an innovation strategy has become increasingly critical for adaptation to environmental change. Opportunities for developing innovative customer offerings are typically greater under turbulent conditions. To develop superior customer offerings, a sea change needs to take place in the capability of new service development systems to generate differentiated customer offerings. A pivotal factor in response to environmental dynamism is the formation of a cross-functional group responsible for developing innovative offerings. Consolidating stakeholders responsible for NSD fosters the adoption of organic practices which stimulates innovation.

259

The need and capability for innovation drives the adoption of practices that provides the platform for the emergence of the composite model.

13.1. Flowcharting Transformational Change

Large-scale bureaucracies are operational machines that perform best in stable environments where customer offerings are relatively standardized and predictable. They tend to become introverted in order

> The speeding up of practically everything is hazardous for mechanistic bureaucracies

to maintain the efficiency of their internal operations. This internal focus is often associated with a lack of awareness of external changes. Case studies in textbooks on business strategy are littered with the road kill. Successful enterprises failing to reconnoiter their environment are often struck down by unanticipated changes. One reason is because companies have egos somewhat analogous to those of humans and consistently overrate their position relative to competitors within their own industry.[i] Their myopic vision means they are even more likely to miss threats from outside their industry. For example, several studies have documented that goods companies almost always fail to adopt emerging technologies supplanting their existing core competencies in businesses such as vacuum tubes, propeller aircraft engines, mechanical watches, analog electronics, etc.[ii]

Extensive research documents that as competitive environments become more dynamic and complex, successful enterprises adapt by shifting their practices away from mechanistic bureaucracy toward the organic end of a continuum of organizational design options.[iii] However, for transformation to begin, environmental changes must be recognized and the need for adaptive response accepted as necessary by top management. Often willingness to change only arises after environmental changes affect performance.

Crises in performance often opens cracks in operations into which organic practices may be infused. Adaptive responses to the challenge of change requires a coordinated approach for creating value in new ways. For example, the most successful service enterprises are those which form an explicit NSD function instead of relying upon functions departments to differentiate their offerings. The pivotal shift to an integrated approach to NSD is associated with change in strategy and the structure of development operations. If the transformational journey runs its full course, the development system evolves into a hybrid development system synergistically melding the best features of organic and mechanistic designs to achieve cost-effective innovation.

A hypothetical scenario for transformational change is depicted in Figure 13.1. An optimal first step is the establishment of a function responsible for NSD in recognition of the need for trans-departmental integration of development operations. Often the establishment of a focal point for coordinating development operations represents a pivotal response to environmental change. The formation of a NSD group is significantly correlated with environmental dynamism. However, some enterprises fail to organize cross-functional development operations even though evidence shows this practice is associated with high performance, particularly in complex, dynamic environments.

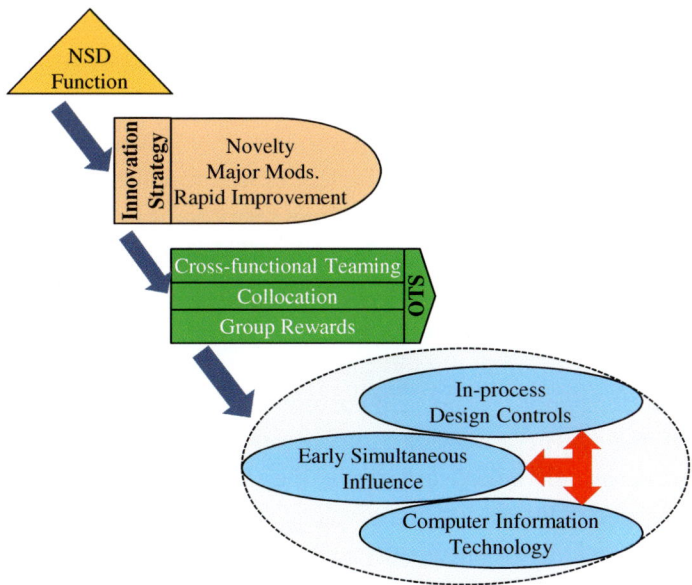

Figure 13.1.   Flowchart of Transformational Change in Innovation Practices

A centralized point of coordination for development in large enterprises is needed because the creation and delivery of new offerings entails complex business operations. Enterprises with an NSD function are more likely to adopt a strategy of innovation and to deploy the elements of OTS which provides a foundation for the composite model. The strategic decision to integrate responsibility for the development of service offerings by cutting across the functional chain-of-command is a necessary step for transforming mechanistic bureaucracy to a relatively more project-based organization.

13.2. Market Challenge and Turbulence

Attracting and retaining customers has become ever more competitive in a globalizing economy where the pace of innovation and change is rapidly accelerating in many sectors. Electronics industries have set the pace and exerted pervasive effects on business activities in services as well as goods industries. Although Moore's law was devised in the semiconductor industry, applications of more powerful and cheaper computer chips have rippled throughout global economies. Service as well as goods industries have been affected. The speeding up of just about everything has driven lower costs down mostly because time compressed is easily converted to money saved.[iv] The pervasive effects of computer-based technologies have contributed to exponential increases in choices for customers. For example, customers of yesteryear choose from a delimited variety of automobiles and credit cards. Today customers encounter what sometimes seems to be bewildering array of offerings. Formerly customers made trade-offs between cost and quality. Today quality is becoming ever more standardized globally after Japanese manufacturers began offering reliable products at relatively low cost in the 1980s. As methods of Total Quality Management (TQM) began to pervade services as well as goods, providing customers with innovative features has become increasingly necessary for competitive differentiation. Goods companies have increasingly added services to their offerings. Service companies have introduced new features as well as improved the quality of their offerings in some instances by complementing them with goods.

> New age customers want it all, now, but are reluctant to pay more

13.3. Transformational Change in Services

To improve performance, many service companies have looked to goods industries where formal methods of product development are more common and institutionalized in everyday operations. One of the industrial paradigms indirectly influencing service companies innovating in product development methods is TQM. Concurrent engineering is an application of TQM that focuses specifically on integrating the horizontal value creation stream. Concurrent methods have proved to be faster, cheaper, and better for product development than serial alternatives.[v] A concurrent strategy focuses on rapid cycles of continuous development that are not only cost-effective, but also innovative.[vi] Concurrency overlaps with a bevy of less comprehensive methods for performance improvement such as business process re-engineering, six sigma, and lean.

Many services are quite traditional. In some instances enterprises are able to continue pretty much as they did in the past with few downside consequences. However, others must strategically adapt their operational capabilities for meeting new demands in order to survive. Many enterprises face difficult decisions under changing environment contexts. To succeed, they must transform their development systems to provide more innovative offerings faster.

Adaption to Environmental Dynamism at Merrill Lynch

A senior Vice President at Merrill Lynch remarked that "when I came to work here 50 years ago we offered two products, stocks and bonds, which is what we still have today". Yet, the variety of these two basic services exploded during the next decade in myriad of innovative offerings. To respond to environmental challenges, Merrill Lynch began to develop a NSD function to help evaluate new ideas for creating differentiated customer offerings despite resistance. Yet the shift to a centralized NSD approach was halting because many of the old guard did not recognize the need for change while others wanted to introduce new features without any corporate oversight. An array of independent brokers preferred to make judgments on their own. But the exponential increase in online trading required a centrally coordinated approach to development of customer offerings. The economies of scale achieved by program trading, algorithms, simulation modeling, hedge bets, and other methods of investment diminished the role of broker dealers. Moreover, online services have increasingly enabled investors to by-pass Merrill Lynch broker dealers.

The case of Merrill Lynch illustrate how modes of service delivery may be affected by environmental change. Deciding how to respond to change in services is sometimes more complex than in goods because delivery processes are critical features of the service offering and may be integrally intertwined with it. Relationships between brokers and customers became much more impersonal in the wake of online trading.

13.3.1. *Reconnoitering environmental changes*

Environmental changes affect enterprises in the diverse service sector in varied ways. The first step is assessment of the environment followed by any adaptations appropriate for optimizing performance. Some enterprises, especially in long established lines of business, may be able to continue pretty much as they have in the past without making concessions to environmental shifts. Others, however, must strategically adapt their operational capabilities for meeting new demands in order to survive. Failure to adapt to changed circumstances may be fatal.

In the services data analyzed herein, an association was observed between environmental dynamism and differentiation performance ($r = 0.45$) and delivery performance ($r = 0.31$). What explains these associations with performance? What distinguishes enterprises that capitalize on the challenges of change vs. those that do not? One possibility is that some types of services are more advantaged than others, such as those with offerings valued because of tacit and/or explicit forms of knowledge. However, no significant relationships were observed between environmental dynamism and type of knowledge exploited. Alternatively, some enterprises make strategic choices to innovate by adopting new business models and development systems to succeed.

13.3.2. *Adaptation by forming a NSD group*

Environmental dynamism has a strong correlation with formation of a functional group responsible for NSD ($r = 0.49**$). This relationship presumably indicates recognition of the need for a strategic shift in operations from functional departments to relatively more integrated approach for developing new offerings. A cultural sea change is needed in response to environmental challenges. Agility may be gained by shifting to a development system where functional departments are better able to collaboratively respond to environmental challenges by strategic innovations.

Most large service enterprises, however, do not have an explicit NSD function. Enterprises retaining departmental structures may not have needed to change either because they were unaffected by environment shifts or because a key department was able to manage adaptive responses.

> Increasingly complex service offerings require simultaneous rather than serial coordination of diverse functions for transforming inputs into outputs

Alternatively, some enterprises may encounter resistance from functional departments reluctant to cede responsivity for NSD to a central group. However, enterprises failing to diagnose dynamic, complex changes in their environment may endanger their survival, unless they adapt accordingly.

13.3.3. *Strategy of developing radical offerings*

Innovation in product and/or process is often required to remain competitive. A central NSD function has opportunities for building collaboration in development across departmental functions. The formation of heterogeneous development teams is a springboard for cross-fertilizing ideas for innovative customer offerings. As shown in Table 13.1, the creation of a NSD function is associated with the adoption of three tactics for innovation.

Enterprises with an NSD function are more likely to target radical innovation. However, enterprises typically use a portfolio approach for funding innovative projects. The bulk of most budgets is spent on making modifications to existing offerings. A major modification strategy,

Table 13.1.   Correlations of NSD Function with Innovation Strategies

Innovation strategy	NSD function
Developing novel service products (Radical Strategy)	$0.35; p < 0.05$
Major changes to existing service products	$0.56; p < 0.01$
Rapid changes to existing service products	$0.66; p < 0.01$

especially when coupled with rapid cycles of change, may cumulate sustainable competitive advantages.

13.3.4. *Structuring development for innovation*

The strategic decision to target the development of radically new offerings is extraordinarily consequential for the design of the enterprises. A radical innovation strategy is significantly correlated with differentiation performance ($r = 0.45$; $p < 0.01$) and delivery performance ($r = 0.34$; $p < 0.05$). One way high performing enterprises succeed is by adapting the structure of development operations to support strategic intent of developing radical offerings.

The adoption of a strategy of radicalness demands a more organically integrated structure. As shown in the right column of Table 13.2, the more radically innovative the strategic intent of enterprises, the more likely they are to deploy Organic Team Structure (OTS) which provides a foundational platform for the troika comprising the composite model.

The adoption of such a strategy is also correlated with all three components of the troika of components of the composite model. The strongest correlation is with IDC. Devising ways of guiding the creation of new kinds of customer value is demanding. Ironically, the more novel the development, the greater the need for flexible plans as emergent opportunities and obstacles often emerge during the innovation journey.

Table 13.2.   Correlations of Structure and the Composite Model with Function and Strategy

OTS	Radical strategy
Cross-functional teaming	0.48; $p < 0.01$
Collocation	0.40; $p < 0.01$
Group rewards	0.42; $p < 0.01$
Composite Model	
Early simultaneous influence (ESI)	0.26; $p < 0.05$
In-process dynamic control (IDC)	0.56; $p < 0.01$
Product development tools (CIT)	0.35; $p < 0.01$

13.4. OTS and Performance

The advantage of the composite model is its benefit for performance. As shown in Table 13.3, the troika of components of the model. The elements of OTS and the troika of components of the composite model all have significant correlations with both types of performance.

Although the correlation between a radicalness and ESI is significant, its weight in moderated regression analyses is much greater because of synergies. Radicalness triggers the interaction effects between CIT with ESI and IDC. Radicalness has many interaction effects with the input of various kinds of human capital, not only at the concept phase, but throughout the development cycle. The need to develop novel offerings is the principal drivers of organic practices upon which the composite model is founded.

Benefits of the Composite Model

Synergies among the troika provide benefits for both time and cost and innovative features, both of which are captured in the performance measure of differentiation. The mutual reinforcement of the troika provides development systems with the capability of generating more holistic offerings. Enterprises lacking the benefits of synergies are lower performers and are less capable of offering their customers a portfolio of competitive advantages.

Table 13.3.　Correlations of Structure and the Composite Model with Performance

Performance:	Differentiation	Delivery
OTS		
Cross-functional teaming	0.52	0.47
Collocation	0.50	0.38
Group rewards	0.35	0.43
Composite Model		
Early Simultaneous Influence (ESI)	0.49	0.31
In-process Dynamic Control (IDC)	0.60	0.45
Development Tools (CIT)	0.39	0.26

Some elements of the composite model are of exceptional importance for exploiting types of knowledge for creating value. A strategy of exploiting tacit knowledge is demanding of human capital in general and ESI in particular. Pursuing an explicit knowledge strategy disproportionately relies upon CIT.

13.5. Conclusions

This chapter provides an integrative overview of a hypothetical flow from environmental stimulus to the design of a very capable development system. The strategic decision to integrate responsibility for the development of service offerings outside of the functional chain-of-command is a necessary step for transforming mechanistic bureaucracy to a relatively more project-based organization.

The pattern of transformation from mechanistic bureaucracy to the composite model starts with environmental change. Responding to the challenge of adaptation, requires a more coordinated approach to creating value so that some enterprises form an explicit NSD function instead of relying upon functions departments to differentiate their offerings. The pivotal shift to an integrated approach to NSD is associated with a shift in strategy and structure which progresses to a hybrid of organic and mechanistic design in a composite model. The pattern of this transformational flow is depicted in Figure 13.1. Enterprises with an NSD function are more likely to adopt a strategy of innovation and to deploy the elements of OTS which provides a foundation for the composite model.

Notes

[i] Caplow, T. 1964. *Principles of Organization*, Harcourt: New York.

[ii] Thushman, M. L. and Anderson, P. 1986. Technological Discontinuities and Organizational Environments, *Administrative Science Quarterly*, 31(3), 439–465.

[iii] Lawrence, J. and Lorsch, P. R. 1967. *Organization and Environment*, Harvard University Press: Cambridge.

[iv] Moore, G. E. 1965. Cramming More Components onto Integrated Circuits, *Electronics Magazine*, p. 4.

[v] Fleischer, M. and Liker, J. K. 1997. *Concurrent Engineering Effectiveness*, Hanser Gardner Pubns: Cincinnati; Hartley, J. R. 1992. *Concurrent Engineering: Shortening*

Lead Times, Raising Quality, and Lowering Costs, Productivity Press: Cambridge; Liker, J., Collins, P., and Hull, F. 1999. Flexibility and Standardization: Test of a Contingency Model of Product Design-Manufacturing Integration, *Journal of Product Innovation Management*, 16, 248–267; Nevins, J. L. and Whitney, D. E. 1989. *Concurrent Design of Products and Processes*, McGraw-Hill: New York.

[vi] Collins, P. and Hull, F. M. 2002. Early Simultaneous Influence across Stages of the Product Development Cycle: Impact on Time and Cost, *International Journal of Innovation Management*, 6(1), 1–24; Smith, P. 1994. *New Products in Half the Time*, John Wiley: Hoboken.

CHAPTER FOURTEEN

CHAMPIONING TRANSFORMATION WITHIN YOUR ENTERPRISE

Overview

This chapter provides leaders with actionable practices for transforming their value creation systems from mechanistic bureaucracies to concurrent systems. The need for a concurrent system based on the composite model is driven by demanding customers who seek multiple performance advantages simultaneously. Increased variety in customer demand is typically associated with changes in competitive environments. Transformational leaders help reconnoiter changes in the strategic environment and rally enterprise stakeholders to envision a more effective development system for creating and delivering value. They facilitate the co-creation of a common vision of an improved system state capable of delivering greater value to customers as well as increased profits. Enacting the role of transformation leader is challenging because it's typically an extra job so influence is exercised instead of command and control. A transformational assurance process (TAP), a proven method for leading change, is outlined in this chapter. A transformation workbook provides supplemental exercises for championing and guiding change.

14.1. Strategic Foresight and the Role of Champion

Champions take on a great variety of tasks, mostly voluntary, to fulfill unmet needs of enterprises. One of the most challenging opportunities for champions occurs prior to any serious consideration of transformation. Alerting the enterprise to impending dangers is a valuable, but risky role.

The great majority of business failures are due to a lack of strategic foresight. Successful businesses as they grow typically become more introverted with narrowed vision. Almost no businesses that established pioneering technologies survived after disruptive innovations altered the structure of their industry. For example, RCA was a dominant player in television sets, but failed to shift to transistors from vacuum tubes. Companies that were dominant in chemical photography such as Kodak and Polaroid filed for bankruptcy because electronic technologies were outside of their core competencies. Some managers at Kodak realized this and established a ventures group. However, once revenues began to decline Kodak rapidly divested itself of over 40 entrepreneurial ventures, mostly dealing with electronic technologies. Had the managers of chemical lines of business adopted electronic options earlier, the corporation might have avoided bankruptcy. A case study of Polaroid reveals a similar pattern where sunk costs in an existing core business inhibited adoption of innovative alternatives in electronic photography.

Polaroid and the Tar Baby

Polaroid's core business was based on instant photography using chemicals. Although they subsequently invented many electronic enhancements, the rivalry between chemical and electronic divisions within the corporation hampered adaptive collaboration in crafting a revised business model. Ultimately the company filed for bankruptcy because champions of electronic options failed to persuade management early enough to avoid catastrophe.

Champions need to be harbingers of the future. Reconnoitering the environment for dynamic changes is essential for proactively assessing potential threats. Successful champions not only warn of impending dangers, but also proactively help lead enterprise transformation to achieve greater capabilities for innovation if needed. One reason vigilance is needed is because the context of service operations is often turbulent. Champions and other guardians of an enterprise need to remain alert to shifts the competitive landscape. In the services data, "environmental dynamism" is measured as an index of change, regardless of direction, in six items: (1) technological complexity, (2) rate of new product introduction in the industry, (3) compatibility (interoperability) of your product with others, (4) customization, (5) globalization, and (6) quality.

> As the pace of change accelerates, champions of proactive development help enterprises innovate to survive

After identifying potential threats, champions face the challenge of justifying the need for change. Stakeholders in the existing business typically resist calls for change so long as cash flow continues. Once margins begin to decline, a typical response is to adopt methods of cutting costs by increasing bureaucratic controls. A mechanistic system is cost efficient, but if innovation is required to increase the value of the offering, it is only a short-term fix which often marginalizes innovators. By contrast, the advantage concurrency is cost-effective innovation which offers the prospect of simultaneously increasing top line profits from improved value as well as reducing bottom line costs.

14.2. Championing Concurrent Enterprise

Champions lead their enterprises in transforming functional structures into project-based operations. They cut across hierarchies to better integrate contributions to product development by diverse disciplines within and/or outside the enterprise. To accomplish this, they often coach product development teams on new processes and reorganized responsibilities. Essentially they are infusing organic practices for horizontally integrating work along the value stream into the bowls of a mechanistic hierarchy. To succeed, they must champion the project as as an activity requiring resources that transcend the authority of functional department heads. Department heads are a huge source of resistance because champions lack the authority of a formal position in the hierarchy and must rely instead on persuasive influence.

Champions take on an "extra-role" that is only informally recognized within the bureaucratic hierarchy. Their influence relies on dotted lines relationships with persons in authoritative positions. Their interstitial position therefore relies more on their capability to persuade than to wield authority. Persons with authority make decisions that others will follow regardless of personal sentiment. Influence rather than authority is required for persuading people to go along with a new plan of action. Champions must rely heavily upon influence because the transformation from serial to simultaneous methods involves organizational and cultural changes that counter the authoritative power of department heads.

> The effectiveness of champions depends on capturing the hearts and minds of those willing to make extra efforts to improve in small ways so diverse that are beyond the command of micro-managers

The transformation from serial to simultaneous methods of product development involves organizational and cultural changes that counter the norms of large-scale bureaucracies. The differentiation that occurs with growth in size means that specialists are located in different parts of the corporation and often lack close relationships. For example, those developing services are often physically segregated from those delivering services who usually hold positions of relatively low status and have little input in decision-making. In serial development systems, functions normally involved only at late stages of a cycle, such as customer service, are placed in reactive roles that limit their potential contributions.

To drive the transformation from serial to concurrent methods, education and training are needed to change attitudes. The first step is to change attitudes by raising awareness of concurrency and the principles behind it via training in the skill-sets required for its practice. A second step is leading employees in executing the new practices. Champions are needed for changing attitudes and reinforcing behavioral changes.

> Champions are entrepreneurs of new forms of development capability

14.3. Influencing Transformational Flow

A champion takes inordinate interest in engaging and motivating others to band together to achieve objectives that are beyond extant standards. Typically champions focus on influencing the execution of a given project, or more broadly, a project-based form of organization which is a horizontally integrated alternative to mechanistic bureaucracy.

Champions need to build strong project manager roles which are essential for the deployment of Organic Team Structure (OTS). Project managers have to garner specialists from functional department heads, preferably deploy them in collocated space, and provide incentives for achieving collaborative objectives that transcend those of subject matter disciplines. Resistance from hierarchical authorities responsible for managing functional departments is often fierce. Champions are levelers of hierarchical barriers. The horizontal dimension of organization often needs to provide a stronger thread of integration than the vertical dictates of department heads.

A general rule of thumb devised by participants in user groups is that concurrency is difficult if not impossible to execute unless over 60 percent of people and finance are committed to the project independently of direct control by hierarchical authorities. Otherwise the project leader is constantly running around with a begging bowl to department heads for resources to carry work forward.

In the services data, the role of a champion is measured by two intercorrelated practices: Strengthening the role of project managers and flattening the hierarchy in the organization chart. In combination, these two measures assess the tilt from a vertical to a relatively more horizontally integrated enterprise. Building teamwork across the base of the organization at the workflow level diminishes hierarchical authority.

These two practices in tandem are powerful predictors of system transformation from mechanistic bureaucracy to the composite model. Shown in Figure 14.1 are the correlations for the champion role with practices at each phases of the transformation flow.

All the correlations are statistically significant. The consistency and scope of these associations suggests that the champion is a kind of Leviathan except transformation is not achieved by dictatorial powers. Champions are typically delegated referent power from more senior managers because of the need for transformation to relatively more organic practices for fostering innovation.

14.4. Strategic Innovation and Project-based Leadership

The promise of benefits from innovation is the carrot champions' proffer to garner resources from functional departments. Mechanistic bureaucracies are slow and ineffective for achieving innovation strategies. Therefore, champions argue for stronger project teams to achieve more rapid and innovative execution which is the reason their efforts are so strongly correlated with cross-functional teaming and early simultaneous influence as shown in Figure 14.1. Often champions get their start by abetting a key project vital for the success of the enterprise which then becomes the beachhead for further transformation.[i] A classic example occurred at Eli Lilly which reluctantly allowed a champion to help guide the formation of their first two cross-functional teams to make rapid breakthroughs critical for the survival of the corporation.[ii] Success is critical as champions need to show results quickly by executing development projects as rapidly as possible.

Seldom is the authority of those responsible for value creation commensurate for the task. Role strain is particularly great for integrators taking on the challenge of bundling goods and services because managers responsible for each sector are often housed in hierarchically separate departments of a corporation or in external enterprises. Organizational fragmentation, internally and externally, is a barrier for collaborative input by stakeholders in goods and services. To extend Early Simultaneous Influence (ESI) to include the integration of stakeholders in value creation in goods and services over the life cycle from concept to customer, cross-functional teams representing both sectors need to engage all relevant stakeholders in up-front decisions and throughout the value stream.

High performers are more likely to adopt a project-based leadership for developing new and improved offerings than rely upon coordination among departments within a functional hierarchy. The issue with matrix organizations, where employees report to two managers, is control over resources. On the one hand, functional departments need to domicile experts to develop specialized knowledge required for competitiveness. On the other hand, without a project focus, knowledge remains hierarchically ordered instead of deployed along the value creation stream at the horizontal base of the organization. To motivate cross-functional collaboration at the base of the organizational pyramid, champions do their best to regard the group as a whole. The correlation between championing and group rewards is quite strong (0.70, $p = 0.01$).

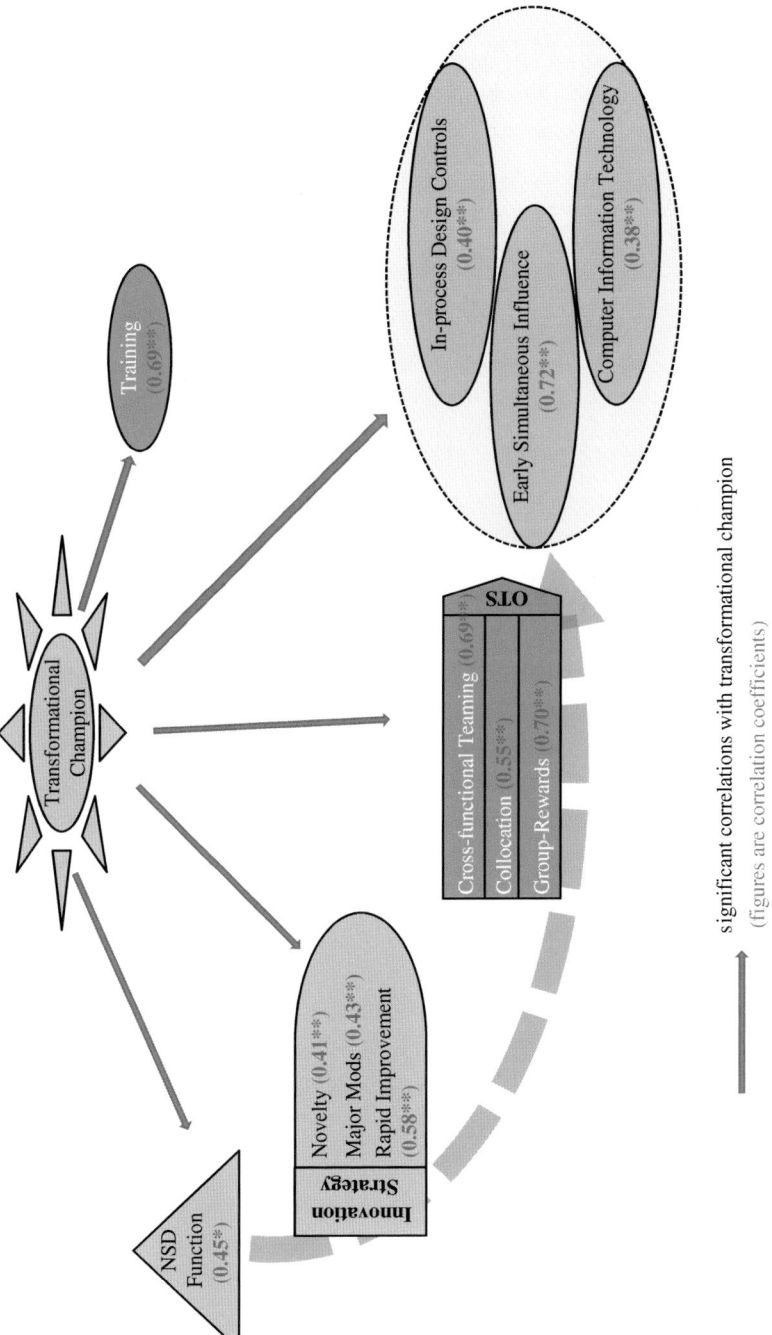

Figure 14.1. Correlation of Championing with Each Stage of Transformation

*p < 0.005; **p < 0.001.

The tension between project leaders and functional managers in matrix organizations is typically associated with considerable ambivalence, ambiguity, and shifting plate tectonics. The balance of power often tethers between decentralization to projects vs. centralization to functional departments.

Empowerment for developing new offerings is greater if a team is formally established with dedicated stakeholders representing various functional departments. Unless relevant functions are engaged up-front by a well-respected leader supported by senior management, integration across departments and sectors is difficult to achieve. Large enterprises, however, often have a portfolio of projects underway at any point in time for which different structures are appropriate. Some projects can be managed within the confines of a mechanistic bureaucracy. Others may need to be unleashed as an organic sprout tantamount to a temporary stand-alone business endeavor. A four-fold typology of leadership alternatives is suggested by Clark and Wheelwright (see Figure 14.2).[iii]

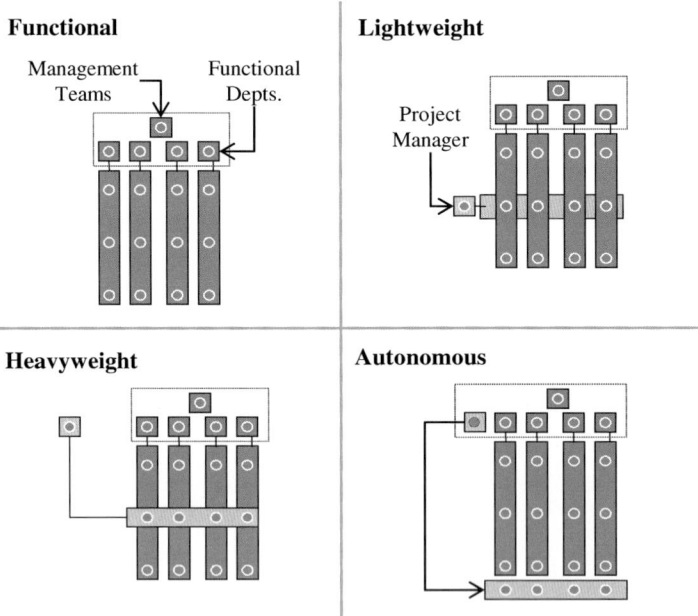

Figure 14.2.   Four Types of Project Leadership and Teaming
Source: Adapted from: Clark and Wheelwright, 1992.

(A) Functional Teams

One of the four types is a functional organization where responsibility for differentiating offerings resides within the authoritative domain of the heads of functional departments. In a "functional" organization the lead in development is usually taken by a representative from a single department. The key department relies upon the authority of upper management to ensure its prominence in the dominant coalition so that other departments may be commanded to contribute resources. A problem is often that departments retain their best talent and allocate those with relatively less competence to projects falling outside of their purview. Functions within mechanistic bureaucracies may suffice for development if traditional offerings require only minor adaptations or if a single subject matter expertise drives competitiveness. Examples include staff in the IT department writing programs for computer automated transactions or marketing staff repositioning offerings by targeting new segments of customers with advertisements for minor variations on existing offerings.

(B) Lightweight Team

A lightweight manager has no authority, but can use the reference power from higher ups whose support augments personal influence. The lightweight project manager is a kind of shuttlecock serving as a conduit for interdepartmental exchanges. The project liaison may serve adequately as a go-between so long as departments do not closely retain authoritative control over whatever resources are shared in developing a moderately complex offering. A common problem is that liaisons often have difficulty in garnering sufficient resources from multiple departments simultaneously at any given point in time, especially over the course of development of the offering. Liaisons often frequently report that they feel as though they run around with a begging bowl and only when senior managers intervene on an ad hoc basis do they obtain sufficient interdepartmental resources for developing the offering. Liaisons across functional departments have only influence and no authority for project execution. Consequently cross-functional integration of new value creation is usually inadequately resourced and sketchily rewarded.

(C) Heavyweight Team

A "heavyweight" team has a project manager with principal responsibility for the work of people on the team representing diverse functional departments. This responsibility includes discretion over the bulk of required resources starting at the concept phase of the development cycle where the voice of the customer is defined. Heavyweight teams resolve the tension inherent in matrix organization in favor of project managers. However, project managers must also work with functional managers so the scales do not tip entirely in one direction. Subject matter expertise resident in functional departments usually needs to be maintained and updated as knowledge for developing competitive offering often grows in complexity over time. To the extent heavyweight teams also deploy flexible processes for guiding development activities, they epitomize the realization of the composite model.

(D) Autonomous Team

An "autonomous" type of team has a project manager with full authority over the work of members of functional departments as well as budget authority. This type of team approximates an entrepreneurial enterprise with stand-alone capabilities. At the extreme these autonomous teams are "skunk works" that are able to operate as quasi-independent businesses for a temporary period of time. Intrapreneurship is an extreme form of autonomous teaming whereby champions risk all by attempting to realize radically new business opportunities.[iv] The downside of autonomous teams is that an organic culture emerges that eschews process discipline without which innovative solutions may prove impractical. Even if successful, the personnel reassigned to their former jobs may have some difficulties in adjusting and even quit.[iv] Reining in the cowboy mentality of those unleashed from disciplined processes to rapidly develop an offering may result in subsequent resistance to due diligence. Lack of deployment of the discipline of process erodes synergies with organic practices that are the cornerstone of the composite model. Thus, autonomous teams are usually best as one-off trials as they are difficult to institutionalize as a mode for sustained operations. However, sometimes the best option for achieving total value development (TVD) is to establish an intrapreneurial venture within an existing enterprise or to launch an external venture either as a strategic partnership or as a stand-alone business.

Champions attempt to build horizontal collaboration across functional boundaries between departments to integrate the value creation stream. A barrier champions confront is the authority of department heads; especially those who are principally responsible for introducing new offerings within the domain of their subject matter expertise, such as marketing or IT. In mechanistic bureaucracies launching new offerings is often within the discretion of a single department, but can lead to sub-optimal results. Therefore, champions often push for the establishment of a cross-functional group to take principal responsibility for NSD. To the extent an NSD function is established that transcends the authority of hierarchical departments, the initial work of the champion has been accomplished.

Champions of concurrency need to shift the balance of power from hierarchical functions to horizontally integrated collaborators. Project leaders need to have a majority of the say over personnel assignments. Empowerment for developing new offerings is greater if a NSD group is formally established with dedicated stakeholders representing various functional departments. Unless relevant functions are engaged up-front by champions of transformation, cross-departmental and trans-sector integration is difficult to achieve.

Lightweight teams coordinated by liaisons are a start in the direction of new service development, but only as a beachhead toward the establishment of heavyweight teams. Liaisons from functional departments have only influence and no authority for project execution. Champions need to help foster the creation of successful heavyweight teams a proof of the principle justifying the establishment of a formal NSD function. Success offers proof of the principle that the predominance of control over people and financial resources for developing complex offerings should reside with the project team relative to functional departments. However, champions of the transformation of concurrent development practices should ensure that hierarchical departments have a shared stake in collaborating in the development of new offerings by influencing NSD activities.

Champions of the NSD function should take a portfolio approach to the project management as not every development project requires a heavyweight team taking over control of personnel from functional departments. The need for heavyweight or autonomous teams is contingent upon strategic needs. Enterprises transitioning from functional to concurrent NSD systems should strive to have an appropriate number of heavyweight teams in their portfolio of funded projects, but not so many as to erode state-of-the-art expertise resident in supporting departments. Transformational leaders need to operate in an infrastructure that is flexible enough to deal with unanticipated obstacles and seize emergent opportunities whilst relying upon steady-state forms of management for routine projects. On the upside, functional experts working in teams may find their expert capabilities broadened by collaborating with people from other disciplines. On the downside, too much firefighting and cross-functional teaming can put the quality of technical competencies for which functional departments are responsible at risk. Over time the depth of functional expertise in enterprises may degrade to the extent heavyweight team members are unable to keep up with new knowledge continually generated beyond the focus of their project assignments. Therefore the project and departmental managers need to share responsibility for the balance of breadth and depth in human resource management in matrix organizations.

14.5. Championing the NSD Function

Champions help lead a shift toward a project-based development system. But a project by project-approach is impermanent. Recognition of the need for a centrally coordinated NSD function needs to be institutionalized. Helping the enterprise make a cultural shift to a focused NSD group has pivotal effects on the strategy and structure of the enterprise which enhances its performance capabilities. Successful firms adapt their strategies and structures to environmental change while others do not. The shift to NSD is associated with the deployment of OTS, the foundation of the composite model. As shown in Table 14.1, the NSD function is correlated with cross-functional teaming, collocation, and modestly with group rewards. NSD is also correlated with the troika of components of the

Table 14.1. Correlations of the NSD Function with OTS and the Composite Model

	NSD Function
OTS	
Cross-functional teaming	0.52
Collocation	0.53
Group rewards	0.33
Composite model	
ESI	0.36
In-process Dynamic Control (IDC)	0.33
CIT	0.51

composite model. Interestingly, its strongest correlation is with Computer Information Technology (CIT), an enabler of dynamic process change as well as rapid cycles of redesign. An environmental factor in stimulating the need for innovation has been revolutionary advances in computer information technologies. However, the emergence of new technical capabilities is a somewhat necessary, but far from sufficient cause of innovation.

14.6. Championing OTS and the Composite Model

The champion is the spearhead for the deployment of OTS. The shift does not occur readily because project-based team is resisted by authorities in mechanistic bureaucracy. It is the persuasive and sometimes charismatic influence of the champion that results in a beachhead for OTS which must be reinforced constantly. Otherwise project resources quickly revert back to hierarchical departments unless the OTS approach is institutionalized and preferably protected by a NSD group. As Jack Welch remarks, bureaucracy is spring loaded and will snap back into place unless resisted. The correlations of the champion role with all three components of OTS are particularly significant for cross-functional teaming and group rewards, but somewhat less so for collocation which is often resisted because of relocation expenses.

Lacking hierarchical authority, the champion must ensure discipline because the guardians of mechanistic bureaucracy are very control oriented. Moreover, a common team process provides a way of unifying the work of disparate functional specialists hitherto guided by departmental rules and procedures. Therefore the formation of a NSD function is associated with the deployment of processes many of which are explicitly embedded in computer information tools and technologies.

14.6.1. *Championing process at UBS*

New service development often requires improvements to processes that are tantamount to innovations in the service product itself. A champion of operational improvement with an innovative mind-set found a myriad of opportunities for improving customer value via processes. For example, when a major client stopped trading with the bank, a cross-functional team was dispatched to the client site to understand the issue. The client demand seemed simple, a more immediate confirmation of the execution of trades. However, the speed requested was at odds with the standard operating procedures of the bank. To retain the client, however, processes which seemed impossible to improve at first turned out to require only some relatively minor tweaks that would not otherwise have been implemented without direct feedback from customer experience. This example is one of the many ways the bank providing customer value by continual process improvements that were often proactively rather than reactively implemented.

The creation of a NSD function is a huge driver of OTS. But to increase effectiveness, functional departments need to contribute to the formation of the development team up-front. ESI is the cornerstone of the composite model. To optimize the benefits of ESI, a synergistic bond with IDC is needed to form the axis of the composite model. To the extent the NSD function seeks to emulate the advantages of the composite model, the group not only needs to garner human resources from hierarchical departments, but also design processes providing integrative discipline transcending functional domains of subject matter expertise. CIT also needs to be deployed to help not only in designing services, but also for synergistically enhancing collaboration among cross-functional team members and electronically tailoring processes.

NSD groups need to consider the advantages offered by the composite model for two principal reasons, multiple performance capabilities and robust capability. Although enterprises may deploy improvements to drive *either* cost or innovation, our research suggests that the composite model has the capability of delivering both competitive advantages simultaneously. Another selling point for the composite model is its robustness in that it is predictive of development performance in both goods and services. This enables NSD groups to consider from the outset what goods may enhance customer experiences derived from the offerings they propose for development. A "composite" provides synergy because the combinatory impact of the troika of practices is greater than the sum of each separately. All interactions among the troika in the services data are synergistic to the extent the enterprise targets the development of new offerings.

Champions need to provide a vision for the benefits of transformation to a more capable future system. Transforming mechanistic bureaucracies into concurrent systems does not just happen! Systems must be changed from serial, bureaucratic methods of product development to operations where all relevant stakeholders for realizing the total development cycle are engaged from the outset. This requires the articulation and continual co-creation of a vision of a future system that garners support from the depth and breadth of the enterprise.

Strategic advantage is the carrot champions need to use to engage stakeholders in thinking about the future capabilities that will be required for sustainable gains in competitiveness. Champions perform a complex and dynamic role to:

- Influence the debate on the features and mode of operation of the ideal development system of the future.
- Inspire key leaders to influences their subordinates to undertake the transformational journey.
- Elicit broad support for transformation from the depth and breadth of the organization.
- To assess the benefits/costs of transformation from all points of the compass so that the downsides are understood from the outset to reduce resistance, such as the reluctance of department heads to cede control over some of their resources.

14.6.2. *Role of education and training*

To overcome bureaucratic barriers, education helps employees engage in practices that enable cross-functional integration. Especially important is training in process, which has a strong correlation with the championing role as shown in Figure 15.1. Training includes formal workshops and courses designed to transmit information regarding concurrency and related skills to its participants. Training plays a vital technical and cultural role in the institutionalization of concurrent practices, such as cross-functional teaming and new product design protocols. Education and training helps firms embrace organic, team-based structures that, in turn, enable members to effectively adopt practices of concurrent product development.

The difficult role of the champion is made easier if reinforced by education and training. Once champions have established a beachhead for change, education and training helps employees become aware of the need for change and the rationale behind it. However, training, especially if classroom-based, is more useful for institutionalizing and solidifying the seismic shifts in plate tectonics initiated by champions.

14.7. Five Steps for Championing Transformation

Transformational leadership starts with envisioning what the enterprise should do and culminates in a continually improved capability for developing and delivering cost-effective, innovative offerings. Championing the transformation from a functional, serial approach to NSD to a concurrent approach with the capabilities of a concurrent system requires a vision.

Champions of change must co-create a vision of improved capability with the people whom they lead. Although vital, envisioning is only the initial step of a five phase process of transformation as illustrated in Figure 14.3. This approach to change management is similar to many

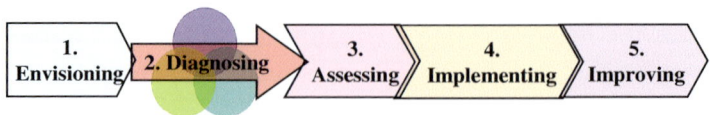

Figure 14.3.   Transformation Assurance Process (TAP)

others, including basic quality management methodologies, an eight-step process by Kotter,[vi] and a transformational learning approach espoused by Senge.[vii] A somewhat unique feature of TAP is its specific focus on improving the capability of value development systems.

14.7.1. *Envisioning*

Champions of change help people envision a state-of-the-art development system offering significantly greater capabilities that extant ones. Because overcoming inertia is a challenge, champions need to persuade others that the improved system stage offers benefits which are necessary for competitiveness over the long if not the short term. However, the need for transformation needs to be understood as urgent so that the design of an improved system state is a co-created vision valued by most if not all stakeholders in the enterprise. Leaders often inspire the enterprise to undertake the transformational journey with the understanding that the future state can only be partially specifiable at the outset and will emerge more clearly as progress is made.

Champions of transformation engage stakeholders in building a collaborative vision of a future system state. This leadership process is surprisingly complex and demanding. The leader needs to communicate the vision over and over again while incorporating input from stakeholders into each generation so that it is a collaboratively-owned destination that offers characteristics valued by most if not all. A vision is a "big picture" image of the way we would like our systems to operate.

The composite model provides a relatively comprehensive design for a system capable of developing offerings in services and/or goods that are simultaneously innovative and cost-effective. However, the model is a framework and the stakeholders in your system will decide on the extent to which concurrent methods of development on which the model is based are those they wish to adopt. They will also need to design a development system that is best capable of achieving targeted strategic objectives. Therefore, envisioning an improved future system is a dynamic process champions need to lead, not dictate.

Champions lead by profiling future capabilities. They need to articulate a vision of improved system capability without dictating too many specific details. One reason is that any future state involves many unknowns. Another is that stakeholders need to buy-in and shape the actual design of the vision. This helps motivate them to undertake the journey and overcome unanticipated obstacles during their transformation journey. Nevertheless, champions need to communicate a somewhat fuzzy version of the vision they recommend over and over again. Rapid cycles of communication and feedback are essential for getting buy-in from stakeholders and building a collective vision. Ideally the vision is shared by influential leaders who may become sufficiently committed to change to reach a tipping point in favor of transformation. To accomplish this level of buy-in, champions must make a compelling argument for the benefits of transformation and its feasibility. As these are seldom realized quickly, the benefits of the profiled end state system need to be constantly communicated as it is easy for anyone to lose sight of a hypothetical, distant destination. Lack of constant communication and reinforcement of the vision puts the journey in jeopardy.

Champions need to deploy a panoply of communication skills. Communication for leading transformation involves more than rational appeals. Auxiliary tactics include ingratiation, bargaining, and co-optation. Although negotiation and compromise are constants, champions must nevertheless hold steadfastly to the core dimensions of the vision they espouse.

This book argues for the use of the principles of concurrent development in formulating a vision of a more capable future system. To the extent champions choose concurrency and the composite model as a foundation for helping build a shared vision, some knowledge and ground rules are helpful.

14.7.2. *Diagnosing*

An assessment of present reality provides champions with a powerful rationale for making compelling arguments for change. Benchmarking not only against competitors, but especially vs. Best-in-Class practices will almost invariably identify gaps. To the extent best practices can be associated with enterprise performance, these leaders have blazed a trail for provent methods of improvement. Of course, emulating practices of

---

Envisioning Improved Development Capability with Concurrency

1. The people you lead need to believe that the principles of concurrency and the composite model is a feasible option that will provide future benefits.
2. The promise of concurrency is a cost effective innovation!
3. *This means bottom line profits (less cost).*
4. *This means top line profits (more revenue).*
5. To realize this simultaneous benefit, you must synergistically meld the creativity of people to get innovation with the discipline of process to get cost reductions.
6. Concurrency is actually fairly simple, but hard to do. The cornerstone is building early and continuous engagement of key stakeholders in product development decisions.
7. Concurrency is systems engineering done right for a whole business enterprise and should not be confused with lower order tools for quality, process improvement, or computer automation.

---

best-in-class leaders may require adaptation for application within a given enterprise. But taking an external perspective in viewing one's own enterprises is invaluable for dispelling complacency.

Transformational Workbook, Exercise A
Benchmarking Your "As Is" Development vs. Best-in-Class

To participate in a benchmarking experience, use score sheets to locate where your enterprise ranks vs. the top ranking firm in the service database and/or a recent database of goods industries. For each of the 10 images illustrating concurrent systems in Chapter Three, questions from the respective surveys were extracted which describe aspects of each practice depicted. Insert your scores into a bar chart arraying firms from lowest to highest in order to estimate the overall gap your enterprise has vs. the best-in-the-databases.

14.7.3. *Assessing*

According to Senge, a powerful driver of transformation is the building of an appropriate level of creative tension between a vision of an improved future

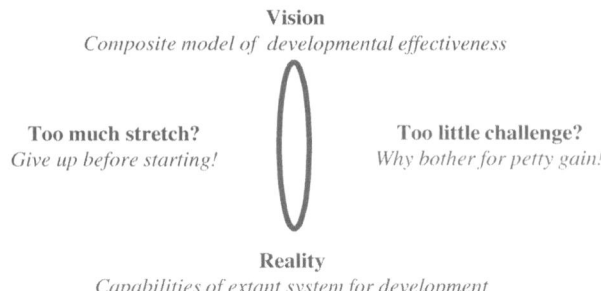

Vision
Composite model of developmental effectiveness

Too much stretch?
Give up before starting!

Too little challenge?
Why bother for petty gain!

Reality
Capabilities of extant system for development

Figure 14.4. Creative Tension for Transformation: Gap between Future System and Present Reality

state vs. present reality. For example, a rubber band is useful only within a restricted range of tautness. If the stretch between present reality and aspiration is too great, the band risks snapping as illustrated in Figure 14.4. People are unwilling to strive for an objective perceived as unattainable. Alternatively, if the aspirational goal is only a small improvement over existing capabilities, the rubber band lacks useful tautness. People are unlikely to strive to make changes in established routines for a negligible gain.

Alternatively, if the aspirational goal is only a small improvement over existing capability, an unstreched rubber band is useless as indicated by the flabby short arrow upward. People may be less motivated to strive to make changes in their established routines for petty gains representing less than an appreciable step improvement.

The prerequisites for assessment are a vision and a diagnosis of present reality. Analysis is the critical step for resolving the creative tension between aspiration and extant capabilities. Analysis is a back and forth process of brainstorming features of the "should be" system state coupled with identifying the root causes of inadequacies in the present system using methods such as fishbone diagrams. Such interwoven analyses help the enterprise prioritize which gaps vs. best-in-class practices need closure and select strategies and tactics for implementing change. Champions help stakeholders *create a vision of an improved system stage and help map how to get there.* Without analysis, progress is difficult if not impossible as implied by two well-known aphorisms:

- If you don't have a vision, a map won't help.
- If you don't have a map, any road will do.

The beauty of the Senge approach is that formulating the vision and assessing which practices are optimal for closing gaps becomes a collaborative endeavor by stakeholders within the enterprise. The role of the champion in what Senge terms a "learning organization" is to help orchestrate a process whereby stakeholders collaborate not only in designing an achievable vision of a future system state, but also assessing which gaps are most important to close for making the transformation.

Benchmarking exercises help readers envision alternative future system states because most enterprises are introverted. Most employees in large mechanistic bureaucracies are relatively unaware of what others have achieved that might be worthy of emulation. The 10 images depicted in Chapter Three, coupled with the benchmarking exercise in the Transformational Workbook, should stimulate thinking about future development system states that may be more capable than extant ones. Potential leaders of a transformation journey are encouraged to co-formulate a vision of an improved system state in follow-on Exercise B.

Transformational Workbook, Exercise B
Envisioning a "Should Be" "Development System"

Criteria of strategic visions are profiled. Steps for championing the co-creation of a strategic vision for enhanced development capabilities are provided.

Champions in learning organizations help lead a structured process for assessing the benefit vs. cost of practices to close gaps between reality and a shared vision of a future, more capable development system. Steps champions may take in helping lead the analysis phase of transformation include:

1. Brainstorming capabilities of your "should be" future development system.
2. Analyzing root causes of problems with the capabilities of the extant development system.
3. Identifying gaps providing the greatest leverage for enhancing the capabilities of the future development system?
4. Prioritizing potential action based on stakeholder ratings of:
   a. Benefit closing a specified gap will likely provide for performance relative to the extant system.

    b.   Empowerment to enact changes for closing gaps.

    c.   Measurability of progress from the baseline "as is" to the "should be" state.

5.   Identifying people in the enterprise who are enablers and blockers. Form a coalition of enablers to co-champion the transformation and attempt to preempt blockers as naysayers often exert outsized influence on opportunities for a successful transformation.

Many methods and tools are available for analyzing the benefit/costs of actions to transform systems. Greater detail about diagnosing and assessing is provided in Exercise C.

Transformational Workbook, Exercise C
Closing Gaps between "As Is" and "Should Be" Development Systems

Assessing is an analytical process for prioritizing actions to close gaps between your "As Is" system vs. a "Should Be" development system. Champions need to lead brainstorming sessions to flesh out the vision of the future state. They need to start the journey by fixing problems with the extant system as a step toward a broader and more comprehensive transformation. The exercise provides an overview of the process and methods for deploying it.

14.7.4. *Implementing*

The flywheel of change is difficult to get moving, as Jim Collins argues in reviewing many business cases.[viii] Therefore, champions should steer initial actions toward those that have benefits that are obvious to most, which also require relatively little effort to change. A quick win that is celebrated and shared helps solidify the transformational coalition and train people for larger challenges. For each improvement action, champions should enlist support from specific senior managers to gain their commitment to the change regardless of the extent of resources required.

Tracking progress is an essential feature of a good many successful transformation stories. Visual management may help stakeholders be constantly aware of progress or the lack thereof. Given that transformational journeys may be long and complex, "intermediate" performance indicators should be tracked as well as final outcomes vs. the baseline. Identifying intermediate performance indicators is tricky because most are relatively soft. However, many research studies have shown that development teams often know when they are off track typically well ahead of realization by managers. Champions can use group meetings to discuss progress as well as one sentence anonymous ratings to monitor perceived progress.

Diagnosing is a continual activity along transformation journeys, not just at the outset. As shown in the diagram of the five steps of TAP, the implementation phase requires diagnosis to ensure that the actions initiated have effects as intended. Often the best laid plans go awry for reasons that were unanticipated at the outset. Champions are able to help stakeholders identify blockages and either alter the intervention or abandon it for a more propitious alternative. On the upside, unexpected opportunities sometimes emerge during the transformational journeys that need to be seized.

Implementing change requires a continual feedback loop of *Plan-Do-Check-Act* for ensuring the quality of outcomes (see Figure 14.5). A *Plan-Do-Check-Act* approach ensures diagnosis is part of the cycle to trial testing prior to a full roll-out of a plan.[ix] Most transformation as well as strategic plans fails.[x] One reason is because planning needs to be rethought as a dynamic process rather than a one-off event conducted by

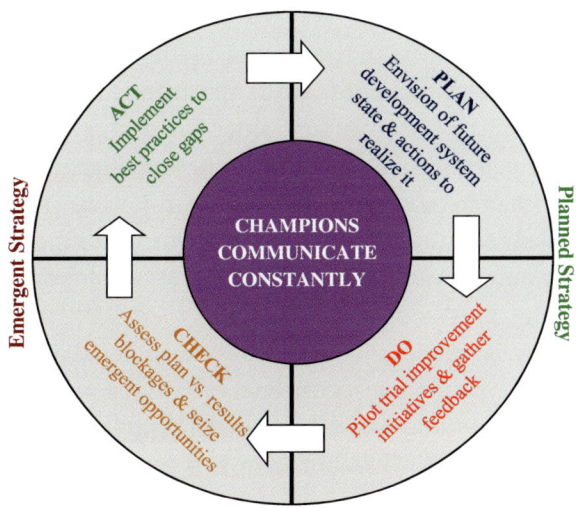

Figure 14.5. Rapid, Reiterative Redesign of Strategic Plans

senior managers and their staff. Changing the operations of development systems affects a large number of people and the doers in the enterprise need to be continual participants in ensuring the transformation provides net benefits.

14.7.5. *Continuously improving*

Achieving all the features of a vision is a difficult mission. Often initial attempts fall short in some regards, which means that cycles of continual improvement need to be renewed after understanding the root cause of blockages. But even if the new system exceeds expectations, complacency is dangerous. Even when an improved system seems to be of proven effectiveness, some may be reluctant to embrace and occasionally attempt to sabotage it. Moreover, the baseline benchmark that was used as a reference for envisioning improvements has likely not only moved within your enterprise, but also in competitor firms as well. In many sectors benchmarking needs to be supplemented by so called "bench trending" because the pace of improvement is often fairly continuous.

The *Plan-Do-Check-Act* approach used in implementing changes becomes institutionalized as a way of life in many leading corporations. One of the culminating tasks of champions is inculcating the norm of continuous improvement as a way of life. To the extent significant improvements were achieved in the development system, the commitment and level of energy that brought about the transformation needs to be maintained. If cycles of improvement slow down, it is usually even more difficult to renew commitment to envision new challenges.

The pace of change that stimulated the need for transformation in the first place is unlikely to subside. Successful enterprises competing in complex dynamic environments raise the bar after every successful cycle of improvement. Champions must do what they can to ensure that momentum becomes culturally accepted as a daily routine rather than an exceptional kind of behavior. Developing new customer offerings is extraordinarily complex in many instances and opportunities for improving elements of the system are easy to identify. Collaboration is a continual need because the complex developments systems have many interdependencies requiring continual adaptations and improvements.

14.8. TAP vs. Alternative Improvement Methodologies

The five steps of TAP are similar to many other approaches to change. TAP is somewhat distinctive as it was devised specifically by executives responsible for development activities to improve them. The subject matter discipline for devising TAP was concurrent engineering, which has broadened its scope to resemble systems engineering and instilling the principles of concurrency throughout enterprise-wide operations. By contrast, most other methods are derived from manufacturing and have been subsequently adapted for application to development.

(A) Computer automated behavior controls

The need for discipline in development is widely recognized. Perhaps the most well-known process for controlling development is stage-gate systems with entry and exit criteria at each step from concept to outcome delivery, which has also been demonstrated to work in financial services.[xi] An issue with the stage-gate approach is that it is often deployed as a serial, lock-step process. Although phases may overlap, the temptation to rigidly automate the development process with software management tools like product life cycle management has been great. The deployment of such tools is diffusing from goods to service development. In both sectors, the use of product life cycle management tools runs the risk of supplanting human judgment and hampering opportunities for employees to add value by generating creative features for which customers are willing to pay.

(B) Total quality management (TQM)

One of the best known improvement approaches in manufacturing is TQM. A method for reducing defects with the acronym of Define, Measure, Assess, Improve, and Control (DMAIC) is similar to TAP in many ways. However, TAP focuses on envisioning rather than defining as a first step. Envisioning usually broadens the scope of change targeted. Sometimes quality problems can be defined in relatively narrow dimensions so that a delimited feature is targeted for improvement that may provide only modest benefit or occasionally suboptimize the system because of interdependencies. Another contrast is that TAP emphasized continuous improvement as a way of life in operating development systems instead of control, which implies the curtailment of outliers. Of course DMAIC methods may be dynamically redeployed, but the provenience of the method is rooted in the standardization of manufacturing operations. Deploying DMAIC and six-sigma quality methods in upstream development operations is tricky because of greater degrees of intangibility. For example, 3M deployed DMAIC and other six sigma methods, but found that their rate of innovation significantly declined.[xii]

(C) Process excellence

Process improvement is a major handle for a wide variety of improvement initiatives. Some of the earliest processes for complex product development projects were propagated by NASA. Blueprinting of processes was a pioneering parallel in services.[xiii] ISO has propagated worldwide guidelines to help ensure that processes are repeatable and delivery reliable results. Business process reengineering focuses on taking waste and cost out of operations as does it popular successor, *lean production* methods from Toyota. Lean focuses on reducing seven kinds of waste: transportation, inventory, motion, waiting, over-processing, over-production, and defects.[xiv] Value stream mapping is a key method for identifying unnecessary actions for which customers are willing to pay.[xv] By evaluating each step of a process in terms of value added, waste is eliminated. Lean and Business process reengineering methods often save money in manufacturing and sometimes in development, at least in the short-term. But the risk is that much of the value in upstream development operations involves intangible ideas that may be too readily eliminated as waste, thereby resulting in lower levels of creativity. For example, Business process reengineering often attempts to automate process steps, which may attenuate the scope of human judgment and dampen innovative options.

Table 14.2 shows the correlation of alternative improvement methods with differentiation and delivery performance. Available measures of alternative interventions to improve performance provide little or no support for their contribution to performance with the exception of TQM. As noted in Chapter Nine, enterprises exploiting a strategy of tacit knowledge

Table 14.2. Correlation of Alternative Improvement Methods with Performance

Improvement methods	Differentiation	Delivery
Total Quality Management	0.33	0.47
International Standards Organization (ISO)	0.27	0.22
Business Process Reengineering	0.16	0.07

were reliant on TQM to help ensure performance. Thus, TQM methods need to be considered by champions as a way of augmenting performance in service delivery. However, the measures available in the service dataset analyzed herein suggests that concurrent practices, as portrayed by the images used for benchmarking provide a basis for shaping a vision of a highly capable development system.

Notes

[i] Markham, S. K. and Griffin, A. 1998. The Breakfast of Champions: Associations Between Champions and Product Development Environments, Practices and Performance, *Journal of Product Innovation Management*, 15, 436–454.

[ii] Clark, K. B. and Wheelwright, S. C. 1993. *Managing New Product and Process Development: Text and Cases*, Free Press: New York.

[iii] Clark, K. and Wheelwright, S. 1992. Organizing and Leading 'Heavyweight' Development Teams, *California Management Review*, 34(Spring), 11–28.

[iv] Pinchot, G. 1985. *Intrapreneuring: Why You Don't have to Leave the Corporation to Become an Entrepreneur*, Harper and Row: New York.

[v] Kidder, T. 1981. *The Soul of a New Machine*, Little, Brown & Co.: New York.

[vi] Kotter, J. 1996. *Leading Change*, Harvard Business Press: Marvand.

[vii] Senge, P. 1990. *The Fifth Discipline: The Art & Practice of the Learning Organization*, Century Business: London.

[viii] Collins, J. C. 2001. *From Good to Great*, William Collins: New York.

[ix] Demming, E. 1992. *Out of Crisis*, MIT: Cambridge.

[x] Mintzberg, H. and Quinn, B. 1996. The *Strategy Process*, Prentice-Hall: Englewood Cliffs.

[xi] Cooper, R. G. and Edgett, S. 1999. *Service Product Development: Lessons From Market Leaders*, Perseus: Cambridge.

[xii] Hindo, B. 2007. At 3M, A Struggle Between Efficiency And Creativity, *Bloomberg Business Week*, June 10.

xiii   Shostack, G. L. 1982. How to Design a Service, *European Journal of Marketing*, 16(1), 49–63.

xiv   Taiichi, O. 1988. *Toyota Production System*, Productivity Press: New York.

xv   Martin, K. and Osterling, M. 2013. *Value Stream Mapping: How to Visualize Work and Align Leadership for Organizational Transformation*, McGraw Hill: New York.

CHAPTER FIFTEEN

INTRAPRENEURIAL AND ENTREPRENEURIAL VENTURES FOR TVD

Overview

This chapter invites you to participate in thought experiments about creating new kinds of value to differentiate offerings in radically new ways. Championing radical designs may require transforming your employing enterprise, establishing strategic partnerships or launching external ventures. Your target is the realization of an offering with a compelling value proposition for customers. Taking a customer-centric point of view helps map ways of adding value which may transcend the goods vs. services dichotomy. The key is envisioning a future development system capable of generating innovative new offerings satisfying customer needs in unique ways. This approach attempts to achieve more holistic solutions for customers based on the meaning they impute to their experiences. Methods for stimulating creativity are helpful for generating new ideas that exceed the boundaries of conventional paradigms. However, generating ideas for your value proposition is only the beginning of a lengthy process. Innovators of new business models may need to deploy a composite model to develop and deliver complex, dynamic new offerings. To realize radically new designs, assessment of capabilities of your existing development system for achieving objectives is a pre-condition. If the proponents of radically new designs are employed by an enterprise lacking in the capabilities for Total Value Development (TVD), internal or external venturing may be required. Development activities may be configured as a semiautonomous team or autonomous group depending on the extent to which the target offering lies within the core capabilities of the enterprise. To the extent the enterprise recognizes the need for developing radically new offerings, support may be garnered for piloting an internal venture. A successful new venture may help further transform development capabilities from mechanistic to a system more capable of TVD. In the face of entrenched bureaucratic resistance to transformation, however, proponents of radically new designs may need to consider entrepreneurial options for external ventures. Regardless of the choice, guidelines are provided to stimulate thinking about how to design radically new offerings as well as ways of configuring human capital and building operations to support development and delivery of holistic value.

15.1. Assessing the Capabilities of Your Development System

For targeting radically innovative design options, a primary consideration is the extent to which new offerings fit within the core competencies of your employing enterprise. Internal sponsors are much more readily obtained if proposed offerings enhance or complement existing lines of business. Investment costs are lower if extant knowledge-bases and distribution processes may be utilized in development. By contrast, offerings which require new kinds of knowledge and/or delivery often require greater up-front investment as well as risk.

To the extent new offerings are complex and varied, the robustness of the development system should be considered. Mechanistic systems are often narrowly focused and constrained by sunk investments. Although organic systems may be receptive to radically new ideas, they often lack disciplined processes necessary for realizing them. By contrast, composite systems have capabilities for developing complex offerings because heterogeneous stakeholders are engaged up-front in evaluating strategic options. The diversity of knowledge and resources on the table for

> The more complex new customer offerings become, the greater the need for robust development systems

decision-making in concurrent systems allows for early evaluation of alternative ways for achieving multiple competitive advantages simultaneously. The composite model has the capabilities for developing offerings that are innovative and cost-effective as well as holistically integrative of services and goods.

15.1.1. *Typology of development system options*

Proponents of radically new designs need to consider not only competitive advantages in the marketplace, but also how to garner capabilities for developing them. A typology of options for realizing radically new designs considers fit with existing core competencies as well as the extent to which the development system is robust. Four analytically distinct alternatives are illustrated in Table 15.1.

(A) Pilot transformation project

To the extent radically new designs fall within the boundaries of core competencies, winning sponsorship is a relatively promising prospect. Regardless of the extent of fit, however, novelty requires changes in thinking and capabilities for development and/or delivery which may trigger bureaucratic resistance to proponents of new ideas. Managers in the dominant coalition often achieved their power based on sales from established offerings and eschew risks. Development systems typically become more mechanistic concomitant with growth. To the extent development operations are serial operations for achieving cost efficiencies, opportunities for achieving (Total Value Development) TVD are limited. Unless

Table 15.1.   Development System Options for Radically New Designs

	Design within core competencies	Design outside core competencies
Pre-TVD Capability	A. Pilot Transformation Project	C. External Start-up Venture
TVD Capability	B. Semi-autonomous Heavyweight Team	D. Intrapreneurial Venture Team

growth is faltering or margins slimming down, champions of designs for TVD in mechanistic systems are likely to face an uphill battle. To the extent the competitive environment of the enterprise has become more dynamic, however, opportunities for promoting innovative designs are greater. If proponents of the new design are able to gain sponsorship from top management, a pilot project may be launched to pioneer concurrent practices conducive for innovation.

Most enterprises successfully undergoing transformation begin by piloting concurrent methods to increase the probability of success of critical projects. For example, top management at Eli Lilly permitted the establishment of two semiautonomous teams to speed the development of critical new offerings. However, proponents of radically new designs need to champion not only the value their offering *per se*, but also concurrent methods for managing its development. If top managers support the building of a heterogeneous team up-front, a beachhead for the transformation to concurrent systems is underway.

Winning a battle by demonstrating the advantages of concurrency for one project does not win the war. Unless the enterprise has a culture of continuous improvement, a successful pilot project may be treated as a one-off accomplishment. The effort to expand the beachhead to encompass the enterprise as a business system now begins. However, if top management fails to provide up-front resources for subsequent projects and resists further transformation, relatively more autonomous options should be evaluated for realizing radically new designs.

(B) Semiautonomous, heavyweight teams

If new designs fall within the core competencies of an enterprise with the robust capabilities of the composite model, proponents of new designs have an easier time building heavyweight teams to support radical developments. Heavyweight teams are able to garner the bulk of resources needed for development up-front, e.g., a leader championing the project, people, and funds. The more radical the proposed offering, the more heterogeneous the team needs to be. The more tacit knowledge entailed, the more some kinds of functions, especially those associated with delivery processes, need to be engaged pre- and post-launch.

(C) *Autonomous teams and the challenge of intrapreneurship*

If new designs lies outside of the core competencies of a mechanistic enterprise or tradition-bound establishment, one option is to take an intrapreneurial approach. The more radically different the new design is from those in existing lines of business, the more necessary autonomy becomes. Allowing teams to operate autonomously, however, has some risks. To succeed, the discipline of flexible processes is needed in tandem with creative input from heterogeneous stakeholders. If the autonomous project is successful, an attractive option is to merge the advantages from TVD offering with existing lines of business to leverage extant resources. However, the relative freedom enjoyed by members of autonomous teams is constrained by normal bureaucratic operations. If the window for greater innovation is to be widened, some of the practices used for achieving radically new offerings need to be infused into the extant enterprise, which often proves difficult.[i]

The need for internal ventures is painfully realized by large corporations because so many creative people leave to establish entrepreneurial ventures. Hewlett-Packard is famous for the number of entrepreneurial startups by its former employees in Silicon Valley, the total revenues from which are colossal. If Xerox had commercialized all of its inventions from its Parc lab, it might be the largest corporation in the world today. Opportunities for establishing an external venture are exemplified by a frustrated employee at DuPont who left to found a Gortex. The start-up venture grew to become a multibillion dollar rival. Large corporations need to be more accommodating to radically new ideas generated by their employees. Pinchot popularized the concept of "intrapreneurship" and suggested Ten Commandments beginning with the exhortation to "come to work each day willing to be fired", for pursuing their idea.[ii] Large corporate enterprises have struggled to become more supportive of new designs and entrepreneurial ideas. 3M has been one of the most successful with the strategic goal of a vitality index in excess of 30 percent sales from new products every 2 years. Funding from its Genesis program is famous for sponsoring intrapreneurs such as the creator Post-it Notes. Although many corporations provide seed money for new ideas, some spend more on advertising to promote an innovative image than on actual seed money for new ventures. As R&D budgets have been decentralized under the control of established lines of business, the challenge of intrapreneuring has become more risky than ever as strategic business units often cling tightly to established core competencies and known practices regardless of their effectiveness in rapidly changing environments.

Intrapreneurs may attempt to have their enterprise establish a new line of business. However, building new strategic business units is often expensive as well as risky. Managers of existing lines of business often regard resources as scarce and are unlikely to be supportive unless they are persuaded of potential benefit in the long if not short term. Champions of newly established strategic business units, however, need to ensure that internal sponsors are continually appraised of progress against plan and remain committed stakeholders.

An alternative option is to spin out the intrapreneurial venture as a strategic partnership. Strategic partnerships may provide an excellent method for enabling large corporations to retain a stake in an intrapreneurial venture that offers an uncertain promise. Intrapreneurs that are spun out as venture capital investment are liberated from much of the bureaucratic red tape of large corporations. For example, Exxon Enterprises knew how to pick winning technologies, but not how to manage them within their own bureaucracy. All but one of their internal ventures died while their investment in entrepreneurial start-ups paid back over 40 to 1.[iii]

The advantage of strategic partnerships is that the start-up has access to capital, knowledge resources, marketing distribution, and credibility by association with an established corporation.[iv] Large enterprises that have melded organic with mechanistic design practices in the composite model make better partners for entrepreneurs than mechanistic enterprises. Ideally, the entrepreneurial firm is relatively more mechanistic that normal for its size, the large partner relatively more organic that typical. This reciprocal adaptation enables inter-enterprise exchanges to occur within a framework consistent with the synergistic advantages of the composite mode melding the advantages of both mechanistic and organic forms of design.

(D) External venture options

If the new design lies outside of the core competencies of a mechanistic enterprise or traditional business that is successful, the prospects for gaining support for innovation are probably low. Consideration of new business models is rare for enterprises already successful in a given line of business. To the extent understanding and capability for TVD is lacking, proponents of radially new designs may be wise to consider leaving to establish an entrepreneurial start up.

The option of obtaining venture funding from the former employer should be considered. It is often a difficult sell. But if the risks to the sponsoring corporation are low, it is may be a feasible source of support. Moreover, the process discipline of working with a larger corporation in a stra-

Large bureaucratic enter- prises may achieve greater returns from investment in external than internal ventures because decision- making is focused and rapid

tegic partnership may be helpful so long as the entrepreneur retains the majority of say over development decisions. However, large mechanistic enterprises often find decentralization of decision-making difficult and attempt to control entrepreneurs with overly rigid procedures. The rapid growth in new designs of service offerings strains the boundaries of traditional enterprises and opens up opportunities for establishing relations with external entities such as suppliers and customers.

15.1.2. *Value added by supplier relationships*

Proponents of radically new designs are unusually needy of various kinds of human capital. Requisite knowledge from subject matter experts may be configured in development teams from internal employees. However, the exponential growth of knowledge means that enterprises are increasingly dependent on externally sourced knowledge. Some prominent firms own only a small percentage of the intellectual property embodied in their offerings. Increasingly, providers of services and products are reliant upon inputs from a variety of external entities. In some instances, suppliers are treated as strategic partners, especially if they provide proprietary knowledge and/or unique capabilities. More commonly, companies attempt to mechanistically control suppliers by contracts that are more rigid in some ways than procedures for internal employees.

External suppliers may make huge contributions to enterprise success, especially if they provide significant proportions of the value added to

Table 15.2. Correlations of Supplier and Customer Engagement with Differentiation Performance

	Differentiation performance
Supplier Involvement	0.58
Customer Involvement	0.52

Table 15.3. Correlations of Composite Model with Supplier and Customer Engagement

Composite model (OPT)	Supplier involvement	Customer involvement
Organization (OTS)	0.65	0.61
Process (IDC)	0.75	0.59
Tools/Technology (CIT)	0.16	0.23

customer offerings. Whether suppliers were engaged in the development of service offerings was measured along with 10 internal functions. As shown in the top row of Table 15.2, supplier engagement has a statistically significant correlation with differentiation performance.[v]

To ensure the quality of their offerings, service providers need to manage external relationships with suppliers. Organizational and process practices melding organic with mechanistic management have significant correlations with supplier engagement in decision-making about new service development (NSD) as shown in the left column of Table 15.3. However, the relationship for tools and technologies is insignificant. One reason may be that attempts to enforce impersonal controls over suppliers outside of collaborative framework are often successful. If suppliers are part of your up-front development team, competitive advantages may be gained such as proven in cases for some auto corporations like Toyota and Chrysler.[vi]

Organic team structure is an internal practice which may help enterprises form partnering relationships with external suppliers. Processes provide a common framework for suppliers to engage in co-development. Tools and technologies are more likely to be beneficial if deployed in concert with the other components of the troika.

15.1.3. *Value added by customer involvement*

Customer experience is the ultimate arbiter of value added. Providers of services need input from customers to design offerings that are valued. As shown in the bottom row of Table 15.2, input from customers in development decisions is significantly correlated with differentiation performance. As shown in the right column of Table 15.3, OTS and IDC are strongly correlational with differentiation performance although CIT has only a modest relationship.

Intimate engagement with customers helps enterprises understand how to design offerings adding value for which customers are willing to pay. An exemplar is Intuit, which provides software for performing a myriad of services for individual consumers as well as corporations. They employ ethnographers to empathize with customer experiences. They engineered a software to monitor eye movements and facial expressions indicative of emotions when using their software on computer screens in their lab. Intuit provides an example of pay-off from customer empathy. The founder, Steve Cook, argues for the need of being humble with customers. His best insights and breakthroughs in design thinking occurred when he listened to customers and found out he was wrong.[vii]

Customer Empathy at Intuit

A software provider, Intuit, is noted for customer empathy. This approach began when its founder, Steve Cook, followed customers home to observe how they used his software in actual practice. Today the corporation employees a bevy of researchers dedicated to understanding and improving customer experiences. A permanent team of researchers use anthropological field methods and computer design tools to empathize and analyze customer experiences. If Intuit's growth can be attributed to any one managerial practice, it would be the now tired cliché about listening to your customers — which, cliché or not, still too few companies understand or act on with any faith. Is there a smarter, simpler, cheaper, or more telling example of the practice than Intuit's "Follow Me Home" program? It called for an Intuit employee to hang around the local computer store until someone bought Quicken off the shelf (this was back when people did that sort of thing). The employee would then ask the buyer to take him home so he could see how difficult the product was to install.

(Continued)

Customer Empathy at Intuit (*Continued*)

He would watch the process silently, noting everything from how easily the shrink-wrap came off, to which lines of direction bred that confused look on the new users face. If there were problems, every pause and every source of frustration were evidence of something Intuit needed to fix. Cook was a radical simplifier. He knew, right from the start, that Intuit did not need only to make Quicken better and easier than every other software program; it needed to make Quicken better and easier than the pen in your hand and the paper check-writing process that Quicken aimed to replace. And Cook knew that if he and his company could just be alert and creative and open-minded enough, then making it so was possible, because would-be customers could tell them how.

An observational approach to empathetic understanding customer needs and how this orientation drives the management of development is well documented at IDEO, a world renowned design shop. IDEO's methods have been widely adopted by many companies, including Intuit.[viii]

Authentic partnerships between providers and customers are relatively rare. One reason is because many companies, especially in high-tech, have solutions dictated to them by customers that are suboptimal. Many companies want to avoid giving their customers a ring in their nose. However, if the provider company deploys the composite model, significant gains from customer partnerships are possible.[ix] An exemplar in customer led innovation is 3M which has succeeded in innovating for decades. 3M engages in many partnerships with customers focusing, in particular, on fulfilling unmet needs that are sticky and difficult to articulate.[x] Such a partnership approach helps result in a democratization of innovative processes and co-creation.[xi]

Customer Led Innovation at 3M

3M is a very service-oriented goods company that excels in empathizing with customer problems. They have a huge customer service center which hosts many thousands of visitors per year staffed by sales and engineering personnel. Their 60,000 diversified offerings gives them options for configuring many kinds of solutions from off-the-shelf products. However, they are quite willing

(Continued)

(*Continued*)

> to collaborate with customers in developing unique solutions to their problems. The 3M sales force is trained to explore unarticulated needs customers experience. For example, they probe for activities a customer company performs which lies outside of their core competencies. If this activity is compatible with core capabilities, the sales person attempts to initiate a collaborative venture.

15.2. Nonlinear, Open Designs

Service designs are rapidly evolving from linear solutions of rationally defined problems to exploration of open, multifaceted opportunities. For example, agile scrum is a software method that inspired the metaphor of organic development as a swarming of players in rugby. Instead of a serial relay race where one specialist hands the baton to another, every player takes responsibility for moving the ball regardless of formal role. Examples in development include set-based design for pursuing orthogonally differentiated approaches simultaneously.[xii] Similarly, 3P methods engage diverse stakeholders, including production employees, to progress designs from easily modified materials such as cardboard to steel so that plasticity in thinking is encouraged.[xiii] Recently ISO standards have included design processes with feedback loops relatively more human-focused on users and the context of use.

Some critics, however, argue that the bulk of design methodologies presume rational boundaries within a confined problem space which results in solutions that are essentially serial in character despite feedback loops.[xiv] Such critiques parallel the contrast between explicit and tacit modes of knowledge. Much of industrial design is reliant upon explicit knowledge at varying levels of codification. By contrast, designing disruptive new offerings requires insights that are essentially intuitive and thereby largely tacit.

Exploiting tacit knowledge requires designers to break out of delimited frameworks by using intuitive approaches that open up options precluded in typical definitions of market opportunities. This requires designers to toggle between explicit and tacit modes of knowledge. The most reliable predictor of innovation is heterogeneity of input.

Exposure to unknowns helps designers react intuitively and generate speculative ideas that closed loop design processes are unlikely to explore. Designers processing information lying outside of the paradigms within which they normally work experience the challenge of dealing with a diversity of tacit knowledge. Tacit knowledge challenges designers to rethink the value of customer offerings in new ways.

15.2.1. *Virtual networks and TVD*

The perspective of the sole source corporation needs to be complemented by the notion of a network of collaborative providers. A simple example is a startup like Uber which disrupted existing markets. Their business model for providing transportation services on demand was changed by enabling a myriad number of owner providers to link with customers through their website. More complex examples involve configuring multiple kinds of value into single offering. For example, e.g., GE Capital leases goods as well as supplying various services ranging from finance to maintenance as a holistic package.

Opportunities for configuring radically new offerings have been considerably enhanced in recent years by the growth in availability and capability of electronic communications for networking. The capability of partnering with others to configure multiple inputs from a variety of suppliers to provide customers with solutions enhances the power of designers within corporations. Designers of services are relatively less dependent on the financial recourses of their employing corporation and thereby better positioned to launch intrapreneurial start-ups. Start-ups usually need to include external stakeholders in an environment of open exchange where ownership of intellectual property is relatively non-contentious. The key to maintaining a proprietary position in an open environment increasing depends of designing offerings to enhance customer experiences whilst retaining a position in the network as a principal point of contact for customers. However, serving as a hub in a network demands rapid, extensive communications.

15.3. Unmet Customer Needs

Key for NSD, especially for radically new offerings, is a compelling value proposition. Your value proposition should focus on fulfilling unmet customer needs. Many books and websites offer help in formulating them.[xv] Value propositions range from incremental improvements of existing offerings to radical new ones fulfilling unarticulated or even unanticipated needs. Some of the most disruptive offerings restructuring markets met needs that were unanticipated, e.g., computers, portable music players, search engines, mobile phone apps, etc. While it is tempting to try to design disruptive new offerings, it is obviously not an easy first step. Fortunately a lot of the insights for making big leaps emerge from working within existing paradigms so long as designers are alert on new options transcending the boundaries of existing systems. Another advantage of making major modifications to existing products is the prospect of considerable profit in relatively short time spans. However, dynamic processes need to be used for achieving synergies from a strategy of major modifications.

To the extent enterprises target radically new designs, the need is heightened for the robust capabilities of the composite model. Development systems based on the principles of concurrency emerged to enable the realization of novel features and/or modes of delivery. Concurrency development systems have an advantage for helping designers generate potentially disruptive ideas because heterogeneous inputs of human capital occur at the conceptualization phase of development and exchanges of ideas continue among diverse functions along the value realization stream. The notion of concurrency connotes simultaneous engagement from multiple stakeholders from design concept to delivery. Reciprocal, recurrent feedback among diverse stakeholders stimulates ideas that have the potential to burst the bounds of conventional thinking.

15.3.1. *Designing outward from customer experiences*

Among heterogeneous inputs to the design process, the most important is often the interpretation of experiences from the customer's point of view. One of the best methods is direct observation of how customers actually use existing products and services.[a] Taking the perspective of customers is doubly difficult because designers must not only get outside themselves,

---

[a]The correlation between observing how customer use products with innovation in the follow-on study of goods industry is quite strong, $r = 0.79$.

but also emphasize with the experience of customers. Solecism is an especially tricky barrier because empathy has non-rational, emotional facets. To empathize, designers need to get inside the heart and head of potential customers. The designer as empathizer typically encounters difficulty in interpreting the meaning of experiences to customers as they are dynamic and multidimensional. Taking the third person perspective of customers requires integrating a trove of tacit knowledge which is difficult to codify. One reason is that the experiences of customers include intuitive pre-reflective meanings that are semi-conscious, emotionally charged and tacit in nature. Only subsequently do customers construct these subjective feeling and facts in rationally articulated forms.

15.3.2. *Creative design methods*

Dynamic methods of industrial design have proliferated in recent years that are relatively more open and nonlinear than rational, closed loop approaches compatible with serial development in mechanistic bureaucracies.[xvi] However, the legacy of a sequential development procedure approach is difficult to overcome. Although a growing number of industrial firms have deployed *design for service*, they often lack an authentic customer perspective.

Customer-oriented development has recently been boosted by the emergence of service design. A growing number of books are devoted to the subject along with online support services and toolkits such as QFD (Quality Function Deployment).[xvii] Recent literature increasingly approaches service design thinking from a humanistic perspective which includes not only providers, but also customers. Many designers in services engage customers from the outset in collaboratively seeking solutions to their needs. Human factors are salient in many kinds of service, especially intangible offerings involving interpersonal interactions.

Many service designers build networks to collaboratively design customer offerings, e.g., ethnographers, market researchers, behavioral scientists, strategist, etc. Creativity is enhanced by heterogeneity of input into the design process. There are many categories of contributors such as subject matter experts, stakeholders in the provider enterprise, significant others affecting customer context, and customers themselves. Internal human capital needs to be supplemented by collaboration with suppliers, customers, and even strategic partners. A seemingly simple category for a functional roles may include many complex activities. For example, market research departments may include ethnographers, audio–visual analysts of customer interchanges, dramatic reenactors of customer interchanges, etc. A wide variety of specialized roles are increasingly pertinent for service design.

Technologies for analyzing customer experiences have grown more sophisticated in recent years. One of the most obvious methods is to analyze video tapes of interchanges between providers and customers. Many analyses of customer survey data can be analyzed using a variety of methods to infer deeper emotions providing the gestalt behind a given response. The gestalt of customers affects the emergent reality of customer experiences. Context includes fellow-users, friends and relativities, situations depicted in sitcoms, advertising, and a whole variety of interpersonal as well as impersonal context. Buying patterns are increasing analyzed using trolling methods for mining so-called "big data".

Contributors are not limited solely to the venture. Increasingly many new ventures are one unit within a wider networked ecosystem. App developers and contributors to crowdsourcing may become vital contributors to developing and delivering value. For example, networks of contributors are often asked to respond to challenges and offer ideas for solutions to customer problems.

A great variety of creative methods have proliferated recently that go beyond variants of brainstorming. Many of these methods are particularly appropriate for services where interpersonal interactions involving tacit knowledge are critical for adding value. Many kinds of methods and tools are used for visualization of prototype situations and constructing scenarios adapted to the context stakeholders involved in service processes.[xviii] The goal is to visualize and choreograph behaviors to foster empathy with the latent emotions of customers. Observing hypothetical scenarios helps service designers dig into the meanings customers construct of their experiences so that service designs may better fulfill existing needs that are difficult to articulate. The development of offerings providing extraordinary value builds on insights arising from reciprocal interactions between the interpretations of designers and their read of the subjective experiences of customers.

15.3.3. *Value from systems engineering perspective of service design*

The service perspective is a valuable complement to an engineering-centric approach. For example, a world renowned corporation developed a multibillion dollar monitoring system for NASA, but neglected to engineer the service maintenance needs of the ground stations. These could have been designed for electronic monitoring, but did not. The cost of sending humans to check and maintain the land-based stations over the next 30 years far exceeded the expense of the engineered installation. Systems engineering needs to encompass a life cycle perspective of customer value to provide holistic solutions.

Co-creation of offerings with customers is increasingly used in experimental development. Although many large engineering-based offerings have recently tried to take a customer-centric point of view, many are technically complex and must consider reliability dimensions that risk being neglected by focusing on experiential episodes of customer experience. An example is Galileo, a global satellite navigation system built by the European Space Agency that has many applications with the potential for improving life experiences. However, a lot of due diligence is required for developing the service as well as the product side of Galileo. Some of the mandatory engineering-oriented checks also have potential relevance for selected kinds of service design, especially large-scale systems with interdependencies.[xix]

- Service-Oriented Architecture;
- Service Level Agreement;
- Systems Requirement Document;
- Concept of Operations;
- Key Performance Indicators;
- Total Cost of Ownership;
- Balance between non-recurring and operating costs.

TVD demands that the customer perspective be sufficiently encompassing to include the context of use during the entire life cycle. This may be one reason why engagement by the finance function as well as sales is so beneficial for service enterprises developing offerings based on tacit knowledge. Tacit knowledge offerings are often idiosyncratic and difficult to systematize. But the principles used in goods may also be applied although with less actuarial precision.

15.4. Designing TVD Systems

Development systems exploiting TVD capabilities are better able to fulfill unmet customer needs by developing radically new offerings. To generate disruptive ideas designers need to build on speculative ideas that might fulfill unanticipated as well as existing customer needs. From the customer perspective, initial experiences with offerings are typically covert and tacit as shown on the right-hand side of Figure 15.1. Subsequently customers may articulate their needs, but some of the most successful radically new offerings strike an emotive dimension in customer experiences that is initially difficult to express even *sotto voce*.

From the company perspective, designers thinking out of the box, so to speak, often have flashes of insight springing from so-called gut reactions prior to post hoc analysis that seed radical designs as shown on the left-hand side of Figure 15.1. These intuitive insights are more likely to sprout if designers empathize with customers in the netherworld of diverse meanings they give to their experiences which are not entirely rational. Subsequently insights may be transformed into rational explicit knowledge. But to configure radically new offerings, the greater the

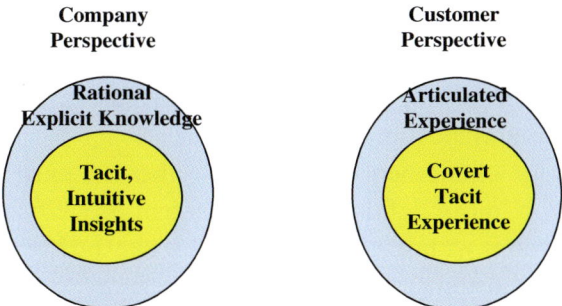

Figure 15.1.   Customer vs. Customer Perspective

reliance on intuition as well as rationality at least initially, the more likely designs are to fulfill an unmet need.

Systems engineering deployed at the enterprise level provides guidelines for busting paradigms which may serve as rigid gestalts shaping our thinking. Systems engineers focus first on brainstorming myriad solutions that transcend past options. For example, a customer may need transportation, but this does not necessarily require an option with four wheels. Taking the customer's perspective of what might constitute a solution is a more open, systematic approach holistic design thinking that gets below the surface of conventional approaches to development.[xx]

Once a service designer has articulated their intuitive insights of the customers' needs and how these are to be satisfied the organization needs to make this explicit by developing the prerequisites of the service. This requires the development of the service system development and the service process. The development system represents static resources required for the service. These consist of the service company's staff, the physical/technical environment, and the organization in terms of its structure and administrative support systems. The service process is the chain of activities which must occur for the service to function. Thus, the service concept requires considerable resources for transforming insight in ways that can be actualized in rationally explicit systems.

15.4.1. *The emergent customer experience*

The realized customer experience determines value added. This is because service development does not result in the production of the service itself, rather it produces what has been termed the service "prerequisites".[xxi] The actual service offer is only produced when the customer interacts with these prerequisites as illustrated in Figure 15.2.

According to phenomenological approaches to understanding the human condition, meaningfulness is an emergent property arising from a person's interactions with sensory inputs which may be from other people, data, or things. Customers usually react to sensory input emotionally and then rationally. The experiences of customers include intuitive prereflective meanings.

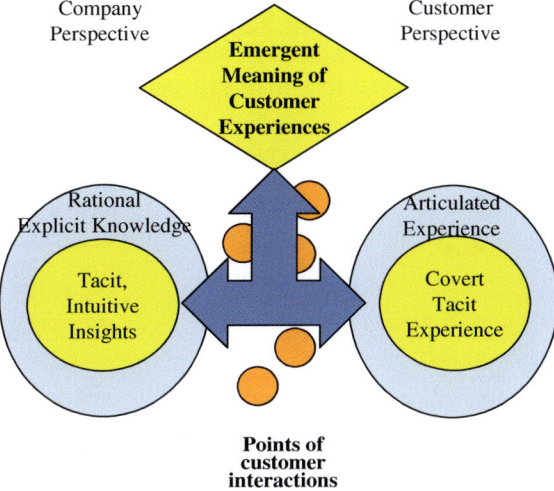

Figure 15.2.   Emergent Meaning of Customer Experiences

Customers construct a social reality from sensory touchpoints regardless of the arbitrary categorization of offerings as services and/or goods. The non-objective nature of experiences makes interpretations of customer needs necessarily conjectural.[xxii] This existential approach regards customer experiences as arising from inter-subjectivity.

The dynamic between external inputs and internal processing means that experiences of customers are altered by the flow of stimuli and are constantly renewed. This complex dynamic nudges the design of services to become an ongoing activity. The need for ad hoc adaptations and innovation in services is greater if tacit knowledge is intertwined in interpersonal interactions between provider and customer. Idiosyncrasies emerge from the dynamics of exchanges in which tacit knowledge is delivered. The value of many kinds of services is largely due to augmentation of offerings in ongoing ways that exploit tacit knowledge.

The service product does not completely represent the total offering that customers perceive when purchasing and consuming services. A customer-oriented model of a service should include not just what the customer receives but also how the customer perceives the quality of the interaction with the service provider.[xxiii] The customer's interactions are with the firm's physical resources and service systems, with employees, and possibly with other customers. The core service product is augmented by facilitating and supporting services that add value and enable the service to be delivered.[xxiv] Service augmentation is not an added extra but an integral part of the total offering. Unlike tangible products, where the physical product can be sold without any elements of augmentation, the service product cannot exist without service augmentation, in one form or another, as the service is not created until the customer interacts with the service organization, its systems, and/or staff.

15.4.2. *The networked experience*

The emergent customer experience is created, or rather co-created, each time the customer encounters a point of interaction. However, the interaction is not limited to the direct interaction of the customer with the providing firm. Interactions are exponentially increased by the network of customer communities on the customer side and the network of partners in the service delivery ecosystem on the company side as shown in Figure 15.3.

Touchpoints internal to customer organization may be quite numerous. The emergent property of customer experience (emotive and rational,

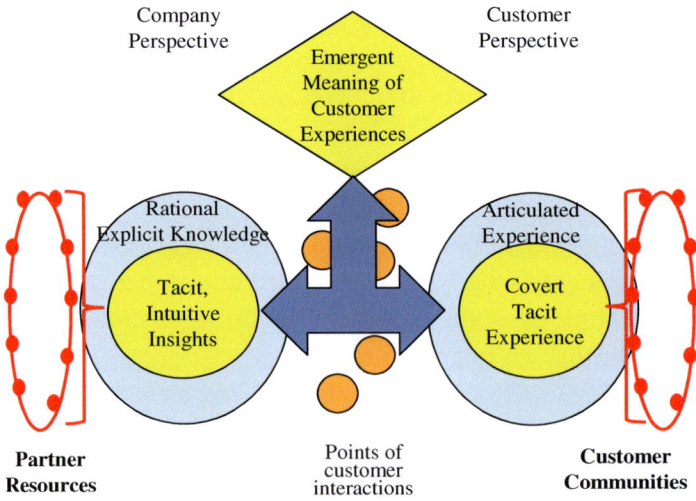

Figure 15.3.   The Networked Experience

pre- and post-reflective) indicates the fact that consumption occurs within a network of customer communities, e.g., friends, referent groups, fellow users, etc. as well as social media that influence the customer experience of value. For example, recommendations by friends or persuasive advertisements may nudge customers to choose offerings with suboptimal value for money spent according to so-called "objective" criteria.

Customers are not only individuals, but often organizational enterprises with many stakeholders who may experience services from providers from varying points of view, e.g., direct users, support staff, purchasing officers, quality managers, administrators, etc. Designers of service offering are more likely to please corporate customers if they understand the enterprise-wide needs the service may provide. For example, Access Technologies, a division of Stanley Works, grew rapidly to achieve multibillions in annual revenue because they designed a photoelectric door that pleased many stakeholders with ancillary service benefits, e.g., the reduction of lawsuits pleased the legal department maintenance liked lower cost of use, security staff used the videos to reduce theft, etc.

Service providers may also have various internal personnel as well as external partners that are integral for developing and delivering services. Many services offer multifaceted features and diverse experiences over time. Functions having touchpoints with customers have direct as well as indirect impacts on value as experienced by customers, e.g., sales, delivery, customer service, marketing, development staff conducting as well as

---

Transformational Workbook, Exercise D
Realizing NSD ventures

Formulating a compelling value proposition is a reiterative process. It helps to engage a diverse network in drafting value propositions until customer needs are better fulfilled compared with alternative offerings. Configuring an appropriate venture team is essential for capitalizing on the potential of a value proposition. Contributors may be external as well as internal to the enterprise. Capabilities for developing new offerings vary depending on the fit between the venture and the host enterprise. An open approach to sources of input helps in developing a holistic customer offering which may add extra value if services and goods are holistically integrated.

capital resources for a new offering is a challenging task. Too often ventures fail not so much because of lack of funding, rather from failure to configure human resources from internal and/or external sources.

Realizing a NSD venture requires formulating a winning value proposition and configuring a team with the right kinds of human capital to bring it to life. Exercise D provides some guidance for building a venture team to capitalize on new kinds of customer offerings that offer compelling value.

Providers of services, like their counterparts in goods, often outsource many intrinsic features of their service *per se* as well as aspects of delivery. For example, credit card companies often outsource customer service to calling centers. IT solutions may be externally sourced as well as developed. Companies may incent app providers to jump on their bandwagon as mobile phone companies do. Just as many large goods companies source as much as 80 percent or more of the components of their product from suppliers, so also do a growing number of service enterprises. These providers of the augmented service must be carefully managed so the various touchpoints are consistent from the customers point of view.

Strategic partnerships often provide ways existing enterprises as well as entrepreneurial start-ups can design valued offerings with less up-front investment and risk. The prospect of combining the resources of one enterprise with a network of others may enhance opportunities for designing disruptive offerings. As Christianson notes, most disruptive innovations consisted of "off-the-shelf components put together in a product architecture that was often simpler than prior approaches. They offered less of what customers in established markets wanted and so could rarely be initially employed there". Therefore, the avenue of strategic partnership among a network of enterprises may offer exciting prospects for configuring new offerings to fulfill unmet customer needs at relatively low cost and risk. However, building intercompany partnerships is froth with obstacles. Importantly, the more entrepreneurial firm in the partnership needs to retain the bulk of responsibility for decision-making, otherwise delays risk realization of the market opportunity.[xxv] To make partnerships between entrepreneurial and incumbent firms work, the entrepreneurial ones need to be relatively more structured and disciplined by processes than average. Correlatively, the incumbent firm needs to practice a higher degree of organic flexibility than typical for established bureaucracies.

15.4.3. *Managing customer experiences*

The growing awareness of the need to serve customers from the perspective of their experiences is reflected in the rise of executive positions responsible for them. Titles include Chief Customer Officer,

> Designs of new customer offerings are increasing eclectic architectures of disparate elements

Chief Client Officer, and recently Chief Experience Officer. Although only a small minority of enterprises have such formal titles, the growing number of such positions indicate recognition of the importance of dynamic customer relationships. However, the emergent nature of provider–customer relationships, especially in services based on tacit knowledge, risks allocating bureaucratic accountability to a single authority. Responsibility for achieving total customer value needs to be widely distributed and shared from the design concept to realization of the offering and its delivery.

The core competency of many service organizations in managing customer experiences can help bring new capabilities to value creation. One way is by building on Aristotle's insight that people derive more pleasure from the use of physical objects than their ownership. Already many enterprises provide physical goods through concierge services and leases. Yet many services result from ad hoc developments. A purposive cross-functional organization of value creation commonly deployed in goods industries has proved useful in many services especially those establishing central responsibility for NSD.

Configuring total customer experiences by integrating mixes of goods and services is a capability that can be further enhanced. Can enterprises consider ways physical accoutrements may enhance the value of their services up-front in their development? Many providers focus on developing their service and its delivery without parallel consideration of how goods may augment value. Yet many interpersonal services may be enriched by architectural surroundings, artistic images, mnemonics, computer information technologies, and all sorts of devices and equipment.

A cautionary note on attempting to design holistic offerings is that considerable analysis needs to be done up-front. A great variety of business planning methods and tools should be considered. One of the most reliable is QFD. This requires rating the attractiveness of your offering relative to competition and estimating the extent to which customers will be willing to pay for whatever differentiating features are offered. The notion behind QFD is fundamental and its logic compelling and applicable to the development of services as well as goods. However, to fully deploy QFD methods may be overly consuming time and resources. Nevertheless, the framework provides useful guidance for thinking about how to design holistic offerings optimizing customer value.

Notes

[i]   Kidder, T. 1981. *The Soul of a New Machine*, Random House: New York.

[ii]   Pinchot, G. 1985. *Intrapreneuring: Why You Don't" have to Leave the Corporation to Become an Entrepreneur*, Harper and Row: New York.

[iii] Sykes, H. B. 1986. Lessons from a new ventures program, *Harvard Business Review*, 64(3), 69–74.

[iv]   Hull, F. and Slowinski, E. 1990. Partnering with Technology Entrepreneurs, *Research-Technology Management*, 33(6), 16–21.

[v]   Hull, F., Storey, C., and Edvardsson, B. 2006. Involving Customers in New Service Development, In Edvardsson, B. *et al.* (Eds.), *Customer and Supplier Involvement in New Service Development*, Imperial College Press: London, pp. 281–312.

[vi]   Dyer, J. H. 1996. How Chrysler Created an American Keiretsu, *Harvard Business Review*, July–August, 50–56.

[vii] Hopkins, M. S. 2004. Scott Cook, Intuit, because he learns, and teaches, *Inc.*, April 1.

[viii] Brown, T. 2008. Design Thinking, *Harvard Business Review*, (June) 84–92; Kelley, T. and Kelley, D. 2012. *Creative Confidence: Unleashing the Creative Power within Us All*, Crown Business; Kelley, T. and Littman, J. 2001. *The Art of Innovation: Lessons in Creativity from IDEO, Americas Leading Design Firm*, Crown Business: New York.

[ix]   Hull, F., Collins, P., and Miller, J. 2007, 2008. Integrating the Voice of the Customer, *Concurrency*, 16(1), Fall/Winter, 5–26.

[x]   Kubinski, R. 2004. *Building a Breakthrough Business Through Significant New Business Growth and Profitability*, American Productivity & Quality Center: Houston.

[xi]   Von Hippel, E. 1986. Lead Users: A Source of Novel Product Concepts, *Management Science*, 32(7), 791–806; Von Hippel, E. 2005. *Democratizing Innovation*, MIT Press: Cambridge.

xii   Durward, K. S., Ward, A. C., and Liker, J. K. 1999. Toyota's Principles of Set-Based Concurrent Engineering, *Sloan Management Review*, 40, 2; Nakona, I. 1994. A Dynamic Theory of Organisational Knowledge Creation, *Organization Science*, 5(1), 14–37.

xiii   Coletta, A. R. 2012. *The Lean 3P Advantage: A Practitioner's Guide to the Production Preparation Process*, Productivity Press: New York.

xiv   Hummels, C. and Frens, J. 2011. Designing Disruptive Innovative Systems, Products and Services: RTD Process. In Coelho, D. (ed.). *Industrial Design-New Frontiers*. InTech: Rijeka, Croatia, pp. 145–172.

xv   Anthony, S. D. 2011. *The Little Black Book of Innovation: How It Works, How to Do It*, Harvard Business School Press: Boston, Massachusetts, USA: Osterwalder, A., Pigneur, Y., Bernarda, G., and Smith, A. 2014 *Value Proposition Design: How to Create Products and Services Customers Want*, Wiley; www.peterjthomson.com/2013/11/value-proposition-canvas.

xvi   Sanders, L. 2008. *An Evolving Map of Design Practice and Design Research*, hello@dubberly.com, November 1; Polaine, A., Reason, B., Lovlie, L. 2013. *Service Design: From Insight to Implementation*, Rosenfeld Media.

xvii   Morelli, N. 2002. Designing product/service systems. A methodological exploration. *Design Issues* 18(3), 3–17; Moritz, S. 2005. *Service Design: Practical Access to an Evolving Field*. London, Lulu.com; Stickdorn, M. and Schneider, J. 2010. *This is Service Design Thinking*. BIS Publishers: Amsterdam.

xviii   Hauser, J. R. and Clausing. D. P. 1988. The House of Quality. *Harvard Business Review*, 66(3), (May–June), 63–73.

xix   Lisi, Marco, European Space Agency, February, 2015; Salvendy, Gavriel and Karwowsk, Waldemar (Eds.), *Service Engineering*, Wiley, 2010.

xx   Brown, T. 2008. *Op. cit.*

xxi   Edvardsson, B. and Olson, J. 1996. Key Concepts in New Service Development, *Service Industries Journal*, 16, 140–164.

xxii   Bergman, P. L. and Luckmann, T. 1967. *Social Construction of Reality*, Anchor Books; Mathews, E., Merleau-Ponty. 2006. *A Guide for the Perplexed*, Bloomsbury Academic; Husserl, E. 1970. *The Crisis of the European Sciences and Transcendental Phenomenology*, Northwestern University Press: Evanston.

xxiii   Grönroos, C. 1990. *Service Management and Marketing: Managing the Moments of Truth in Service Competition*, Lexington Books: Lexington.

xxiv   Storey, C. and Easingwood, C. (1998), The Augmented Service Offering: A Conceptualisation and Study of its Impact on New Service Success, *Journal of Product Innovation Management*, 15(4), 335–351.

xxv   Hull, F. and Slowinski, E. (1990). *Op. cit.*

APPENDIX: METHODS OF
RESEARCH AND ANALYSIS

Overview

The principal focus of this book is on new service development (NSD). The goal was to test the extent to which a composite model of proven effectiveness for development in goods industries also applied to NSD. The approach began with qualitative studies of service enterprises to explore how concepts commonly used in studies of development in goods might be translated into the language of services. The bulk of literature on development is based on goods industries despite the fact that most people are employed in services.

1. Services Data

Qualitative methods

1. MBA students at Fordham University in mid-town Manhattan were principally employed in services although most of the course materials dealt with goods industries. The first task was to raise the level of abstraction so that generic terms could be used in courses such as the "strategic management of innovation and technology" to apply more or less equally to both sectors. The initial attempt to translate industrial speak into service speak began with monthly breakfast meetings with MBA students in courses on Strategic Management of Innovation and Technology. Students employed by leading corporations were asked to help translate industrial terminology into service-friendly terms.

Over the course of a dozen meetings, a more abstract vocabulary was devised for teaching how to develop valued offerings for service as well as goods customers.

2. A special topics course was offered on Strategic Business Process Improvement to Fordham MBA students. Students were charged with the responsibility for applying the principles and practices of TQM and concurrent engineering to improving the performance of a service enterprise of their choice. A concept inventory of sorts was provided by a draft of a questionnaire for services adapted from a prior one on goods with measures of concepts that correlated with performance. Students were challenged to help their service clients apply similar practices to improve the performance of their enterprise. Corporations or strategic business units participating in this project included:

- AIG
- American Express Global Process Group
- American Express Travel Services
- American Express Product Development
- Chase Consumer Banking
- Chase Private Banking
- Chase Private Banking
- Chase Syndicated Banking
- Chase Tax Services
- Deutsche Bank IT Services
- GE Capital
- Gemini Consulting
- Jewish Charities
- Mercedes Benz NA
- Milliken Customer Services
- Milliken Financial Services
- New York Times Advertising
- New York Times Custom Publishing
- Paine Webber
- TIAA-CREF
- Verizon Fiber Optic Services
- Verizon Vendor Management

Attempts by students to help host companies implement TQM and concurrency were well received. Gaps in practices were assessed and proposals for one or more major improvements were co-developed by the student and client firm. Over $200 million in potential cost benefits were identified that might be achieved by deploying recommended practices. Specific efforts to realize potential cost benefits were initiated in 14 of the enterprises. Follow-up assessments suggested that the actual amount of financial gain from changes implemented during the next 2 years credibly amounted to well over $60 million. These results tended to validate the notion that the concepts and practices commonly used in goods industries could also be applied to services if operationalized in more abstract, generic terms. Based in part on these results, an improved questionnaire for administration to service enterprises was drafted and administered.

3. A conference with over 100 participants was held at Fordham University to share results of statistical analysis of 70 service enterprises. During workshops, participants were invited to critique the results of the quantitative study paralleling research on goods industries and share information about their efforts to improve NSD.

4. Leading companies from within the sample of 70 enterprises were invited to participate in a user group meeting every 60 days to share best practice with one another. Case study information collected during visits hosted by each of participating companies included interviews, operating documents, and development practices codified by category of behavior.

- American Express
- Bank of New York
- Bankers Trust, Chase
- Chase Bank

- Chubb Insurance
- Citibank
- Morgan Stanley
- Merrill Lynch

5. A conference/workshop on actions for business improvement was held to follow up on how well companies in the user group and others were progressing in applying best practices for NSD.

6. A special topics MBA course in NSD was co-taught with, Beth Hirschhorn, a VP of Chase bank with the requirement that students conduct case studies of their own enterprise. Nine case studies provided further evidence of the applicability of the composite model based on the TQM and the principles of concurrences to services.

7. A booklet integrating quantitative results from the New York study was bound and distributed to user group members and study participants at a final conference to share the results of research applying TQM and the principle of concurrency to services. Follow-on research has continued with selected enterprises from this conference.

Qualitative methods

A service sector questionnaire of service development was adapted from measures used in earlier goods studies. The final measures were drawn from research literature on services and suggestions from leading companies participating in a New York-based NSD user group, students from MBA sources, and conference participants. Measures of practices commonly used in goods industries were recast to better accommodate the diversity of services under study. New measures focusing on the organization of the service function and service delivery were added.

The survey of hypothesized best practices was administered to a top manager in 70 strategic service business units in the greater New York area followed by a subsequent survey in the London area.[1] The categories of enterprises in the US sample in the greater New York area are listed as follows:

Quantitative Service Study: Types of Companies in the US Sample

Category		Number
Banking/Financial services		18
Retail	5	
Credit Card	3	
Lending	2	
Investment Services	2	
Private Banking	1	
Investment Services	5	
Construction		1
Consulting Services		4
Distribution/logistics (*)		6
Education/training		1

(*Continued*)

---

[1] Tidd, J. and Hull, F. (Eds.), 2003. *Service Innovation: Organizational Responses to Technological Opportunities & Market Imperatives*, Imperial College Press: London.

(*Continued*)		
Healthcare		8
Diagnostic services	4	
Hospital	2	
Pharmaceutical services	2	
Insurance		8
Manufacturing related services (**)		4
Non-profit		3
Publishing		2
Retail		3
Travel/Hotel		2
Telecommunications		5
Transportation		5
Total		**70**

* Utilities, Engineering, Distribution of Product, etc.
** Credit, Risk, etc.

Quantitative study measures

- **Performance** was measured not only for differentiation, but also delivery service performance measures are provided in Table 5.3.
- Measures of the troika of concepts of the composite model are provided in chapters on each:
  - **Organization**: Early simultaneous influence (ESI) is measured in the services data as an index of four functions engaged at the concept phase: marketing, process development, finance, and customer service (Chapter Five). Measures of Organic Team Structure are shown in Table 7.1.
  - **Process** measures are shown in Table 8.1.
  - **Tools and technology** measures are shown in Table 9.1.
- **Strategy** measures pertinent to innovative goals are shown in Table 13.1.
- **Knowledge** types exploited for adding value for which customers were willing to pay measured by questions shown in Table 11.1.

- **Championing** transformation is measured by two questions: "strengthen the role of project managers" and "flattening the hierarchy in the organization chart" (alpha = 0.77). The correlations of the championing role with other key measures is shown in Figure 14.1. Championing is also correlated with "training in process improvement" ($r = 0.61$**).
- **Environmental Dynamism** is measured by adding six items: (1) technological complexity, (2) rate of new product introduction in the industry, (3) compatibility (interoperability) of your product with others, (4) customization, (5) globalization, and (6) quality. The index combines standardized scores for change regardless of direction with change toward greater competitiveness.

2. Goods Data

Quantitative methods

A quantitative assessment of 100 goods companies was sponsored by the US Defense Advanced Research Projects Agency. The goal was to identify best practices based on the principles of TQM and Concurrent Engineering predictive of product development that met performance criteria such as time compression, cost reduction, quality, and innovation. Almost all were components of Fortune 500 corporations with approximately 2/3rds engaged principally in the commercial sector. Diverse sectors were represented. Examples of companies from selected sectors are listed as follows:

Automotive	Ford, General Motors
Aerospace	Boeing, Grumman, Northrop, Bell Helicopter
Computers	Digital Equipment Corporation
Consumer products	3M
Electronics	Motorola
Equipment	Black & Decker, Ingersoll-Rand, Westinghouse
Photography	Polaroid
Telecommunications	AT&T

The mix of corporations was mostly commercial, but included significant representations of defense contractors, so that lessons learned could be transferred between civil and military sectors. The results of the study demonstrated most predictors of performance robustly applied to both civilian and defense product development. In combination with many studies showing that the principles and practices of TQM and concurrency were associated with success, the Department of Defense codified best practices in manuals for Integrated Product & Process Development (IPPD).

Additional case study information was gained from survey respondents and participants in user-group workshops. Dozens of leading companies from goods industries were selected to share best product development practices for two decades from 1993. During visits to host companies, case study information was collected and codified.

Quantitative Study Measures in Goods Industries

Measures of Performance
Time & Cost Performance
Σ (Time, Cost)*−1
Time = standardized score of reduction in months tooling time in last 5 years; and
Cost = standardized score of average reduction in labor, material, and machinery

Measures of the Composite Model
Organization: ESI
Σ {Standard score extent of ME participation in design teams at each of eight project stages, arithmetically weighted (research * 8 + development of product concept * 7 + pre-prototype design * 6 + prototype construction & test * 5 + final product design * 4 + tooling & facilities * 3 + ramp-up * 2 + full-scale production * 1) + (level of influence in above eight stages, arithmetically weighted) + (increased influenced of manufacturing in releasing product designs in last five years)}

In-process Design Controls (IDC): To what extent have you engaged in the following activities during the past 5 years in the development of new products? • Use of design documentation • Increased use of design standards • Increased use of product design reviews in the last 5 years • Level of manufacturing participation in design reviews in eight stages of product development process	

Computer Information Technology (CIT): To what extent have you emphasized the following kinds of activities during the past 5 years? (alpha = 0.82) • Increased use of electronic databases • Increased use of Computer Automated Design (CAD) • Increased use of Computer Automated Manufacturing (CAM) • Automaticity of manufacturing capability, i.e., extent of computer controls • Increased use of electronic databases • Increased coupling of CAD/CAM	

Measures of Organic Team Structure (OTS)	
To what extent have you emphasized the following kinds of activities during the past 5 years?	
Cross-functional Teaming	• Increased use of cross-functional teams in last 5 years. • Extent Manufacturing Engineering assigned to cross-functional product design team on full-time basis
Collocation	• Extent to which the use of collocation has increased in last 5 years • Design and Manufacturing Engineering collocated at the same physical site
Group rewards	• Extent to which groups vs. individuals rewarded for new designs, and design implementation
Training	• Change in level of promotion of CE practices • Change in CE education and training

(Continued)

(Continued)

Championing	• Strengthening the role of project managers • Reducing levels in the hierarchy
Measures of Strategy	
Innovation Strategy: Percentage of design changes in product X in last year that were new designs.	

Methods of statistical analysis

Pearson correlation coefficients designated by "*r*" range from 0.0 to 1.0. The closer to 1.0, the stronger the co-variation. However, association does not mean causation. However, one may speculate that practices are causal drivers of performance if there is a conceptual framework that makes associations between actionable practices and performance seem plausible based on experiences. This is why case illustrations coupled with probabilistic associations are mutually reinforcing.

Levels of statistical significance show the likelihood that associations are due to chance alone. Correlations range from 0.0 to 1.0 and indicate the strength of association between two measures such as practice as a performance outcome as a hypothetical consequence. Unless otherwise noted, all correlations shown in the services data are statistically significant at least at the 0.05 level of confidence, i.e., coefficients of 0.32 or higher. This means that the probability of a happenstance relationship is less than 1 in 20 as illustrated in Table 5.1.

Many relationships between hypothetical causes and effects are moderated by interrelationships with a third variable as shown in Table 5.2. Moderated regression analyses is important for testing the effectiveness of the composite model because it is based on synergies amongst a troika of key sets of practice. For example, the impact of ESI by multiple functions on performance is greater if processes are dynamic rather than inflexible procedures. This synergy between cross-functional organization and process is the axis of the composite model which boosts capabilities for cost-effective innovation, e.g., 1+1 = more than 2. Another important moderator is the adoption of a strategy targeting the development of radically new products. Given the contingency of radically new development, collaboration among diverse functions has a greater impact on performance.

The strength of associations in multiple regression analyses is indicated by "betas," the significance of which is indicated by asterisks.

Qualitative methods

The text offers case examples of goods industries to parallel those in services. Similarities are consistent with the notion that the composite system of development is robustly capable of transforming inputs into outputs regardless of sector. Most case studies of goods corporations were participants in user groups formed to share best practices with one another in hosted visits of product development operations at their headquarters location. The initial dozen companies were selected from top performers in the sample of 100 US companies. Each of those listed below contributed to the definition of the composite model and provided over 200 pages of documented best practices.

- 3M
- AT&T
- Black & Decker
- Eaton
- Ford
- GE Aerospace
- Lockheed-Martin/Unisys
- Motorola
- Sun Microsystems
- US Army Research
- Westinghouse
- Xerox

Over 50 additional strategic business units from more than 30 corporations participated in following-on user groups. Some of the cases providing information relevant for illustrating the composite model included:

- Agilent Technologies
- Applied Materials
- Chrysler
- Colgate

- General Dynamics
- Genie Industries
- Hewlett-Packard
- Honeywell
- IDEO
- Ingersoll-Rand
- Intuit
- Lucent Wireless
- Rolls-Royce Aerospace
- Siemens
- Solectron
- Stanley Works
- Steelcase
- Tecumseh
- TRW Avionics
- Unisys
- Varian Semiconductor
- Whirlpool

The follow-on quantitative study of goods industries used in the Transformation Workbook, Exercise A, was based on the analysis of over 100 strategic business units such as those listed above.

TRANSFORMATIONAL
WORKBOOKS

Overview

These workbooks provide the readers with guidance for envisioning a new service development (NSD) venture and delivering on its value proposition. Exercises start with benchmarking and envisioning development systems with greater capabilities for TVD. Readers may engage in thought experiments about championing enterprise transformation and designing new kinds of offerings to exploit the capabilities of the composite model. Developing and delivering a new offering is extraordinarily complex. The great majority of efforts fail. The food for analysis is these exercises is the meat sandwiched in the gap between your top slice of bread, the vision of your "should be" development system capability, and the bottom slice, your "as is" capabilities. The condiments enhancing your new offering are external resources needed to transform your concept into reality.

Contents

A. Benchmarking "As Is" Development Systems vs. Best-in-Class

This exercise enables readers to benchmark an enterprise against best-in-class scores in the services dataset and/or strategic business units in a goods study that expanded upon the industrial study used herein. A total of 10 images of concurrent systems in action that apply to development systems in services and goods is provided in Chapter Three. Wording is extracted from the surveys that correspond approximately to the contrasting practices depicted in the images. Worksheets enable readers to baseline the "as is" capabilities of extant enterprises. Then readers are asked to rate a "should be" development system using the same 10 images. Understanding gaps in best practices provide a starting point for championing future improvements.

B. Envisioning a "Should Be" Development System

The gap analysis from the previous exercise provides a springboard for the process of leading the co-creation of a vision of a "should be" system state that has greater capabilities for development than the "as is" state. Characteristics of a good vision statement are provided. Guidelines help champions lead the co-creation of a shared vision as a starting point for transformation of the development capabilities of the enterprise.

C. Closing Gaps between "As Is" and "Should Be" Development Systems

The gaps identified using the 10 images exercise is designed to stimulate thinking about "should be" vision that engages the hearts and minds of stakeholders in the development system of the enterprise. Stakeholders are encouraged to brainstorm characteristics desired in their "should be" system as well as analyze root causes of problems in their "as is" system. Methods for prioritizing gaps for closure are provided including feasibility of closure actions, benefit/cost ratios, immediacy of impact, and the identification of leading indicators that others in the enterprise might champion and/or neutralize blockers.

D. Realizing NSD Ventures

Good ideas abound, but translating them into customer offerings in the marketplace is often quite challenging. Readers are invited to design a new service offering with a compelling value proposition. Characteristics of good value propositions are outlined. Mechanistic bureaucracy is the default context for most development systems, which often inhibits receptivity to new designs. Very often

(Continued)

(*Continued*)

the transformation from mechanistic bureaucracies to concurrent development systems with composite capabilities is initiated by a new venture that can only be realized by a heavyweight team or intrapreneurial venture. In some instances the new venture may lie outside of the core capabilities of the enterprise, which increases its resistance to innovative alternatives. In such cases an external venture may be needed with or without ties to the original enterprise. Many new designs are demanding of human capital. Configuring a cross-functional team for a new venture is quite challenging because of scare resources. This means that how functional specialists are recruited and deployed is particularly important. Ten generic functions are profiled in Chapter Twelve to provide indicators in the service sample of the extent to which it may provide competitive advantage based on correlations with performance and the extra needs under contingencies such as the extent to which the strategy is novel and/or tacit knowledge is exploited. Readers are encouraged to add specificity to these generic descriptions appropriate for their proposed venture. A chart is provided to help configure the team pre- and post-launch, which notes that many kinds of specialized knowledge may be externally sourced. The final chart enables the readers to envision the co-creation of holistic offerings integrating the development of goods and services from the outset if relevant to their value proposition.

WORKBOOK A:
Benchmarking "As Is" Development Systems vs. Best-in-Class

1. Benchmarking Qualitatively with Images

Ten images of concurrent vs. non-concurrent development systems are depicted and described in Chapter Three. A cursory benchmarking approach is to decide whether an enterprise operates relatively more like a concurrent or a non-concurrent system for 10 images. Simply refer back to the images and their accompanying descriptions to check the most appropriate category.

Are the practices in development system X concurrent?

3.1 Involve multiple functions throughout	Y	N
3.2 Balance portfolio of advantages	Y	N
3.3 Focus on customer needs	Y	N
3.4 Map processes and continuously improve	Y	N
3.5 Open communication channels	Y	N
3.6 Decide early, with reiterative feedback	Y	N
3.7 Hire and develop ambidextrous capabilities	Y	N
3.8 Pull rather than push designs to the customer	Y	N
3.9 Acquire external and internal knowledge base	Y	N
3.10 Build flexible, reciprocal adjustments in processes	Y	N

Each of the 10 images is supported by survey questions pertinent to the concept depicted. The questions attempt to measure if the facets of system concepts are the same or relatively similar in the services dataset and are a recent follow-on study of goods industries. The principles of concurrency are robust and may be used to guide the design of systems for the development of services and/or goods.

Measures used in the services and goods research surveys are correlated with performance as shown in Figure 3.11 for services. Correlations are described from the goods study. The higher the percentage of time samples of respondents reported observing behaviors related to the 10 images, the higher their performance score was likely to be.

Emulating the behaviors suggested in the images may or may not help an enterprise achieve higher levels of performance because association is not causation. Therefore, benchmarking is an exercise requiring analytical and insightful thinking. One needs to think of a plausible explanation as to why a given practice might lead to higher levels of development performance. To the extent readers are able to link practices implied in the images with efficacious actions, emulating the operations implied in the images might have a causal link with performance and would be worth considering for deployment.

Readers may benchmark an enterprise of their choice vs. top scores in either the service dataset analyzed in this book and/or a data from a follow-on goods study. The questions extracted from each of the surveys to indicate the 10 images are similar, but not always exactly the same. However, the overlap should be sufficient for gauging how measures of concurrent vs. non-concurrent practices may be linked with development performance in both sectors.

A Note on Comparing Services and Goods

Service enterprise X participated in surveys of both sectors. Enterprise X ranks at the 94th percentile in the services data, but only on the 71st percentile in the goods database. Service enterprise X is a globally renowned corporation. Enterprise X was among the first in the service sample to appoint a vice president of product development and assemble a group of over 50 stakeholders from diverse disciplines to systematically design and deliver new offerings. The pioneering initiatives taken by Enterprise X are chronicled in some of the case examples in this book. Although their efforts to establish a formal NSD function took some trial and error, they ultimately succeeded brilliantly. However, most of the other enterprises in the services data did not take the crucial step of establishing a formal NSD group. Comparisons of these and other data suggest that the formation of an explicit development function is a practice that is more widely and proficiently deployed in goods than services.

2. Benchmarking Quantitatively with Survey Questions

Benchmarking Service Enterprises

The following ten questions are extracted from the survey of 70 service enterprises analyzed herein. Each question was selected to correspond as closely as possible to the 10 images 3.1–3.10 shown in Chapter Three, as depicting facets of a concurrent development system in operation. Using observations of your own enterprise, or another one with which you are familiar, rate the frequency that the 10 behaviors occur in actual practice in the Service Questionnaire.

Table A.1. Rate the "As Is" State for 10 Practices, Then Divide by 10 and Insert on Bar Graph				
Facets of concurrent systems in Services *To what extent does your enterprise systematically observe the following practices, 0 to 100% of the time?*	Not At All	Just a Little	Somewhat	A Great Deal
3.1 Increasing the influence of downstream functions in upstream decisions, e.g., customer service input in product development	1	2	3	4
3.2 Balance portfolio of competitive advantages for which customers are willing to pay such as low cost and novelty	1	2	3	4
3.3 Align competing product requirements by focusing on the Voice of Customer (VoC)	1	2	3	4
3.4 Transfer lessons learned from previous activities to succeeding project so that they build upon an existing base to reach ever higher future targets	1	2	3	4
3.5 Open communication channels to all functions and ranks in the organization	1	2	3	4
3.6 Review projects early and often to ensure conformance with plan	1	2	3	4
3.7 Cultivate staff to provide holistic, system-wide thinking as well as specialized knowledge for multi-tasking	1	2	3	4
3.8 Involve customers early in the service product development process, pulling the product design in the direction of customer needs	1	2	3	4
3.9 View knowledge as a paramount competitive advantage to be gained from outside as well as inside the company	1	2	3	4
3.10 Act as a good partner with others, such as internal customers, suppliers, external service providers, alliance partners and customers, in creating and maintaining mutual win/win scenarios	1	2	3	4

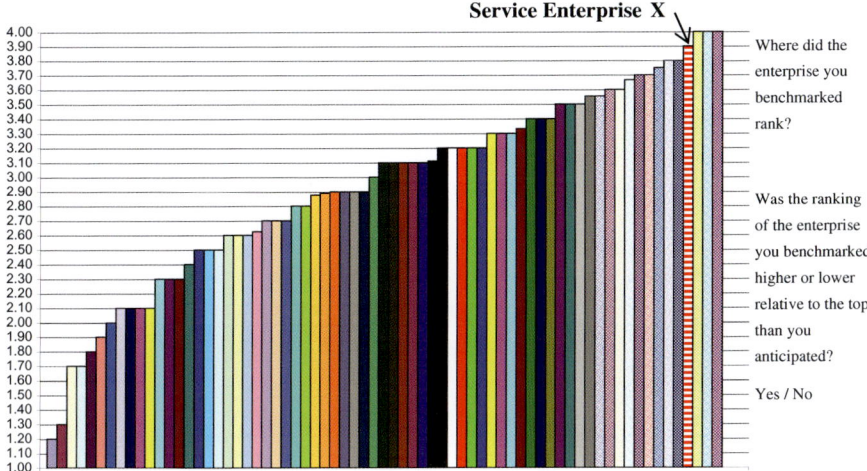

Figure A.1.   Service Enterprise Bar Chart: Ratings of 10 Practices Observed in Service Enterprises (1 = low/4 = high)

Table A.2.   Rate the "Should Be" State for 10 Practices in Services, Then Subtract Your "As Is" Score

To what extent does your enterprise systematically observe the following practices?	Should Be, 1–4	As Is, 1–4	Gap, 0–3
3.1 Increasing the influence of downstream functions in upstream decisions, e.g., customer service input in product development			
3.2 Balance portfolio of competitive advantages for which customers are willing to pay (cost-novelty)			
3.3 Align competing product requirements by focusing on the VoC			
3.4 Transfer lessons learned from previous activities to succeeding people so that they build upon an existing base to reach ever higher future targets			
3.5 Open communication channels to all functions and ranks in the organization			
3.6 Review projects frequently to ensure conformance with plan			
3.7 Cultivate staff to provide holistic, system-wide thinking as well as specialized knowledge			
3.8 Involve customers early in the service product development process, pulling the product design in the direction of customer needs			
3.9 View knowledge as a paramount competitive advantage to be gained from outside as well as inside the company			
3.10 Act as a good partner with others, such as internal customers, suppliers, external service providers, alliance partners and customers, in creating and maintaining mutual win/win scenarios			

Gaps of Concern

What were the three largest gaps you think the enterprise should consider closing vs. the best?

Circle your most urgent three below.

A	B	C	D	E	F	G	H	I	J

Describe the gaps in terms appropriate for the benchmarked enterprise.

Gap 1 _____

Gap 2 _____

Gap 3 _____

How do these gaps affect performance?

Gap 1 _____

Gap 2 _____

Gap 3 _____

Benchmarking Goods Industries

The following ten questions are extracted from the survey of 91 strategic business units in goods industries. The ratings are behaviorally anchored based on the percentage of time the practices were actually observed. Each question was selected to correspond as closely as possible to the 10 images 3.1–3.10 shown in Chapter Three as depicting facets of a concurrent development system in operation. Using observations of your own enterprise, or another one with which you are familiar, rate the frequency that the 10 behaviors occur in actual practice in the follow-on study of goods firms.

Table A.3. Rate Your "As Is" Development System 1–5, Add and Divide by 10, then Multiply by 20 and Plot on the X-axis of the Goods Chart					
Images of concurrent systems in Goods *How frequently do the following behaviors occur?*	Rarely (0–19%)	(20–39%)	Half the Time	(60–79%)	Nearly Always
3.1 Downstream functions such as manufacturing or customer service are involved in early product development decisions	1	2	3	4	5
3.2 NPD projects focus on achieving a balanced portfolio of competitive advantages, e.g., time and cost as well as novelty	1	2	3	4	5
3.3 Customer needs provide the major focus for our product development projects	1	2	3	4	5
3.4 Once targets have been reached, lessons learned are used to help us reach even higher targets	1	2	3	4	5
3.5 Communication channels are open to all regardless of function or level in the organization	1	2	3	4	5
3.6 Multiple internal functions participate in product development reviews	1	2	3	4	5
3.7 Generalists as well as specialists are cultivated to provide holistic, system-wide thinking about product development practices beyond their own discipline	1	2	3	4	5
3.8 The "Voice of the Customer" drives the unification of disparate functions and levels within the organization	1	2	3	4	5
3.9 Knowledge is viewed as a paramount competitive advantage and is sought from outside sources as well as cultivated in house	1	2	3	4	5
3.10 People try to anticipate the needs of their internal customers and rapidly adjust their behavior to fulfill the requirements of others in the value stream	1	2	3	4	5

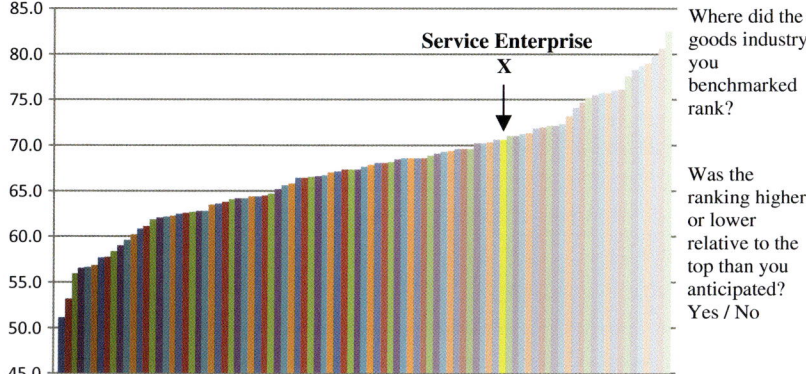

Figure A.2.   Goods Industries Bar Chart Percentage of Time 10 Practices Behaviorally Observed in Goods Study

Table A.4.   Rate the "Should Be" State for 10 Practices in a Goods Industry, then Subtract Your "As Is" Score

How frequently do the following behaviors occur?	Should Be, 1–5	As is, 1–5	Gap, 0–4
3.1 Downstream functions such as manufacturing or customer services are involved in early product development decisions			
3.2 Product development projects focus on achieving a balanced portfolio of competitive advantages, e.g., time and cost as well as novelty			
3.3 Customer needs provide the major focus for our product development projects			
3.4 Once targets have been reached, lessons learned are used to help us reach even higher targets			
3.5 Communication channels are open to all regardless of function or level in the organization.			
3.6 Multiple internal functions participate in product development reviews			
3.7 Generalists as well as specialists are cultivated to provide holistic, system-wide thinking about product development practices beyond their own discipline			
3.8 The "Voice of the Customer" drives the unification of disparate functions and levels within the organization			
3.9 Knowledge is viewed as a paramount competitive advantage and is sought from outside sources as well as cultivated in house			
3.10 People try to anticipate the needs of their internal customers and rapidly adjust their behavior to fulfill the requirements of others in the value stream			

Gaps of Concern

What were the three largest gaps you think the enterprise should consider closing vs. the best?

Circle *your most urgent three below.*

A	B	C	D	E	F	G	H	I	J

Describe the gaps in terms appropriate for the benchmarked enterprise.

Gap 1 _____

Gap 2 _____

Gap 3 _____

How do these gaps affect performance?

Gap 1 _____

Gap 2 _____

Gap 3 _____

WORKBOOK B:
Envisioning a "Should Be" Development System

The 10 images shown in Chapter Three depict facets of best practices for high-performance systems. Benchmarking other enterprises in services and/or goods should stimulate thinking about features of your "should be" development system. This exercise builds on back and forth comparisons of our "as is" system state vs. what it could be, to help visualize a better future alternative.

A champion of transformation needs to co-create a vision of a future system state and influence stakeholders to help bring it to fruition. This exercise profiles characteristics of good visions and prompts readers to generate a hypothetical version of one. Co-creating a vision of an improved system state with other stakeholders motivates everyone to share the journey toward a better future.

What is a Transformational Vision?

A vision is the *image* we hold in our heads and hearts of our *desired future*. It is our *big picture aspirations* of the *future* of our business or organization. Most corporate visions are general statements. However, the Stanley Works devised a vision specifically for inspiring and guiding improvements in their product development system:

> *Continually deliver incremental, profitable growth, ever faster and at lower cost, through innovative products that raise customer expectations and industry standards.*

A strategic vision formulated by Starbucks for the corporation also focuses on the nature of the customer offering. The vision implicitly deals with the development and delivery of their service offerings:

> *To become the premier purveyor of the finest coffee in the world while maintaining our uncompromising principles while we grow.*

A good vision needs to be anchored in values commonly held by stakeholders. Visions tap into our sense of purpose beyond just making money. They have unique powers to inspire and motivate and breed commitments. Key characteristics of good visions are aptly described by Senge.[1]

- Visions that are shared change a company by changing us individually.
- Shared visions emerge from personal visions; the only vision that motivates you is your vision.
- At its simplest level, a shared vision is the answer to the question, 'What do WE want to create?'
- A vision is truly shared when you and I have a similar picture and are collaboratively committed to its realization.
- Champions need to help guide behavior as people move toward their vision of how to realize a purpose that is commonly valued.

1. Formulating a Transformational Vision Statement

Exercise in Writing a Vision Statement, Draft #1
Write a vision statement for approval by top management Your 1–3 sentence statement should profile advantages that may accrue from a more capable development system for creating and delivering value to customers. ***Insert your vision statement below***

Question: How well does your statement meet the 10 criteria listed below? Circle those that your statement covers explicitly or implicitly. Are any vital elements omitted? It is difficult to touch all bases as a vision statement needs to be relatively cogent and pithy. If necessary, redraft your vision statement until you have.

A Good Transformational Vision

1. Identifies direction and purpose.
2. Builds loyalty through involvement.
3. Sets standards of excellence that reflect high ideals and a sense of integrity.

---

[1] Senge, P. 1990. *The Fifth Discipline*: *The Art & Practice of The Learning Organization*. Deckle Edge.

4. Is persuasive and credible.
5. Inspires enthusiasm and encourages commitment.
6. Is well articulated and easily understood.
7. Is ambitious and calls for a shared commitment.
8. Challenges and inspires people to align their energies in a common direction.
9. Fits with the business' unique culture and values by building upon the company's unique strengths.
10. Results in performance advantages such as cost-efficiencies and innovation.

Writing a Transformational Vision Statement, Draft #2

Rewrite your vision statement for approval by top management
Your statement should resemble a so called "elevator pitch", an opportunity of a couple of minutes to persuade someone to embrace a vision. Practice saying it to yourself in a mirror and/or close colleagues until you are able to articulate it persuasively and convincingly.
Insert your 2nd draft of your vision statement below

---

2. Communicating your Vision Statement and Beginning the Co-creation Process

Realizing a vision requires support from top management. Sometimes the vision starts from the top and needs buy-in from subordinates. Without the opportunity for authentic input, subordinates will perceive the vision as imposed which makes its realization problematic. Ideally, top management engages champions to lead a collaborative process in building a shared vision, e.g.: "Let's create the future we individually and collectively want".

Exercise in the Process of Co-creating a Collaborative Vision

Further rewrite your vision statement in five sentences after collaborating with three or more colleagues at least one of whom is a ranking manager
Be sure to include corporate values and features that will be appreciated by a broad swath of potential stakeholders in the proposed transformation.
Insert your co-created vision below

WORKBOOK C:
Closing Gaps between "As Is" and "Should Be" Development Systems

Champions usually need to start the transformation journey by fixing problems with existing development systems. Almost all stakeholders in development encounter frustrating barriers and roadblock in using the extant system effectively. A good first step toward transformation is to eliminate "pebble in the shoe" kinds of problems. Starting on small, relatively easy to fix issues, however, should be used as a springboard for kindling aspirations for further and more expansive improvements. People need to believe change is possible as well as wish for it.

1. Brainstorming Features of Your "Should Be" Development System

Provide a group of stakeholders with a vision statement of future development system capabilities (Excerpt from Workbook B).

Brainstorming your "Should Be" Development System
1. Ask participants to brainstorm the positive features they feel are explicitly or implicitly included in this statement by writing their top three on post-it notes.
2. Affinitize the post-it notes (a good way is to have people circle a white board or table until there is a consensus about categories).
3. Ask each person to write one feature they would like to see included that is missing or inadequately stated.
4. Affinitize missing features by adding categories as necessary.
5. Redraft a vision statement with two levels of detail.
• 1–5 sentence overview that may be persuasively stated.
• A brief paragraph profiling each key feature of the "should be" system.

Select one or more strategic capabilities that key stakeholders would like to see in a future system more capable of delivering. Commonly chosen categories include:

- Meeting customer requirements
- Faster development cycles
- Lower cost
- Reduction of late-phase quality issues
- Innovation
- You name it: _____

2. Identifying and Prioritizing Problems with Your "As Is" System

Select a performance capability your "As Is" development system fails to deliver as needed. Your selection may be influenced by comments made during the prior discussions of capability issues. Select problems to address based on criteria such as:

- Root cause?
- Would solving the problem kill more than one bird with a single stone?
- Is the problem an issue that will require systematic transformation to solve?

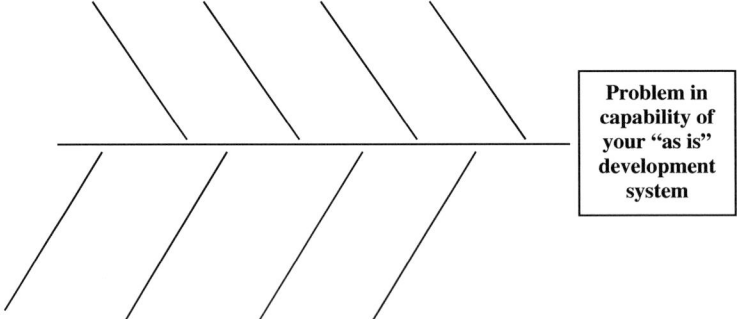

Problem in capability of your "as is" development system

Figure C.1. Fishbone Diagram for Brainstorming Problems with Your "As Is" Development System

Brainstorming Problems with your "As Is" Development System
1. Place a commonly agreed upon problem your "As Is" system has in delivering desired performance outcomes at the head of a fishbone diagram (see Figure C.1).
2. Ask participants to brainstorm causes impeding the effectiveness of the development system (*Brainstorming norm: no criticism, just encourage the free flow of ideas without questioning or negativity. Focus on behavioral actions that are problematic while avoiding personalities*).
3. Affinitize the post-it notes (a good way is to have people circle a white board or table until there is a consensus about categories).
4. Ask members of the group to select their top three negative features and place results of voting in a rank order.
5. Redraft problem statements as positive actions that need to be taken to improve.

Causes of problems in system capability need to be categorized. Some of the gaps in practices surfaced during benchmarking exercises with the 10 images of development systems may be used. The practices measured representing these images are positively correlated with development performance outcomes such as requirements, time, cost, quality, innovation, etc. A more generic approach commonly used for grouping causes of performance issues in manufacturing use four categories beginning with the letter M: Manpower, Methods, Machines, and Materials. These categories may be adapted to capture upstream development issues.

Prioritize positive actions for improving your "as is" development system in the following table. Rate them in terms of three criteria:

1. Trackable, i.e., it is a line in the sand you will be able to use as a baseline for measuring progress that will be acceptable to the bulk of stakeholders.
2. Doable, i.e., the action is something that can be undertaken without either a huge investment of time and money or without a major shift in thinking by top management.
3. Effective, i.e., stakeholders believe that benefits will accrue from deploying practices associated with performance.

Prioritization of Actions to Close Gaps			
Redrafted Action Statements (Top 5)	Trackable	Doable	Effective
A.	Yes No	Yes No	Yes No
B.	Yes No	Yes No	Yes No
C.	Yes No	Yes No	Yes No
D.	Yes No	Yes No	Yes No
E.	Yes No	Yes No	Yes No

3. Benefit/Cost Ratings

Some worthwhile actions have higher benefit/cost ratios than others. While this calculation can become very complicated, the collective wisdom of stakeholder usually suffices for making an approximate ranking. For the top five improvement actions under consideration, estimate benefits/costs on a 1–5 scale.

Benefit/Cost Rating

A. Action: _____ Benefit _____ - Cost _____ = _____

B. Action: _____ Benefit _____ - Cost _____ = _____

C. Action: _____ Benefit _____ - Cost _____ = _____

D. Action: _____ Benefit _____ - Cost _____ = _____

E. Action: _____ Benefit _____ - Cost _____ = _____

- BENEFIT such as faster time, lower costs, higher quality, more radical innovation, etc. 1–5 (high).
- COST such as resources required, e.g., people, money, etc. 1–5 (high).

4. Solution Circle

Champions need to focus on quick wins at the outset of the development journey. The ultimate goal is transformative actions with high benefit/cost ratios. But in the action queue, benefits from quick fixes needs to take an early priority as suggested in Figure C.2.

Order positive actions by placing them in a "solutions circle".

1. The first circle = solutions with the most immediate benefits.
2. Second circle = solutions with more intermediate term benefits.
3. Third circle = large contextual solutions with longer term benefits.

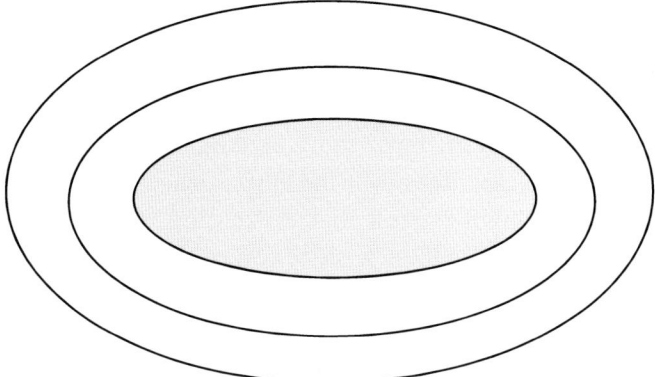

Figure C.2.   Improvement Circle Prioritization

5. Enablers and Blockers and the Need for Champions for Moving Leading Indicators

Leading metrics as a critical component of a dynamic vision

The vision statement needs to be continually co-created as your transformation journey gathers the resources to begin. Along the way, the vision should be subjected to revisions as unanticipated barriers are likely to be encountered as well as emergent opportunities.

The benefits from undertaking the transformation journey need to be continually defined and restated in operational terms. Most changes take persistent effort over extended periods of time. Therefore, it is prudent to identify "leading indicators" that are like blazes on a trail for tracking progress. An example of a leading indicator is the percentage of key functions actively participating in development meetings. In goods companies projects where any of 4–5 key functions are absent often predicts subsequent problems. Another leading indicator is the one question survey administered at the end of a team event, "my voice was heard at this meeting." Almost all should answer "Yes", and any "No" should be a concern. It is important to have the right people at the meeting and ensure they are appropriately engaged. Whatever leading metrics are used, they should be easily understood, transparent, and visually shared.

Champions to enable backers and neutralize blockers

For all proposed actions, identify one or more executives of rank who may serve as enablers of implementation. Draft a similar list of people who are potential blockers. Favor strongly those actions lacking a blocker and/or other barriers to implementation. Techniques such as "force-field analysis" pioneered by Kurt Lewin suggest that restraining forces are three times more powerful as obstacles than positive forces. Some blocking forces are technical, but most are associate directly or indirectly with stakeholders in your enterprise.

Shown in the following table is a chart that illustrates elementary considerations for ensuring progress in implementing the transformation from mechanistic bureaucratic forms of development to concurrent systems. State your leading indicators for tracking progress along your way in the first column. The next two columns identify enablers and barriers fostering or hindering your journey. The last column identifies a champion or sponsor who will serve as an enabler for achieving targeted progress and/or helping to neutralize a barrier.

Indicators of Success, Enablers, Barriers, and Champions			
Leading Indicator/Outcome Metric	Enablers	Barriers	Who will Champion?

WORKBOOK D: Realizing NSD Ventures

Often proponents of radically new designs challenge the culture and capabilities of their extent development system. Proponents of change need not only champion the competitive advantages of a design, but also transformations of the development system adding capabilities that may be required for its realization. Many case studies show that the initiation of transformation from bureaucratic to concurrent systems of development begin with the realization that the extant system is incapable of supporting the new design and its realization, e.g., ATMs in banking or blockbuster drugs at Eli Lilly.

In this exercise, you are asked to engage in a thought experiment as to how to advocate on behalf of a radically new design and challenge your enterprise to support its development. You will need to develop a compelling value proposition on whether to launch an intrapreneurial development or external venture.

There is a rapidly growing literature on NSD and the exercises in this workbook attempt to call your attention to some of the kinds of information you may wish to seek out. A final recommendation is to seek a mentor who has prior experience in NSD within an extant company as a new venture. Do not be put off by anyone who has experienced failure. Many of the most successful champions of NSD are those who learned from their failures in order to succeed.

1. Formulating Your Offering and its Value Proposition for Customers

Exemplars: How would you describe the value proposition of a company you admire? Select an enterprise and either extract it from conversations with their employees, their website, or draft your own version based on your experiences with their offerings:

359

The TVD framework proposed in this book argues that the composite model is capable of developing customer offerings with at least two kinds of competitive advantages. The *first* is cost-effective innovation because up and downstream stakeholders collaborate at the outset to ensure ideas are transformed effectively into value customer offerings. The second is the robust capability for simultaneously developing services and goods in a robust development system. The value of your proposition is enhanced to the extent you are able to collaboratively engage the entire value stream in simultaneous development and integrate services and goods in holistic customer experiences.

Hypothesize a behavioral scenario whereby customers experience a service *per se* or a product which is enhanced because of embedded services. What are some of the ways you would like customers to value your offering relative to others?

- Requirements met
- Unanticipated needs met
- Faster delivery
- Lower initial cost
- After purchase reliability
- Innovative features
- Pleasure in using
- Trustworthiness
- Lower operating costs during use
- You name it: _____

1. What emotions you would like for customers to experience in using your offering?

_____
_____
_____

2. How you would like your customers to describe their experience with your offering to others?

_____
_____
_____
_____

3. How would you describe the value proposition of your company?

Stating your Value Proposition for Customers
Your 2–5 sentence statements should profile advantages customers may experience from your offering.
Insert your value proposition below

Question: How well does your value proposition meet the five criteria in the following list? Circle those that your statement covers explicitly or implicitly. Are any vital elements omitted? It is difficult to touch all bases of a value proposition as it needs to be relatively cogent and pithy. If necessary, redraft your proposition until you have a 1–2 minutes version that can be spoken persuasively and cogently written up.

1. Do you focus on how your customers are likely to experience your offering?
2. Did you devise a catchy question or issue enabling potential customers to engage with the features you offer?
3. Do you fulfill an unmet customer need?
4. Is it clear how your offer differs from competitive alternatives (even if outside your industry)?
5. Can you credibly provide easy-to-grasp examples of demonstrable benefits?
6. Have you provided a context denoting or connoting trust in you and/ or your company?

2. Internal NSD

Proponents of the development of a radically new offering should usually try at least initially to do so within the enterprise employing them. To the extent an offering is new to the enterprise, forming a heavyweight team will likely be essential. This is more feasible to the extent existing lines of business may receive synergistic benefits from the new offering.

Does development of an offering require cross-functional teaming? • If yes, does the enterprise have a cross-functional NSD function? • If no, do you have executive sponsorship to support the formation of a heavyweight team?	Yes/No

A heavyweight team will require an executive sponsor and cross-functional team members drawn from requisite departments up-front. Enough funds needs to be committed to get the team to the point where proof of principle can be established.

3. Internal Venture Sponsors

Sometimes enterprises need to expand their range of offerings beyond so called "line extensions". These may be radically new products that offer high levels of customer benefit, but may lack commonality with the core competencies of the extant enterprise. Garnering the requisite resources is often difficult. Assuming the enterprise is willing to make the investment, the venture is often best managed as a semi-autonomous unit within the larger structure.

Is your offering radically different than extant lines of business in terms of core competencies? • If yes, do you have sponsorship for an intrapreneurial venture? • If no, consider strategic partnership options or an external venture.	Yes/No

Devising a winning-value proposition from the customer perspective is a necessary first step for any radical development. But convincing managers of an enterprise to fund development of a new kind of product line takes time and a lot of extra effort.

First, you must convince internal sponsors that the design of the offering you propose is likely to be enthusiastically received by customers. Especially, if the customer base differs from existing ones, the value proposition may need to be translated into terms customarily used by your potential sponsors. Second, there are many questions that you will need to answer to persuade potential sponsors.

Does the design:

1. Complement or enhance existing offerings?
2. Provide a superior alternative to existing offerings even at the expense of cannibalization?
3. Fall within the core competencies of the enterprise?

   a. Customer base
   b. Distribution network
   c. Knowledge and technological capabilities
   d. Other compatibilities, specify: _____

4. If a design falls outside of the core competencies of your enterprise, you must justify why the value of your offering warrants additional effort and expense, e.g., advantages of diversification, potential for enlarged market scope, cost sharing through strategic partnerships, etc.
5. A business plan will need to be drafted that includes targeted market segments and cost/revenues, preferably over the life cycle of use.

4. External NSD Venture

To the extent an enterprise lacks NSD capabilities and/or an offering falls outside of the core competencies of your employing enterprise, the more likely it is that you will need to venture externally. One option is for your employing enterprise to partner with the external venture or make an investment in it.

Do you have internal sponsors willing to consider forming a strategic partnership with an external entity for realizing a radically new customer offering?	Yes/No
• If yes, consider becoming an internal champion within your enterprise of the external partnership relationship which you may help lead from an internal or external position?	
• If no, consider establishing a solo entrepreneurial venture?	

New ventures in services vary in the extent to which capital investment is required. Often less cash up-front is required for new ventures services than for goods. If your employing company does not choose to partner or invest in your venture, external sources of support will be needed. Of course, you will need to develop a comprehensive business plan. You may find ways of financing your own venture or attracting investors. Venture capital is available, but often at a considerable price. Alternatively, one of the fastest and more reliable paths to success is by securing partners for your venture with one or more enterprises that might obtain complementary benefits from your start-up firm.

Are you able to partner or contract with other enterprises to help support the launch of your new venture? There are many kinds of partnerships, contractual relationships and network options, e.g., <ul><li>Will you purchase components for bundling with your offering so they might invest in your success?</li><li>Will your offering be bundled with theirs so they will be motivated to invest in helping you supply them?</li><li>Are you able to contract with others to supply components of your offering at discounted prices?</li><li>Are you able to integrate external resources into a holistic customer offering?</li><li>You name it.</li></ul>	Yes/No

5. Configuring a Venture Team

Human capital is critical for the development of new offerings. The tendency is for high performers to over-staff relative to average levels at early phases. By contrast, low performers tend to over-manage at later phases because relatively more money is being spent as development nears commercialization. However, return on investment in human capital unusually declines toward end phases of development cycle.

A starting point for assessing how to configure a venture team pre- and post-launch, you may use the results of analyses reported in Chapter Twelve. The role of 10 generic functions are profiled which enables you to use data as an initial basis for prioritizing a team configuration. In the following chart, selected evidence is extracted from Chapter Twelve regarding the deployment of 10 kinds of human capital. The darker the cell, the greater the amount of variation predicted in differentiation performance at pre-launch (including concept) and post-launch segments of the development cycle.

Contribution to Differentiation Performance Pre- and Post-launch[2]

- *Double Circle those functions which you may need for a core team.*
- *Circle those which you anticipate needing over cycle of a development and delivery.*

	Correlation		If Novelty Strategy		If Tacit Knowledge	
	Pre-launch	Post-launch	Pre-launch	Post-launch	Pre-launch	Post-launch
Product dev.						
Marketing						
Process dev.						
Systems/IT						
Sales						
Finance						
Delivery[2]						
Administration						
Logistics						
Cust. service						

	Percent variance predicted
	10% or more
	5–9%
	Statistically significant

These 10 functions analyzed are generic categories. There are many kinds of tasks that may be performed within each. It may be helpful to define what activities function in these categories needed to accomplish to help launch a NSD venture.

---

[2] *Note:* This chart omits savings in human capital that may be precluded by exploiting explicit knowledge. Contingent upon the business model, tools and technologies may substitute for human employees, especially to the extent transactions with customers are automated.

	Description of the Tasks to be performed by functions
Product dev.	
Marketing	
Process dev.	
Systems /IT	
Sales	
Finance	
Delivery	
Administration	
Logistics	
Cust. service	
Others	

Many enterprises lack a full complement of functions for radical NSD, especially in the instance of new ventures. The following chart lists the 10 functions and external as well as internal sources of securing needed human capital.

Opportunities for configuring a team may include:

Source of Functional Expertise:			
	Internal	Partner	Supplier	Customer
---	---	---	---	---
Product dev.	Yes No	Yes No	Yes No	Yes No
Marketing	Yes No	Yes No	Yes No	Yes No
Process dev.	Yes No	Yes No	Yes No	Yes No
Systems/IT	Yes No	Yes No	Yes No	Yes No
Sales	Yes No	Yes No	Yes No	Yes No
Finance	Yes No	Yes No	Yes No	Yes No
Delivery	Yes No	Yes No	Yes No	Yes No
Administration	Yes No	Yes No	Yes No	Yes No
Logistics	Yes No	Yes No	Yes No	Yes No
Cust. service	Yes No	Yes No	Yes No	Yes No
Other	Yes No	Yes No	Yes No	Yes No

6. Opportunities for Simultaneously Integrating Services and Goods in Offerings

To the extent services and goods integration adds value, where is source for value to be integrated from both sectors (check all relevant)?

	Internal	Partner	Supplier	Customer
Services	Yes No	Yes No	Yes No	Yes No
Goods	Yes No	Yes No	Yes No	Yes No

To the extent integration is valuable, at what phase might integration occur for customer?

	Design Concept	Sold Pre-launch	Post-launch
Service enhanced by goods, specify:	Yes/No	Yes/No	Yes/No
Goods enhanced by services, specify:	Yes/No	Yes/No	Yes/No
Commingled holistic experience	Yes/No	Yes/No	Yes/No

Opportunities for holistically integrating services and goods may occur at various points during the development cycle. At what points is holistic value added? At what phase should cross-functional integration occur in development?

	Design Concept	Pre-launch	Post-launch
Service enhanced by goods, specify:	Yes/No	Yes/No	Yes/No
Goods enhanced by services, specify:	Yes/No	Yes/No	Yes/No
Commingled holistic experience	Yes/No	Yes/No	Yes/No

Development of new offerings are complex and requires various modes for integrating diverse functional expertise. How will you bring resource personnel together for developing holistic value?

Cross-functional team	Yes/No
Heavyweight team	Yes/No
Intrapreneurial venture	Yes/No
Supplier contract	Yes/No
Strategic partnership	Yes/No
Strategic Alliance	Yes/No
Networked cooperative	Yes/No
Other, please specify	Yes/No

Index